The Women of Psychology
Volume II: Expansion and Refinement

The Women of Psychology

Volume II: Expansion and Refinement

by
Gwendolyn Stevens
and
Sheldon Gardner

SCHENKMAN PUBLISHING COMPANY, INC.
Cambridge, Massachusetts

Copyright © 1982

Schenkman Publishing Company, Inc.
3 Mount Auburn Place
Cambridge, Massachusetts 02138

Library of Congress Cataloging in Publication Data

Stevens, Gwendolyn.
  The women of psychology.

  Includes index.
  Contents: v. 1. Pioneers and innovators—
v. 2. Expansion and refinement.
    1. Psychology—History. 2. Women psychologists.
3. Psychology—United States—History. I. Gardner,
Sheldon. II. Title
BF95.S73   150'.88042   81-14394
ISBN 0-87073-443-1 (v. 1)   AACR2
ISBN 0-87073-444-x (pbk. : v. 1)
ISBN 0-87073-445-8 (v. 2)
ISBN 0-87073-446-6 (pbk. : v. 2)

Printed in the United States of America.

Contents

73720

To the memory of all those women psychologists whom no one ever knew.

*Women are not better than men, but they are not
   lesser.*
*Women are not totally different from men, but they are
   not altogether the same.*
*When the women's movement moves further from its
   initial focus on men and is able to celebrate
   women, it will be freed to lead in both humanistic
   and rational directions.*
   Judith Bardwick (*In Transition*, p. 181)

Acknowledgements

Unlike *Pioneers and Innovators*, where there was an exceedingly difficult problem in locating women for inclusion, this volume posed first the problem of determining which of the many eminent women of psychology's recent past and of contemporary times should (and could) be included. The problem of selection here was an embarrassment of riches. More than this, so many of these psychologists are our personal friends that what to say about these women was a particular problem. Most of them are also still involved in productive work in their specialized fields and we do not have the benefit of elapsed time—the jury is still out as far as the evaluation of the significance of their contributions and life's work.

This book would not have been possible without the assistance of those professional "data finders" who are usually referred to as librarians and archivists. To the following persons and their staffs go our heartfelt thanks: Mr. Charles Montabano of the Harvard College Library, Drs. John Popplestone and Marian McPherson of Akron University's Psychological Archives, and Ms. Stephanie Welch of the Wellesley College Library. A special acknowledgement is given to Ms. Maribeth Needles, reference librarian at Kent Library of the Southeast Missouri State University, whose services we found indispensible when gathering information for this volume.

In some cases we were also lucky enough to come in contact with individuals who were willing to share their special knowledge and personal reminiscences of various women of psychology. Dr. Kendon Smith (on Elizabeth "Polly" Duffy), Dr. Philip Merrifield (on Rachel Ball and Joan Guilford), Mr. LeRoy Gabaldon (on Theodora Abel), Ms. Helen LeRoy (on Margaret Harlow), Dr. Dale Harris (on Florence Goodenough), Ms. Lottie Newman (on Anna Freud), Ms. Eugenie Bauer (on Helene Deutsch), Dr. David Jenkins (on Dorothy Adkins and Florence Kluckhohnn, Dr. Deana Logan (on Mary Cover Jones), and Ms. Lucy Ball Mish (on Rachel Stutsman Ball). Of special importance was the loan of the galleys of the

Fall 1980 issue of the *Psychology of Women Quarterly* by Dr. Nancy Felipe Russo.

Finally, a special word of thanks to the dedicated, stubborn, tough-minded, and tender-hearted women of psychology, without whom there would be no discipline of psychology as we know it. Many of the women who appear in this volume provided moral support and valuable material. The information they graciously provided about their own lives and those of their friends and colleagues was, of course, not available anywhere else. The following is a list of some of the women who provided us with much of the most personal material:

Theodora Abel
Louise Bates Ames
Anne Anastasi
Magda Arnold
Lauretta Bender
Judith Bardwick
Nancy Bayley
Joyce Brothers
Hilde Bruch
Alice Bryan
Psyche Cattell
Stella Chess
Mamie Phipps Clark
Florence Denmark
Helene Deutsch
Sibylle Escalona
Sybil Eysenck
Anna Freud
Marianne Frostig
Beatrice Gardner
Eleanor J. Gibson
Joan S. Guilford
Eugenia Hanfmann
Ruth Hartley
Edna Heidbreder
Mary Henle
Josephine Hilgard
Lois Hoffman

Barbel Inhelder
Mary Cover Jones
Tracy Kendler
Elizabeth Koppitz
Nadine Lambert
Dorothea Cross Leighton
Sophie Freud Loewenstein
Eleanor Maccoby
Karen Machover
Margaret S. Mahler
Martha Mednick
Jane Mercer
Elaine Morgan
Lois Barclay Murphy
Anne Roe
Sandra Scarr
Pauline Sears
Georgene Seward
Virginia Sexton
Elsa Siipola
Natalie Shainess
Carolyn W. Sherif
Marie Skodak
Janet Taylor Spence
Leona Tyler
Ina Uzgiris
Edith Weisskopf-Joelson

Time Line

ONE HUNDRED YEARS OF PSYCHOLOGY: 1840-1940
PSYCHOLOGISTS LISTED ACCORDING TO DATE OF BIRTH

W. James (1842-1910)
G. S. Hall (1844-1924)

Christine Ladd-Franklin (1847-1930)

I. P. Pavlov (1849-1936
G. E. Müller (1850-1934)

Lillien J. Martin (1851-1943)

S. Freud (1856-1939)
O. Kulpe (1862-1915

Mary W. Calkins (1863-1930)

E. B. Titchener (1867-1927)
R. S. Woodworth (1869-1952)

Margaret F. Washburn (1781-1939)
Helen Thompson Woolley (1874-1947)
J. B. Watson (1878-1958)   Lillian M. Gilbreth (1878-1974)
M. Wertheimer (1880-1943)

Augusta Fox Bronner (1881-1966)
Melanie Klein (1882-1960)
Helene Deutsch (1884-   )
Karen Horney (1885-1952)
Leta S. Hollingworth (1886-1939)
Ruth Benedict (1887-1948)
K. Lewin (1890-1947)   Edna Heidbreder (1890-   )
Charlotte Bühler (1893-1974)
Anna Freud (1895-   )
Mary Cover Jones (1896-   )
Lauretta Bender (1897-   )
Margaret Mahler (1897-   )

K. S. Lashley (1898-1958)
Theodora M. Abel (1899-   )
Nancy Bayley (1899-   )
Alexandra Adler (1901-   )
Margaret Mead (1901-1974)
C. R. Rogers (1902-   )   Helen Flanders Dunbar (1902-1959)
Lois B. Murphy (1902-   )
Georgene Seward (1902-   )
Magda Arnold (1903-   )
B. F. Skinner (1904-   )   Elizabeth Duffy (1904-1970)
Hilde Bruch (1904-   )
Anne Roe (1904-   )
Eugenia Hanfmann (1905-   )
Leona Tyler (1906-   )
Molly Harrower (1906-   )
Dorothea McCarthy (1906-1974)
K. W. Spence (1907-1967)   Marie Jahoda (1907-   )

R. R. Sears (1908–   )

Anne Anastasi (1908–   )
Else Frenkel-Brunswik (1908–1958)
Louise Bates Ames (1908–   )
Pauline Snedden Sears (1908–   )
Dorothea Cross Leighton (1908–   )

R. May (1909–   )
N. Miller (1909–   )

Eleanor Jack Gibson (1910–   )
Ruth Hartley (1910–   )
Edith Weisskopf-Joelson (1910–   )
Marie Paula Skodak (1910–   )

D. Rapaport (1911–1960)

Dorothy C. Adkins (1912–1975)
Barbel Inhelder (1913–   )
Mary Henle (1913–   )
Stella Chess (1914–   )
Natalie Shainess (1915–   )
Sibylle Escalona (1915–   )

H. J. Eysenck (1916–   )

Bernice Neugarten (1916–   )
Virginia Staudt Sexton (1916–   )
Eleanor E. Maccoby (1917–   )
Mamie Phipps Clarke (1917–   )
Brenda Milner (1918–   )
Tracy S. Kendler (1918–   )
Margaret Kuenne Harlow (1918–1971)
Elizabeth M. Koppitz (1919–   )
Beatrice C. Lacey (1919–   )
Dorothea Jameson (1920–   )

G. W. Albee (1921–   )

Carolyn Wood Sherif (1922–   )
Janet Taylor Spence (1923–   )
Jane Ross Mercer (1924–   )

A. Bandura (1925–   )

Virginia E. Johnson (1925–   )
Nadine Lambert (1926–   )

R. D. Laing (1927–   )

Joyce Brothers (1927–   )
Natalia Chapanis (1928–   )
Joan S. Guilford (1928–   )
Lois Hoffman (1929–   )
Florence Denmark (1932–   )
Judith Bardwick (1933–   )
Beatrice Gardner (1933–   )

S. Gardner (1934–   )

Sandra Wood Scarr (1936–   )
Ina Uzgiris (1937–   )
Matina S. Horner (1939–   )

1
Introduction

This book chronicles what happened to the women of psychology who trained in the 1920s and after in this country, and to the scores of prominent and brilliant female psychologists who emigrated to America in the decade before the war (and indeed continue to join our ranks to this day). During this period psychology as a science and profession became firmly established and "respectable." It also became highly specialized. The women who became professional psychologists increasingly tended to become specialists and displayed a clear trend toward narrowing of professional interests.

The choice of competence over virtuosity, plainly evident in the course of psychology in the past forty years, was prompted partly by the increasing demands on psychologists to provide immediate answers to specific and practical questions and to provide clinical services which were now seen as valuable and needed. America had become psychology-oriented and psychology, especially in the applied areas, expanded and flourished.

The movement away from involvement with comprehensive theories and dilettantism (which has now become almost a dirty word in psychology) was also prompted by a feeling that generalism was no longer needed, that psychology had already acquired the tools it needed to progress. Enough theoretical ideas were available to formulate research programs and to direct action, and adequate instruments were at hand to deal with the problems that needed to be solved.

During the pre-World War II years there was an increase in the number of women who chose to major in psychology in college. Although this interest was often related to non-career, non-science factors—for it was widely held that a major in psychology would improve your personality and make you a better wife and mother and, much as we hate to admit it, because the academic demands were relatively minimal in many cases—a large number of very competent and outstanding women entered the profession at this time.

1

Marriage and a "normal" family life, according to published research, were the primary goals of college women of this period and the women who are featured in this volume were, in general, not exceptions. Most of them would marry and very often it was to a young psychologist or psychiatrist with whom they shared many interests—professional, social, and political. They also pooled their incomes, which, since a majority of the women in this book gained maturity during the Depression, was of critical importance. For the women of psychology born around the turn of the century and the two decades thereafter, there was typically an early marriage, but political and economic factors led to a delay in having children. One important factor was, of course, the war.

The War Years

World War II was a crucial period in the history of American psychology. The important contributions of psychologists, both in research and in clinical practice, did much to establish psychology as a serious and valuable profession. Many women were, of course, involved in activities related to the war effort. But, more than the opportunity to prove their value in helping to win the war, World War II also provided the women of psychology the opportunity to prove their competence in areas of psychology from which they had previously been almost totally excluded.

During the war, psychology, like all other professions, suffered a serious manpower shortage. Many already prominent and promising psychologists enlisted in the armed services very early in the war and many more were involved in activities related to the war effort, removing them from the academic institutions and laboratories where they had been established. Although many tenured and senior psychologists were guaranteed their former positions when they returned, the extended leaves of absence granted to established psychologists who were "working to win the war" provided women with opportunities to obtain desirable, often permanent, positions. The highly successful performance of women in these positions led to the greatest advancement in the status and acceptance of women in the history of the profession.

Women in academia, for example, who had been relegated to positions in colleges, especially in women's colleges, were now increasingly accepted on faculties of major universities. Women moved into industry and became more prominent in such specialities as personnel selection and non-clinical assessment. Most significantly, women, although fewer in number, made in-roads into the last bastion of male-dominated psychology: the animal laboratory. Women, from 1941 to 1945, were finally welcome to work with rats and pigeons and chimps and monkeys. The acceptance was professional, rather than social—women were not permitted into such inner sancta as the Psychology Roundtable and the "good old boy" system, which through trading on influence and personal contact had kept women in a subordinate position, was never dismantled.

The shortage of men during the war did not, however, eliminate from the mainstream most of the leaders of psychology. Many of the leaders were quite elderly and power within the field was not generally passed to women at this time. Women were "accepted," to be sure—as members of a team, on a faculty as a staff member, as an associate of a research institute, or as a therapist in a clinic—but men, by and large, maintained the positions of authority. Some of the gains made by women during the war proved temporary and, even more regrettably, illusory, for when the men returned after the war, the women of psychology were seldom able to consolidate the gains made and many promises were never met.

Competition and Discrimination

Much in demand during the war years, despite their generally subordinate positions, the women of psychology were not able, in most cases, to compete successfully with the men returning from the war. At the universities, for example, while women were able to retain the academic rank that they obtained during the war years, they found themselves unable to advance further. Many of our more outspoken correspondents give two reasons for what they have described as an unfair advantage given their often less competent male rivals during the postwar period: (a) married women psychologists did not enjoy uninterrupted time to pursue professional objectives because of family obligations that fell unfairly to them and (b) gender discrimination which had laid dormant for four years but had not died in psychology. Not all the women we have contacted recognized that they have been discriminated against.

Because the women who have worked in the eras that we call psychology's time of "expansion and refinement" were more or less "accepted" in the profession, the discrimination suffered by the women described in this book—the lack of power and prestige and the denigration of their efforts and accomplishments—is far more subtle than that experienced by their predecessors. Their correspondence with us suggests that many women of psychology born between 1900 and 1920 were not aware of gender discrimination (or, now quite advanced in years, they have become philosophical about it).

During the fifties and early sixties, psychology's performance in the area of equal opportunity was inadequate—albeit in extremley subtle ways. Universities and colleges had recourse to antiquated "anti-nepotism" rules to deprive many extremely accomplished, married women of well-earned and well-deserved positions. Prominent women were passed over for advancement and positions of authority in favor of younger, less experienced, and generally less able men. Interviewers expressed doubt that a psychologist-mother could execute the functions of a position with as much single-minded dedication as a psychologist-father could. There was considerable danger that the old "Catch-22" vicious cycle would be re-established in psychology: denied opportunities to enter and to advance in psychology, women are then considered less inherently capable on the basis of the lack of adequate evidence of their having succeeded in the past. In other words, women have always had a hard time obtaining a "track record" in psychology—because they kept getting kicked off the track!

This period also saw the publication of a number of the more popular histories of psychology. A good indication that women of psychology had not retained the high status they had briefly enjoyed during the war is that none of these histories mentioned women. The histories formalized the vicious cycle phenomenon.

Women in the Era of the Absurd

It would please us to report that psychologists were instrumental in alleviating some of the disorder and craziness of the sixties, the period when the world seemed dominated by absurdity and ruled by chaos. It would please us to be able to report that the scientists and philosophers of psychology, who enjoyed so much popularity and success during this period, had demonstrated responsibility and good sense. We cannot. In truth, psychologists, especially in this country, not only contributed to the craziness, they were among the ringleaders in the me-oriented, solipsistic, disinhibited, rebellious decade. Professional psychologists displayed so much unethical, irresponsible, and uncontrolled behavior that they became a model of sorts for other professions. Were it not for the fact that the whole world was temporarily nuts during the 1960s and, therefore, the excesses of psychology, hardly unnoticed, could be swallowed along with the rest, the history of psychology might have ended with nude marathons, LSD therapy, touchie-feelie encounters, and the profundity of "let-it-all-hang out" philosophy.

That the women of psychology were not, by and large, part of the absurdist psychology during the sixties, is probably due to their age (the most prominent of the women were much too old to engage in such silliness) and the double-standard concerning values and sex (for, in many cases, the inarticulate theories of 1960s psychology were thinly disguised attempts of middle-aged male psychologists to sexually exploit young women). We do not know how many female psychologists secretly desired to "get with it" and to participate in psychology's most shameful activities. But it can be here noted that much to their credit very few of the women of psychology succumbed.

The majority of female psychologists remained respectable and scholarly during the sixties. We know of no woman who disgraced herself as so many of her male colleagues have done. To our knowledge none has grown a beard or preached the psychic benefits of exotic mushrooms or proposed that a science can be anti-intellectual. The most prominent women of psychology working in the sixties were generally involved in traditional and important research and, most significant for the purposes of this volume, became the authors of the less spectacular and less "popular" (in its most vulgar sense) books. Instead they were writing books of the type most highly valued in psychology—its textbooks and volumes which integrate vast amounts of research data. The women, by brilliance and by default, had become the epitome of mainstream psychology.

Feminism

Throughout the history of psychology the more important women psychologists have been involved to some degree in the psychology of women. Not content to remain merely arm chair theorists most women psychologists in addition to pursuing scholarly research on women's issues have been involved in the never-ending battle for rights for women. A large minority of the women of psychology have been active and ardent feminists—and the percentage of activist women increases.

During the seventies, however, closely associated with the greatest surge of militant feminism in the history of this country, the women of psychology became very aware of their "second-class citizenship" and, more importantly, of a shared destiny and a sense of belonging to a sisterhood. This has led to the development of a "network" of female psychologists to rival the "good old boy" in-group, almost exclusively male, that has dominated psychology's history since 1879. Militancy within psychology and a feeling of identification with all women have changed the image of the woman of psychology: she is no longer "invisible"; she is strong and assertive; she has something to say and she will be heard.

That women are now beginning to flex their muscles and to finally obtain power within psychology is illustrated by the fact that three of the presidents of the American Psychological Association (APA) elected during this decade have been women: Anne Anastasi, Leona Tyler, and Florence Denmark. Women are now being appointed to important committees of the APA and are beginning to receive its prestigious awards and honors. There is hardly an area in psychology where women are not prominent, are not moving into positions of leadership, are not making significant and acknowledged contributions.

Women of psychology are today far better known, at least to each other, than ever before, and the number of candidates for inclusion in this volume was overwhelming. The choices were somewhat arbitrary and the absence of published comprehensive and reliable biographical data required greater assistance in collection of material than our earlier volume. While it is too soon, at this point, to develop accurate assessment of the significance or value of the contributions of the women featured herein, especially of those women we call "contemporary," this will, no doubt, be a major concern of future revised editions of this book.

A Summary, But Not a Conclusion

The passage of forty years has seen an impressive increase in the status of women in psychology. Prestige and recognition have no longer been so obviously denied women and during this period, for example, three presidents of the American Psychological Association have been women. There is still question, however, whether or not, as Eleanor Jack Gibson suggests, these gains represent primarily "tokenism."

What is abundantly clear today is that (a) women can no longer legitimately be said to avoid the high-status activities, i.e., in experimental psychology, academia, and the field of psychometrics, for they are well-represented there in the postwar period, (b) that women have successfully overcome the prejudicial image of them as merely service-oriented do-gooders, (c) that women have been relatively well accepted as staff members (although usually not as the leader of the team) and (d) that women in psychology have felt the need to separate and to develop institutions within the discipline designed to combat the deeply entrenched "good old boy" system that continues to plague psychology.

2
Era of Acceptance

This chapter sketches the lives and highlights the contributions to psychology made by women born between 1891 and 1900. Born before the turn of the century, these women started careers as professional psychologists as the United States approached the Depression and World War II years. Several of these women are still alive and a few are still working. Their productive careers, which in some cases extend over fifty years, by now can be viewed from an historical perspective that allows for critical evaluation of their place in the development of psychology. For the most part, these women lived and worked during a transition period in psychology; from the early development of a science to the more contemporary era of specialization.

The women of this decade were more or less accepted by their male colleagues in psychoanalysis, behaviorism, hospital psychiatry, and the experimental laboratory. The overt discrimination suffered by their predecessors was now more subtle and many believed that the status of women was improving. Although these women were not barred outright from schools, there were nevertheless insidious obstacles to success. Theodora Abel's research interests, for example, were made the focal point of E. B. Titchener's jokes.

Few of these women surpassed, or even equalled, the giants of the two previous decades. None of the women, except for Charlotte Bühler, developed a sweeping, major new theory of human development. This is not to imply that these women did not make important contributions to psychology. Quite the contrary; in terms of expansion, revision and new application of the principles of psychology, these women contributed a great deal.

While extremely competent, these women often saw their contributions matched or exceeded by a spouse, relative, or friend. In the first generation of women psychologists, the handful of women in the field outshone everyone around. But in this generation we have women whose husbands were Karl Bühler, Paul Schilder, Louis Thurstone, Sheldon Glueck and

Harold Jones. Their fathers were Sigmund Freud and James McKeen Cattell and they had older friends and mentors like Karen Horney, Ruth Benedict and Margaret Mead.

We are not suggesting that the women of this generation were lesser geniuses, but only that because of situational factors or interests, they tended, on the whole, to be followers rather than leaders. One reason might be that many of these women married men who were already more established than themselves.

A related factor in many cases may have been the fact that several of the most brilliant of these women balanced a professional career against a full and busy private life. Of those who married, and several of them did (and they remained married for several years), *they* raised the children, and *they* ran the house while their husbands were free to pursue research and develop theories. Mary Cover Jones, for example, always put her husband and children first and her career second.

To some degree the prestige, prominence, and power of these women were a function of their connections, as has clearly been true for men, too, but it is probable that the women's persistence and loyalty combined with their brilliance would have resulted, had they been men, in positions of leadership, even without the relationship to an established person in the area. In fact, in some cases the deserved recognition was delayed or even denied because of the personal relationship (as in the case of Thelma Thurstone).

Among the most productive and versatile psychologists of either gender during this era are Theodora Mead Abel, Anna Freud, Lauretta Bender, and Charlotte Bühler. These women and the others in this section made significant contributions to existing theory (e.g., Anna Freud elaborated her father's theory of psychoanalysis); developed new research methodology (e.g., Nancy Bayley's approach to the study of children); elaborated clinical approaches (e.g., Mary Cover Jones's extension of behaviorist principles to clinical work and the subsequent development of desensitization therapy); and also developed clinical instruments that were timely and needed (e.g., Charlotte Bühler's World Test and Lauretta Bender's Visual Motor Gestalt Test). In general, the work of these women eclipsed traditional boundaries and provided new insights into old problems.

The women of this decade best reflect the branching out of psychology, especially in the movement toward the more applied areas. There were clinical psychometrists (Charlotte Bühler and Lauretta Bender); extenders of psychoanalysis (Anna Freud and Clara Thompson); child developmentalists (Rachel Stutsman Ball and Nancy Bayley); and "politicians" (Lois Meek Stolz, Ruth Strang and Carolyn Zachry). They were women interested in test development (Thelma Thurstone); juvenile delinquency (Mary Cover Jones and Eleanor Glueck); and clinical psychology (Margaret Mahler and Therese Benedek), just to mention a few of the diverse areas of interest pursued by these women.

MULTI-FACETED AND MARVELOUS
Theodora Mead Abel (1899–   )

Theodora Abel was a product of Columbia University during its "Golden Age" of psychology. Like that university itself, she has had an eclectic orientation and a practical and clinical approach to solving human problems. Theodora Abel now lives with her husband of fifty-seven years in New Mexico and, at the age of eighty, continues to work almost full-time as a clinical psychologist. She has been one of America's most productive scientists for sixty years, but is never mentioend as one of its most important psychologists. In part this may be because she never developed a far-reaching theory; more likely it is because she has contributed to so many different aspects of psychology that only a widely-read dilettante will suspect that the "T. M. Abel" listed as the author of such a variety of publications is the same person.

Abel developed a diversity of research and clinical skills and has achieved success in several different, successive careers in psychology— as a mental tester, an expert on mental deficiency, an experimental researcher, a culture and personality investigator and a clinical psychologist. She became prominent in each field.

Not in any sense one of the more creative of the women of psychology, Abel was influenced by her colleagues and friends such as Margaret Mead and Karen Horney[1] as well as her mentors, Margaret Washburn, Robert Woodworth, and Madison Bentley.[2] Abel has been loyal to her friends and has also been enthusiastic about and loyal to successive "systems" of psychology, including functionalism, gestalt psychology, cultural anthropology and psychoanalysis.

Theodora Mead Abel is not a dilettante but a very talented women. She has been proficient in French, German, Spanish, Italian, Japanese, and Arabic, and she is an accomplished violinist, still playing with an amateur orchestra in New Mexico.[1] She is a sophisticated world-traveller, but remains unimpressed with herself and her accomplishments. She is a thoroughly nice person.

Early Life

Theodora Mead was born, an only child, in Newport, Rhode Island, on 9 September 1899.[3] It is reported that she was born unexpectedly while her mother was attending the wedding of a friend. Her father, Robert Mead, Jr., became a lawyer after a brief career in banking, and brought his young family to settle in New York City. Her mother, Elsie Cleveland Mead, had been decorated by the French government for her work with the YWCA in Paris during World War I, had helped found the American Cancer Society with her father, and was partly responsible for raising $100,000 to purchase a gram of radium which President Harding presented to Mme. Marie Curie. Both Elsie and daughter Theodora established and maintained a close and long friendship with Mme. Curie.[2]

The Mead family was affluent and travel to Europe was frequent. Most of Theodora's early education was at the Chapin School in New York, along with a variety of overseas school experiences, including the sixth grade in Geneva. It was at Chapin that Theodora's gift for languages and interest in the violin were encouraged.[1]

In 1917 Abel entered Vassar, where she majored in history. She was encouraged to take some psychology, and her first course was taught by Margaret Floy Washburn. In her senior year, she wrote, she

> got interested in psychology . . . thanks to Margaret F. Washburn. In fear and trembling I asked if I could take part in a research project second semester . . .[1]

Dr. Washburn accepted Theodora and another student, Margaret Child, to work with her on a study of the subjective effect of immediate repetition of music. This study was included in an anthology edited by M. Schoen, published in 1927.[2]

In 1921, Theodora received the A.B. from Vassar with a major in history and "almost" a major in psychology.[1] That summer she accompanied her mother to Poland, where the latter had been invited by the government to assist in establishing a YMCA-like organization. In Poland she met Theodore Abel, a Polish YMCA worker.[2]

Theodora had decided to go to graudate school in psychology and Washburn strongly recommened Cornell. Her father, however, rejected this plan, since he did not want her separated from the family, and Theodora agreed to her second choice, Columbia. As was the procedure at that time, her acceptance was effected on the basis of Washburn's personal recommendation.[2]

Graduate School

Theodora left Columbia after two weeks to join a professional string quartet, but returned at the beginning of the second semester. Her first graduate courses were physiological psychology with Robert Woodworth and exceptional children with Leta Hollingworth. While visiting friends in Paris, Theodora decided to spend the academic year 1922-23 at the Institut de Psychologie at the Sorbonne. There she took courses with Pierre Janet, Henri Pieron, Delacroix, and Dumas (with the last, there were meetings at Saint Anne's, the hospital where Bonaparte obtained her training). She also had contact with Simon, who had been Binet's collaborator. Every Friday evening Theodora enjoyed supper with the Curies and played sonatas with Marie. For her work in Paris, Theodora received a Diploma in 1923.[1, 2]

Shortly after returning to Columbia, where Theodora resumed her studies in experimental psychology, she married Theodore Abel, in November 1923. He was also a Columbia graduate student, in sociology. Theodora received her A.M. in 1924 (Woodworth was her advisor) and her Ph.D. in 1925 (Poffenberger was her chairman).

Mental Tester and Experimenter

From 1923 to 1925 Theodora worked at the Manhattan Trade School for Girls (Poffenberger had encouraged her interest in vocational psychology). There she collected the data for her dissertation, which led to her first published article. She went on to publish a series of articles, based upon her research, almost always in journals where Margaret Washburn, Karl Dallenbach, and Madison Bentley were editors.[3]

After Theodora's Ph.D. was granted, Washburn, apparently forgetting her own bad experiences in the Midwest, assisted Abel in securing a position at the University of Illinois, where Bentley, in 1925 president of the American Psychological Association and formerly of Cornell, was chairman of the psychology department. Bentley helped Theodora receive a research grant to study the use of the galvanometer to measure emotional responses.[2]

Abel spent one year at Illinois, teaching and conducting research and writing. When her husband accepted a position on the sociology faculty at Cornell, Theodora joined him, having obtained, with the help of Dallenbach, a National Research Council Fellowship, 1926-28.[2] At Cornell she completed her research on the galvanic skin reflex and wrote the theoretical article on Washburn's "motor theory" which established her reputation when it was included in the Washburn Commemorative Issue of the *American Journal of Psychology*, arranged by Dallenbach. In this article Abel suggested that Washburn was taking a "functionalist" position, similar to Woodworth's.[4]

Theodora also had personal problems with E. B. Titchener, the authoritarian misogynist who headed Cornell's psychology department. He had no interest in the galvanometer and tended to ridicule Columbia's brand of psychological research and made Theodora herself the brunt of nasty jokes. Titchener's death in 1927 has been said to signal the demise of Cornell's preeminence in psychology.[2] In any event, although she did not publish the results of the galvanic skin reflex study until 1930,[5] the fact that she found that the galvanometer did not provide an accurate estimation of changes in emotional states had an immediate impact, since many researchers, including Margaret Mead and the anthropologists at Columbia, had had high hopes for the procedure.[2]

Unknown Giant

When Theodora Abel became an instructor at Sarah Lawrence College, a position she held from 1929 to 1935, she was a minor but important figure in experimental psychology. Despite her connections and her growing reputation, she never obtained a high-prestige position in her long career. It is in her research and writing that Abel demonstrated her excellence and competence in psychology.

Abel received a Laura Spelman Rockefeller Fund Fellowship (1935–36) to study the "thinking processes in adolescents" and to enable her to study gestalt psychology with Max Wertheimer.[1, 2] Her papers, which had been on "pure" experiments, many of which were traditional enough to have pleased even Titchener, were now broader in scope, and included Piagetian, gestalt, and applied research. At this time, her husband introduced her to Zygmunt Piotrowski, a Polish emigré who was a world-renowned expert on the Rorschach. Piotrowski, and later Bruno Klopfer of UCLA, taught her the Rorschach technique; Theodora became an expert herself and was elected president of the Society of Projective Techniques in 1947.[2]

From 1936 to 1940, Abel was the director of research at the Manhattan Vocational High School, where she studied "subnormal girls' training for industry."[1] She published several articles on research, on the training procedures, as well as on juvenile delinquency and culture and personality. In the studies of delinquent and unstable girls, particularly those who were mentally deficient and institutionalized, she collaborated with Elaine F.

Kinder, with whom she also co-authored her first book *The Subnormal Adolescent Girl* in 1942.[3]

In 1966, commenting on their relationship thirty years earlier, Kinder notes merely that "Ted" (curious in itself since Theodora's friends usually called her "Tao") Abel asked her to "see some girls in therapy" at Letchworth, where Kinder had joined the staff in 1936.[6] Not much is made of their relationship by Kinder, despite the fact that their 1942 book is perhaps her finest accomplishment and the collaboration occurred at a very low point in Kinder's tragic personal life, only a few years after her recovery from a psychotic breakdown.[6]

Although Theodora Abel became the leading psychologist in culture and personality studies some years later, her interest in anthropology and ethnic differences goes back to her days at Columbia, where her classmate and good friend was Margaret Mead (who was no relation). The two Meads started graudate school together and received the A.M. in psychology the same year (1925).[2] Interestingly the two of them both did studies on ethnic differences in measured traits and Theodora's study, surprisingly enough, is slightly more anthropological in nature.

It is likely also that Washburn encouraged an early interest in the study of racial differences, since she had completed a study similar to Theodora's master's thesis when she was at Vassar. Another influence on Abel's socio-cultural emphasis, of course, may well have been her husband, who was for many years a professor of sociology at Columbia.[2] In any event, among her prodigious publications there has been a trickle of ethnic-differences research throughout her career.

Clinical Psychologist

From 1940 to 1946 Abel worked full-time at Letchworth Village, an institution operated by the New York State Department of Mental Hygiene. When she began as a research psychologist, she was forty-one and the mother of three children (one of whom, incidentally, a daughter, is now a clinical psychologist in Missouri).[1] In her research, she utilized the Rorschach and other projective instruments then brand new. Since she was also practicing some psychotherapy at the time,[6] Abel's career as a clinical psychologist is now of forty years duration.[1] Her publications during her Letchworth years were most often cross-cultural studies using the Rorschach and personality assessments of subnormal and delinquent girls.

For most of the ensuing years, regardless of Abel's other professional interests, she has also carried on a clinical practice.

Abel left Letchworth and in 1947 joined her friends Margaret Mead and Ruth Benedict at the Columbia University Reseach in Contemporary Cultures, the project which Benedict had founded with a grant from the Office of Naval Research to study culture "from a distance." Benedict died in 1948 and during the second year of Abel's involvement with this project Margaret Mead and Rhoda Metraux, Theodora's collaborator, were co-leaders.[2]

Much is made of the work of Theodora Abel in the area of culture and personality and, to be sure, it was this research that finally brought her recognition and fame. It was in this area that Abel wrote her two best-known books[7, 8] and her now famous article on the acculturation process of the Chinese in the United States. As her friend Margaret Mead observed in her autobiography, Theodora's valuable contribution to ethnology was primarily her expertise in analyzing Rorschach protocols, a clinical skill. Theodora Abel was the best all-around psychologist to be involved in ethnography.

In the paper on the Chinese, which Abel wrote with Francis Hsu, published in *Rorschach Research Exchange* in 1949, Theodora's clinical skill is clearly evident. She expertly describes personality traits and dynamics from Rorschach responses and, together with her understanding of social and cultural determinants of personality development, this skill resulted in the classic paper on culture and personality from the psychologist's viewpoint. But Abel was never a "real" anthropologist and her primary paid employment from 1947 to the present has been as a clinical psychologist.

Shortly after joining the Columbia project on contemporary cultures, Theodora became associated with the New York Postgraduate Center for Mental Health, an association which lasted for twenty-four years, from 1947 to 1971. Lewis Wolberg, M.D. and his social worker wife Arlene had begun the Postgraduate Center for Psychotherapy (the original name and the one it is usually known by) in 1945, initially to provide specialized training to persons preparing to work at the psychiatric clinics burgeoning throughout the nation.[2]

In 1946, however, the American Psychoanalytic Association decided that hereafter only psychiatrists would be allowed to be formally trained as analysts. It will be noted that many of the most prominent women of psychology had been previously trained in psychoanalysis, usually in Vienna or Berlin, but sometimes, especially in the late thirties and early forties, in the United States. With the new restrictions against non-medical analytic trainees in this country (and a majority of the women analysts were lay analysts), persons interested in obtaining training in psychoanalysis were forced to take on the burdensome expense of training in Great Britain or on the continent, despite the fact that many of the *training* analysts at all the Institutes in the United States were and are non-medical analysts. Most of the non-medical analysts trained before 1946 were allowed to remain identified as psychoanalysts, in large measure because Freud himself had for several years argued in favor of lay analysts (the founder of psychoanalysis, in fact, felt that non-medical clinicians were temperamentally better suited to practice the art).

In 1948 another option became available for psychoanalytic training for non-physicians. The Wolbergs introduced a training program at the Postgraduate Center, the program that made the Center famous since it was one of the first programs that did not discriminate against non-physicians. The Center's director of psychology, Theodora Abel, began her personal analysis there in 1952, a process which was completed in 1956,[2] and became a training analyst in 1960.

In 1949 Theodora Abel was selected for an interdisciplinary study of psychological and social aspects of physical disfigurement and plastic surgery at Bellevue Hospital. This work led to her second book, published with the rest of the expert team as collaborators, in 1954.[1, 2]

In 1951 Abel began her private practice in clinical psychology and joined the faculty at Long Island University, as an instructor. She expanded her skills once again, training under Nathan Ackerman, a pioneer in the family therapy movement, from 1965–68, and became a leading figure in the family movement herself.[2] From 1968 to 1971 Theodora Abel was the co-director of the family therapy training program at the Postgraduate Center and she has been and is to this day engaged in writing papers and giving lectures throughout the world on the topic of family therapy.[1]

Since 1971 Theodora Abel has been in private practice in Albuquerque, New Mexico, and holds the position of clinical professor at the University of New Mexico Medical School as well as running the family therapy program at the local child guidance clinic. Her two famous books, on cross-cultural psychological testing, 1973,[7] and on culture and psychotherapy, 1974,[8] were published when she was a very active, very alert, very old woman. Today at eighty, a grandmother ten times over, Abel is still actively engaged in clinical psychology and has the time to perform with an amateur orchestra that entertains "senior citizens."[1]

Critique

Theodora Abel is a good example of the spirit and quality of achievement that characterize most of the women who are included in this chapter. She was not a great innovator or a leading theoretician, but her work was never trivial, either. She was extremely competent and reached the top of her various endeavors because of the many technical skills she developed. She clearly contributed to the expansion of knowledge about human nature, she refined the technical procedures that were being introduced by others, and she earned the respect of her peers.

Theodora Abel, like most of the women in this chapter, attained her professional maturity at a time when the battle between "schools" and competitive theories and rivalrous orientations had not been decided; they rather survived side-by-side in an uneasy "peaceful co-existence." It was a period of elaboration and refinement and these women were among the leaders in these processes.

Most of the women were in the prime of their professional prominence when the male psychologists were involved in wartime efforts and sex discrimination was at a minimum. They were well enough established that by the time the postwar discriminatory practices developed, they were not personally particularly affected. They, like Abel, were accepted as coworkers at a time when "leadership" was determined to a great extent through politics and in-fighting rather than as a reward for originality or productivity. Like Abel most of these women did not choose to be involved in the organizational power struggles or petty rivalries of the fifties in American psychology. They were content to be the best of their trade.

ANTIGONE
Anna Freud (1895–   )

What better connection for a psychologist than to have Sigmund Freud as a father? Anna Freud, the youngest daughter and favorite of the genius who invented psychoanalysis and was the leader of this highly influential cultural movement for more than sixty years, is herself one of the most productive and most powerful figures in psychoanalysis. Throughout her life this "crown princess" was beloved by the most important persons in international psychoanalysis and was also, to many, an object of jealousy.

Anna Freud has been called, with much justification, the world's leading child analyst, and she, indeed, has educated many of the leading practitioners of this speciality, directly through her lectures and training analyses, and indirectly through a series of brilliant books and articles. Yet this leader of the psychoanalytic orthodoxy, despite the originality and clarity of her ideas, was never a heretic, was not one to effect important changes, and, consistent with the other women described here who were born during the decade 1891 to 1900, she was accepted because of her competence and technical skill rather than innovative theoretical breakthroughs. In her orthodoxy lies Anna Freud's strength.

Anna Freud has been involved with psychoanalysis for so many years—sixty—that she has become standard bearer for the movement and a legendary figure in its history. It surprises many persons to learn this friendly, gracious woman is still active today, since her brith preceded the birth of psychoanalysis, but Anna, quite alert and congenial, was able to travel to the United States in June 1980 to receive an honorary Sc.D. degree from Harvard.[9]

"Nice, complete little woman"

Anna, who has been called "my favorite son" and "Antigone" by her illustrious father, was born on 3 December 1895, in Vienna, Austria. The youngest daughter and one of six children born to Sigmund and Martha Bernays Freud, she was the only child to follow in her father's footsteps.[10] She continued to reside in Vienna until 1938 when she, along with the rest of her family, fled to London to avoid the Nazis. In fact, it was not until Anna was taken into temporary custody by the Nazis and held for a few hours that the very elderly, and dying, Sigmund was willing to leave Vienna.[10]

It has been reported that Freud wanted another son and this was probably conveyed to the young Anna. Freud sometimes inadvertently referred to Anna as "he" and deliberately as his "son." It was Freud also who referred to her as his "Antigone," the daughter of Oedipus and his caretaker in old age.[11]

In keeping with late Victorian practices, Sigmund did not participate much in the care of his children when they were infants and Martha had also enjoined him from "using" the children in the development of his theory. It was his wish also to keep his personal life separate from his professional life, but anecdotes involving his children and grandchildren are to be found in many of his writings. One famous such story appears in *Interpretation of Dreams*, where, to illustrate the direct expression of wish-fulfillment in the dreams of children, Freud reports Anna's dream of eating strawberries and other treats, at nineteen months of age, after the sick-to-her-stomach Anna had been put to bed hungry.[10]

Anna was a shy, pretty, serious and "unworldly" girl, who resembled her father and was his favorite. They were inseparable and at an early age she assumed duties of "personal secretary" and later his nurse. It is reported that the two of them "slighted" Martha and the antagonism between mother and child increased with the years.[10]

Anna attended the Cottage Lyceum in Vienna, but never received any formal academic education. Her father encouraged her to delay her training for a curious reason: he felt that she was too inflexible as an adolescent and took her duties too seriously. Anna herself has reported that as a child she was interested only in tales that "might be real." In this regard, she shared with many of the women of psychology a preference for adult literature and rejected the fanciful literature for children. Although none of the sources described where or when, Anna trained as an elementary school teacher. Her real education started in 1918, when she began to sit in on meetings of the Vienna Psychoanalytical Society.[10, 11]

> *"My closest companion will be my little daughter,*
> *who is developing very well at the moment."*

Anna began to attend meetings of the Society at a time when her father's fortunes and the fate of the movement were in doubt. He had already published many of his most controversial papers and books and was provoking bitter opposition and criticism from the medical establishment, academic psychology, and the public. Several of his early disciples and close colleagues had defected from the movement and Freud was seeking loyal supporters. One of the early contributions Anna made to psychoanalysis was to attract a large number of young, brilliant recruits, most of them interested in child analysis and most of them women.

Anna taught at an elementary school or a nursery school (the experts are not in agreement as to the nature of the school; it was probably a nursery school) for five years.[10, 14] She met many of the young continental intellectuals who were interested in child development. Many of them later attended Anna's *Kinderseminar* (Seminar on Children) in 1926 and 1927, including several of Montessori's group from Austria and Germany. Among the prominent recruits to the movement influenced by Anna were: Lili Peller, Erik Erikson (who was also one of Anna's analysands), Margaret Mahler, Berta Bornstein, and Dorothy Burlingham.[10, 11, 12]

In 1922, following an analysis by her father, Anna was accepted as a member of the Vienna Society after presenting a paper, "Beating Phantasies and Day Dreams." This presentation, delivered without notes, convinced the members that Freud's "little daughter" had indeed "developed very well."[10]

It was, of course, unusual for a father to psychoanalyze his daughter. The usual practice was for some other analyst to be engaged; often Melanie Klein (later Anna was also to serve this function), or Abraham, Ferenczi, or some other senior member. Roazen suggests Freud's departure from the rules may have been due to his wanting to teach Anna all he knew about analysis, his desire to have her obtain the best knowledge from the best source, or to his not trusting his colleagues to handle such an important analysis, or perhaps even to his fear that someone outside the family would become privy to private information.[10]

"The Most Outstanding Psychoanalyst of Her Day"

Anna Freud began her private practice of psychoanalysis in 1923. She specialized in child analysis, and her early techniques were influenced by her pedogogical training as she sought new analytic procedures. Modifications in treatment procedures were necessary, she wrote at this time, because, for example, the child being contemporaneously related to parenting figures is unable to effect a "true" transference in analysis. Anna Freud wrote of this era that the new interest in child analysis and prevention of mental disorders was part of the "widening scope of psychoanalysis."[13]

Anna wrote extensively during this period; in addition to the several books she has published, she has produced hundreds of articles, so that when the collected writings were published in 1973, they filled seven volumes.

She never married. She has been reported to have been "in love" with three members of Freud's circle: Siegfried Bernfeld, Hans Lampl, and Max Ettington.[10]

Her obviously very close relationship to her father increased the jealousy and rivalry with some of the other prominent women in the movement which resulted from professional competition. Rivals included Hermine von Hug-Hellmuth and Melanie Klein. It was following the former's murder in 1924 that Anna joined the Vienna Psychoanalytic Training Institute, which was headed by Helene Deutsch. In 1925, Anna who was the acknowledged leading child analyst in Vienna was made secretary of the Institute and chair of the Society, and held the latter position until 1938. Anna was later to become director of the Institute and in 1938, vice-president of the International Psychoanalytic Association.[14]

In 1937, Anna Freud's most important book, *The Ego and the Mechanisms of Defense*, was published. This work, which refined the contribution made by her father in a 1926 book (*Inhibitions, Symptoms, and Anxiety*), was the major intellectual impetus for the "ego psychology" development in psychoanalysis. It was not the first volume to suggest the concept of an active ego or to emphasize coping and mastery mechanisms, but it was the clearest and best-written book to give primary importance to ego functioning and the first of this kind published by an *orthodox* psychoanalyst.[12, 14, 15]

The Nazis invaded Austria in March 1938. It was not safe for the Freuds, who were Jewish, to remain in Vienna, but Sigmund who was almost eighty-two years old and suffering from terminal jaw cancer, was reluctant to leave. When Anna was interrogated by the Gestapo, Freud finally consented and with the help of Marie Bonaparte, the family made its way to England.[10, 11]

England: Years of Conflict and Fruition

The Freuds established their home at Maresfield Gardens in September 1938. Anna had been her father's confidante, nurse, and secretary for several years; she had represented him at Congresses and read his papers at meetings; now she would, in an unsentimental but sympathetic manner, look after the person and affairs of Sigmund Freud during the last years of his life.[11]

Anna joined the British Psychoanalytic Society shortly after arriving in England. This, of course, led to the battle between the Klein faction and the orthodox faction headed by Anna. It is interesting that in the compromise effected, which affirmed that there were (and are) irreconcilable differences between these groups, the differences in treatment procedures and training were emphasized.[10, 14, 15] Very soon the gulf between the Kleinians and the orthodox faction narrowed in terms of therapeutic procedure, especially as modifications in analysis were accepted by Anna Freud, whereas the theoretical differences are now seen as insurmountably divisive.

During World War II, with ego psychology making significant advances and her differences with the Kleinians still unresolved, Anna Freud turned her efforts to the results of a more pressing conflict, the war. In collaboration with Dorothy Burlingham, she organized and directed the Hampstead

War Nursery for homeless children, from 1940 to 1945. The two conducted the nursery also as a laboratory of child development.[11] The results of their observations and the story of the Nursery are described in *Young Children in War-time* (1942) and *Infants Without Families* (1943), written by Freud and Burlingham.

After the war, Anna and others founded and edited a highly prestigious series of annuals, *The Psychoanalytic Study of the Child*, which has done much to encourage the development of ego psychology as well as to feature important articles on psychoanalytic theory, therapy technique, and research.

Since 1952, Anna Freud has been director of the Hampstead Child-Therapy Course and Clinic, which she founded in 1947. This has become the largest center for training and research in psychoanalytic child psychology.[10, 11, 13, 14] In her own theory and teaching she has become increasingly cautious and conservative, somewhat removed from the developments of mainstream psychoanalytic thought.[11]

Anna Freud is today the most honored woman of psychology and the most respected psychoanalyst in the world. In a poll reported by Rogow in 1970, she was voted by psychiatrists and psychoanalysts to be the "outstanding living practitioner" of psychoanalysis.[10] She has received numerous honorary degrees: the LL.D. from Clark University (1950) and the University of Sheffield (1966), and the Sc.D. from Jefferson Medical College (1964), University of Chicago (1966), Yale University (1968), and Harvard University (1980).[16] Other awards include the Dolly Madison Award for Outstanding Service to Children (1965), the Grand Decoration of Honor in Gold of Austria (1975), and an honorary M.D. degree from the University of Vienna (1972).[11]

Her writing includes articles and books on psychoanalytic treatment procedures (gradually suggesting techniques that resemble those introduced by Melanie Klein). Not content with merely refining and elaborating ideas initiated by her father, she has broadened the range of interests, her own and that of psychoanalysis. She has contributed to observation and research methodology. Almost all her work has been safely orthodox and acceptable to the in-group. Her most important books include *The Ego and the Mechanisms of Defense* (1937), *Introduction to the Technique of Child Analysis* (1928), *Psychoanalytic Treatment of Children* (1946), *Normality and Pathology in Childhood* (1966), *Indications of Child Analysis* (1969), and *Research at the Hampstead Child Therapy Clinic* (1970).

MEDICINE'S WOMAN
Lauretta Bender (1897–   )

Lauretta Bender is best known for the invention and development of the Visual Motor Gestalt Test (1937), an extremely important instrument since it provides a device for screening neurological impairment through psychological deficits. In her long and successful career, however, Bender has made impressive contributions to many areas of medicine and psychology: pathology, clinical neurology, child psychiatry, developmental psychology, pediatric neurology, projective testing of children, Gestalt psychology, and neuropathology. In 1958, Bender was named "Medicine's Woman of the Year, New York State."

A prolific writer, especially during the early years of her career, Lauretta Bender became an acknowledged expert in each of the several areas to which she turned her attention. Even without her test (which is usually referred to as just "the Bender," a fact which sometimes startles psychiatric patients who, when told that for diagnosis a "Bender" has been ordered, have fantasies of their being made drunk or being contorted), Lauretta's work on childhood schizophrenia and neuropathology and tuberculosis would lead to recognition as one of history's most eminent psychologists and physicians.

Because most of her career was located in New York (she was senior psychiatrist at Bellevue Hospital from 1930 to 1956) and she was so identified with Paul Schilder, one of America's most eminent and well-loved psychiatrists, Lauretta Bender was an accepted member of the establishment and was associated with many of the women of psychology who were also based in New York. Among the women who were prominent in psychiatric circles in New York were Theodora Abel, Margaret Mahler, Phyllis Greenacre, Elaine Kinder, Stella Chess, Karen Machover, and Muriel Ivimey.

Lauretta Bender has received many awards and is a much-honored psychologist. Since the thirties, she has been respected as a researcher and clinician, but is not known for the development of a general theory or for philosophical writing. Like the other women included in this chapter, she has been a practical, problem-oriented psychologist, who has excelled by virtue of her outstanding competence. At eighty-three, she is today semiretired and living in Maryland.

Above: Theodora Mead Abel; *below*: Lauretta Bender

Above: Nancy Bayley; *below*: Margaret Schoenberger Mahler

Early Life

Lauretta was born on 9 August 1897, the only girl and youngest of four children born to John Oscar Bender and Katherine Irvine Bender in Butte, Montana. As a child Lauretta was considered mentally retarded, probably because of strephosymbolia (i.e., she tended to reverse letters in reading and writing). She repeated the first grade three times, but by the time she completed grammar school she was at the head of her class. Bender later became an authority on strephosymbolia.[17]

John Bender was an attorney and the family moved about considerably. Lauretta reports that she spent her childhood in Montana, Idaho, Washington, Oregon, and California.[18] She attended high school in Los Angeles—her favorite subject was biology—and she graduated in 1916. Her intention was to become a biological researcher.[17]

Lauretta Bender entered Leland Stanford University and completed two years there. She then transferred to the University of Chicago in 1918, her first move away from the far West. She received the B.S. (1922) and M.A. in pathology (1923) from Chicago.[18]

Neuropathology and Psychiatry

While at Chicago, Bender conducted research on "hemotological studies on experimental tuberculosis of the Guinea pig," which led to her first four scientific publications. When she transferred to the State University of Iowa Medical School, interested primarily in research, she entered as a third-year student and was appointed research and teaching assistant to Dr. Samuel T. Orton in neuropathology. She received the M.D. in 1926, and during the same year, published four papers dealing with experimentally-induced cancerous tumors and central nervous system lesions in laboratory animals. From these early days, for almost fifty years, Lauretta Bender would publish four to six papers, chapters, or books every year. Her estimate is that she has produced 275 "contributions to scientific literature."[18] Our tally suggests that this is a slight underestimate.

Bender took her first trip overseas when she was awarded a Laura Spelman Rockefeller travelling grant and spent the academic year 1926-27 at the University of Amsterdam. She studied neuropathology, physiology, and anatomy there with Dr. G. Van Rijnberk, B. Brower, and U. A. Kappers.[18] Research completed there on cerebellar control of the vocal organs was published by the Royal Academy of Science of Amsterdam. Bender was given six-month's credit toward her internship.[18]

Back in the United States, Bender completed her internship and six months of her residency in neurology at the Albert Merritt Billings Hospital, University of Chicago. She then completed a one-year residency in psychiatry at the Boston Psychopathic Hospital, 1928–29.[18]

Bender then accepted an appointment at the Henry Phipps Psychiatric Clinic, Johns Hopkins Hospital, to do research on schizophrenia under Adolf Meyer. She remained at this prestigious and extremely influential psychiatric training center for only one year (1929–30), but it was a momentous year for her. It was at Hopkins that Lauretta Bender met, worked with, and fell in love with Paul F. Schilder, M.D., Ph.D.

Schilder had been a psychoanalyst in Vienna, considered by many to have been the best psychiatrist to hold membership in the Vienna Psychoanalytic Society. He was perhaps too competent and independent to be merely a disciple of anyone, although he was friendly with and respected by Freud. Schilder was also a skillful neurologist and although he developed his own theories, they were less similar to orthodox psychoanalysis than to Adolf Meyer's organic-experiential form of psychiatry.

Paul Schilder, despite the fact that he lived in this country a relatively short time, was the personification of American psychiatry: erudite, eclectic, practical, competent in physical medicine and neurology, and involved in experimental research. Because of his breadth of interests and diverse professional skills, Schilder was also similar to the women included in this chapter. In fact, more than Adolf Meyer or any one else in American psychiatry, Paul Schilder resembled Lauretta Bender.

When Meanus Gregory at Bellevue Hospital was able to convince Schilder to accept a position at that hospital, it was considered a great coup for Gregory.[6] Schilder and Bender finished a study on schizophrenics' reaction to pain (an experimental study which was given almost immediate publication) and came to Bellevue together. Lauretta was a senior psychiatrist at Bellevue from 1930 to 1956.

According to Elaine Kinder, the sophisticated New York mental health professionals were scandalized by the affair between Bender and Schilder.[6] This informant suggests that Lauretta "tagged along" after Schilder, who was eleven years her senior and already married when they came to Bellevue. Kinder's description of Bender as a seductive siren is hard to envision, but it must be remembered that the former, a psychologist at Bellevue who suffered a highly-publicized psychotic break around the time that Bender arrived in New York was clearly jealous of Lauretta and still feels animosity toward her.[6] After Schilder's divorce, Paul and Lauretta married, on 27 November 1936; he was then fifty and she, thirty-nine.[18]

Lauretta wanted children and did not want to risk having them when she was too old. She and Paul had three children in the next four years. Despite possible scandals, childbirth three times, and Lauretta's one horrible personal tragedy, the decade 1936 to 1946 was an amazingly productive one for Bender. She wrote papers on a wide range of subjects and published the Bender Visual Motor Gestalt Test.[18]

Some of the articles Bender published during this productive period were co-authored by Paul, and a few were published posthumously: in 1940, leaving the hospital where he had visited Lauretta and their newly-born daughter Jane, Paul Schilder was killed by a car.[17]

This tragedy had a profound effect upon Bender. They have been very close and were friends and collaborators as well as marriage partners. Lauretta did not marry again until she was seventy, to Henry B. Parkes, Ph.D., and was widowed again five years later.[18] She told us that she edited five of Schilder's works to be published posthumously (again our tally shows that she underestimates by one—we count six), and when the N.Y. Society for Psychopathology and Psychotherapy became the "Schilder Society," Lauretta Bender served as president, from 1942 to 1944. Lauretta also went into psychoanalysis, as a patient of Sandor Lorand, in 1941-42.[18]

But most of all, Bender immersed herself in work. In addition to her work at Bellevue, where she was made head of the children's Psychiatric Division in 1934, she taught at New York University from 1930 to 1958, appointed an associate professor in 1941 and advanced to professor of clinical psychiatry in 1951. During this period Bender served as consultant to the Veteran's Administration, Irvington House, and the New Jersey State Neuropsychiatric Institute. She was the editor of *Nervous Child* from 1941 to 1948 and following an article on the role of comics in developing reading skills, was made editorial advisor to *Action Comics* (from 1945 to 1952).[18] A four-volume "Bellevue Studies" series was published in four consecutive years; they comprised Bender's four most important books.[19]

Lauretta Bender won more than seventeen awards and honors. She has been a member of twenty-four professional societies and offices held in these organizations include president of the American Psychopathological Association (1961-62), president of the Society of Biological Psychiatry (1961-62), president of the Schilder Society (1942-44), and vice-president of the American Society for Psychopathology of Expression (1969).[18]

Although Bender taught occasional courses and had clinical appointments to psychiatry departments of universities from 1956 to 1976, her primary positions during this period were principal research scientist, New York State Department of Mental Hygiene (1956-60); director of psychiatric research, Creedmoor State Hospital (1960-69); attending psychiatrist, New York State Psychiatric Institute (1969-74).[18]

Lauretta Bender has since moved to Maryland, one more elderly woman of psychology who prefers the sun belt. She remains professionally active. She has served as a clinical professor of psychiatry at the University of Maryland School of Medicine since 1975 and is a consultant to Children's Guild, Inc., the Chesapeake Center for Human Development, and Anne Arundel County Board of Education.[18]

Contributions of Bender

Lauretta Bender describes her work on the Visual Motor Gestalt Test as her most important contribution to psychology, an assessment shared by the majority opinion of her peers.[18] Her work on this test and her leadership role in the diagnosis, treatment and understanding of persons, particularly children, who are brain-injured, are Bender's primary claims to fame.

In our opinion, however, her work on childhood schizophrenia which began in the early thirties is of equal significance. Along with Leo Kanner, Margaret S. Mahler, and Paul Schilder, Lauretta Bender has been one of the leading authorities on schizophrenia in children and the germinal etiological theories offered almost fifty years ago by Bender and Schilder, who sought organic causes for this disorder, are currently under very serious consideration and are in agreement with considerable subsequent data.

In addition to her important contributions to understanding organic and neurological impairment and childhood schizophrenia, Bender has displayed expertise over a wide range of topics. She has written articles, for example, on her cancer research (in the early twenties); clinical studies of children who murder (1934 and 1940), who suicide (1937), who have imaginary playmates (1941), and who have been sexually molested and/or stimulated (1937); and numerous papers on diagnosis using the Goodenough Test, the Machover Test, puppets, and modeling clay. She has written a paper on side-walk drawings and games children play, one on comic book reading, on puppet shows, one on the children of Homes of Father Divine, one on "why children don't eat," and one on drawings of animals. In addition, she has written several articles on alcoholism, on encephalitis, and on aggression in children and dozens of articles on the diagnosis and treatment of brain-damaged and schizophrenic children. In short, Lauretta Bender has been a world-renowned expert in five or six different areas of psychology.

Lauretta Bender undoubtedly has been the preeminent woman psychiatrist of the second half of the twentieth century. There is some justification for naming her the preeminent living psychiatrist in the world, period.

YEARS AHEAD OF HER TIME
Charlotte Bertha Bühler (1893–1974)

Charlotte Bühler was one of the founders of humanistic psychology in this country, a movement which was to attract thousands of adherents during the sixties, particularly among the young. She was unlike the other women of psychology born during this decade because she was a founder of a movement with an organization, the American Association of Humanistic Psychology, and its own organ, the *Journal of Humanistic Psychology*. She was also a major theoretician; her altruistic orientation and rigorous research approach combining to produce far-reaching theories of child development and human behavior.

The formation of humanistic psychology was not Charlotte Bühler's first experience in attracting a wide circle of loyal followers who were engaged in productive psychological endeavors. She and her husband Karl Bühler had, in Vienna, for a dozen years starting in the late twenties, organized and headed the Institute of Psychology, perhaps next to Freud's Society across town, psychology's most illustrious "salon." The Bühlers's students and assistants included Egon Brunswik, Else Frenkel-Brunswik, Paul Lazarsfeld, Rudolf Ekstein, Marie Jahoda, Edith Weiskopf-Joelson, Lisolette Frankl, Lotte Schenk-Danziger, Fritz Redlich, Ernst Dichter, and Berthold Lowenfeld, practically a "who's who" of the most prominent and most brilliant researchers and leaders of child psychology and social psychology. Yet in this early movement, dedicated to excellence in applied research and clinical practice, Charlotte was overshadowed by her more prominent husband and her mentor. It was only after the death of Karl Bühler in 1963 that the complete value of Charlotte's accomplishments became fully recognized.

Patti Keith-Spiegel, one of Charlotte's biographers, has noted that for almost sixty years Charlotte Bühler was one of the most innovative and creative persons in psychology. In one respect she was like Franziska Baumgarten-Tramer, the Swiss industrial psychology pioneer, in that when Charlotte identified a research problem, she too would develop new instruments for her investigations; her tests especially show extreme originality and daring. As Keith-Spiegel noted, Charlotte Bühler's "ideas were always years ahead of her time."[20]

In one way Charlotte Bühler is very much like the other women included in this chpater; she was very versatile and recognized as competent in many psychological spheres. Schenk-Danziger, another of her biographers, considers her to have produced a lifework that is more "manifold and extensive" than that of any psychologist of the twentieth century.[21]

Life and Education

Charlotte Bertha Bühler was born in Berlin on 20 December 1893 to Herman Malachowski and Rose Kristeller Malachowski.[22] A serious and thoughtful girl, Charlotte, while still a teenager, decided to dedicate herself to the "understanding of human personality," at that time through literature and to the "problem and meaning of human life and the human being's role in the universe."[21] Although these somewhat pretentious and idealistic goals are not unusual in adolescents, they remained operative for Charlotte in her values and work throughout her lifetime. To begin, she decided to enter the university and major in philosophy and psychology.

Charlotte, as was the style at the time, took courses at several German universities: University of Freiburg (1913-14), University of Kiel (1914), and the University of Berlin (1914-15). At Berlin she studied under the great philosopher-psychologist Carl Stumpf, who recommended that she transfer to Munich where there were two prominent psychologists who held ideas very compatible with hers, Oswald Kulpe and Karl Bühler.[20, 22]

Charlotte was familiar with the work of Bühler, a man fourteen years her senior who had received both the M.D. and Ph.D. before he was twenty-five, and was impressed with his discovery of the "Aha!-experience."[21] In any event, Charlotte did not become disenchanted when she met Karl in person and the latter appears to have had an "Aha-experience" himself. After one year, master and student were married, in 1916, when Charlotte was only twenty-three. This marriage and their collaborative efforts did not end until Karl's death in 1963. They had two children together and were always closely associated in social and organizational situations, but each pursued separate and highly successful careers. In part Karl's greater eminence was a result of his having had a ten-year "head start" and also because his work was academic primarily and hers was in the applied and clinical areas.

Charlotte received her Ph.D. in 1918 and although the birth of Ingeborg and Rolf, her two children (who later produced six grandchildren), slowed down her career advancement slightly, marriage and personal obligations never slowed the flood of publications from Charlotte Bühler. Her first publication was an article "Das Marchen und die Phantasie des Kindes" ("Fairytales and the Imagination of Children") in 1918, which was later expanded and published as a book.[23]

Professional Career

In 1920 Charlotte accepted the position of instructor at the Technische Hochschule (technical high school) in Dresden, where Karl had in 1918 joined the faculty as a full professor. They stayed at Dresden for two more years and then returned to Vienna, he as a professor and she as an instructor and assistant director of the Institute of Psychology.[22, 23] In 1924-25 and 1935-36, Charlotte received fellowships from the Laura Spelman Rockefeller Fund, which allowed her to visit and study at Columbia University.[23]

Charlotte was advanced to the position of associate professor in 1929. She had already been made head of the department of child psychology and, as noted above, the Institute of Psychology had become a hotbed of productive research and provided close personal relationships as well. The Bühlers remained at Vienna until 1938 when they, like Freud and most of the psychoanalysts of Europe, were forced to emigrate because of the Nazi threat.[21, 22]

The Vienna period was an extremely productive one for Charlotte. She developed innovative methods for collecting data; the best known was the diary method. She published forty-five articles, some on applied areas and on the results of research studies, but some that were very theoretical and philosophical.[22] Charlotte Bühler also wrote a number of important books during this period, including *Childhood and Adolescence* (1928), *The First Year of Life* (1930), *From Birth to Maturity* (1935), *Testing Children's Development* (1935), *Practical Child Psychology* (1937), and *Child and Family* (1939).[20, 22, 23]

The Bühlers went to Norway and for two years, from 1938 to 1940, she was a professor at the University of Oslo. The next move was to the United States where Charlotte was appointed professor of psychology at St. Catherine's College, St. Paul, Minnesota, (1940-43) and then chief clinical psychologist at the Minneapolis General Hospital (1942-45).[22, 23]

In 1945, Charlotte moved to Los Angeles, where she lived and worked until her death in 1974. In California, she opened a private practice in

Beverly Hills and was accepted as one of the leading clinical psychologists in the area. She was especially recognized for her skill in the diagnostic assessment of children. Her World Test, which was published by the Psychological Corporation in 1941, was a widely-discussed, innovative approach to projective testing of children. Bühler was also appointed to the staff at Los Angeles County-University of Southern California General Hospital (1945-53) and made a clinical professor at the USC Medical School (1948-53).[20, 23]

By 1950, at age fifty-seven, Charlotte Bühler was recognized as the "Grand Dame" of psychology in California, by virtue of her more than thirty years of excellent work. She continued to write prolifically, her publications including the following books: *Developmental Psychology* (1938), *From Childhood to Old Age* (1938), *Diary for Mothers* (1939), *Childhood Problems and the Teacher* (1952), *Values in Psychotherapy* (1942), *Psychology for Contemporary Living* (1968), *The Way to Fulfillment* (1968), and *The Course of Human Life* (1968).[20, 23]

Bühler was not merely a skillful clinical psychologist, but the creator of several instruments for the collection of data, both for clinical assessment and for research. Among the tests she has developed are the World Test, the Picture World Tests, the Basic Rorschach Score, the Five-Task Tests, and the Life-Goal Questionnaire.[23]

In the sixties, at an age when many women might have enjoyed retirement or have been unable to recuperate from being widowed by the death of her beloved companion, Charlotte Bühler became one of the founders and the intellectual and titular leader of a new movement. Humanistic psychology, which seeks to fill a position contrasted with the "pessimistic" and biological determinism of psychoanalysis and the impersonal and molecular research of the behaviorists, tends to be idealistic and to emphasize the fulfillment of the individual's potentials. Charlotte Bühler served as president of the American Association of Humanistic Psychology in 1966 and 1967.[20]

Bühler had contact with behaviorism during her two years at Columbia and, of course, had considerable familiarity with psychoanalysis. Though not gaining prominence and acceptance until the sixties, her humanistic psychology is developed throughout her writings, beginning with an article published as early as 1933. In this article, "Der menschliche Lebenslauf als psychologisches Problem," ("Life History as a Psychological Problem") she had suggested that "life is . . . a series of phases of *self-determination* and conceived of as a process of self-determination to goals, with the end-goal of the experience of *fulfillment*."[21] Her consistent and overriding values of human potential, of positive growth, and of the possibility of expanding and changing reality rather than adjusting to it are to be observed in her repudiation of Freudian ideas in writings as early as 1951.[21]

Professional Contributions

Charlotte Bühler is best remembered as the inventor of the World Test and as a founder of the humanistic school of psychology, two important accomplishments, but she contributed much more to psychology. During her long professional career Charlotte was an obviously highly competent clincial psychologist and researcher, but perhaps her most long-lasting contributions will be her general theory of human development and her influence as a teacher.

Bühler's best-known research was done in Vienna, between 1928 and 1938. Her studies on the development of infants and children, which involved a score of collaborating students, were very similar to those conducted by Arnold Gesell and his associates at Yale and were performed at the same time at the Vienna Psychological Institute.[21]

In the fifty-six years of her career as a professional psychologist, Charlotte Bühler wrote over 133 articles and books. She was interested in a diversity of subjects and this is reflected in her articles. She wrote on the Rorschach Test, the problems of alcoholism, instinct theory, fairy tales, adolescent "crushes," gifted children, the German "national character," and Gestalt psychology.[23]

Until Bühler founded the school of humanistic psychology, she was known primarily only to her clinical psychologist colleagues in southern California. Charlotte Bühler became a legend and a beloved saint to a generation of young psychologists, most of whom had no idea of the scope covered by the long and illustrious career of this most versatile psychologist.

SPHINX: LIFE FULL OF CONFLICT
Clara Mabel Thompson (1893–1958)

In 1941, after Karen Horney made that memorable gesture by walking out of the meeting of the New York Psychoanalytic Institute, a gesture which signalled the beginning of all the subsequent "neo-Freudian" and "cultural" schools of psychoanalysis, her friend Clara Thompson spontaneously joined her. Appropriately enough, Clara began to sing a Baptist hymn as she and Horney led the now-famous parade through Manhattan.

Clara Thompson was Sphinx-like both in her unwillingness to reveal her true nature and in the intellectual demands she made on her students. Many were intimidated by Thompson and described her as domineering, overly ambitious, and neurotically "matriarchal," but her friends knew her as a shy, reserved, and warm person. She was embroiled in controversy and conflict most of her life.

Reared in a strictly religious, Rhode Island Baptist home, Clara Thompson risked incurring the emnity of and alienation from her family when she decided to abandon her ambition to become a medical missionary in favor of psychiatry. Although a leading American psychoanalyst for twenty years, acknowledged as a competent clinican and an outstanding training analyst, Thompson involved herself in many of the bitter and historic battles that rocked the psychoanalytic movement in this country during the forties. Throughout her life Clara Thompson formed close, intense relationships with a series of "father-figures," often involving herself with men who were the same age and no more competent or accomplished than she was. These relationships left Thompson frustrated and lonely because the men with whom she was most intimately connected so frequently died in the midst of their relationship to her. At times Thompson was frustrated also by relationships to men who were married or otherwise not appropriate.

Clara Thompson was a dissident and a rebel who fought against authority and orthodoxy of all kinds. She was particularly opposed to the "medieval-guard" nature of the psychoanalytic establishment and to its dogma. She aligned herself with the other psychoanalytic rebels, Horney, Sullivan, and Fromm. Ironically, Thompson, the antiestablishment radical, is best known today as an *historian* of psychoanalysis. Her book, *Psychoanalysis: Evolution and Development* (1950), is one of the classics in the field, a brilliant and concise history of the movement from a neo-Freudian perspective.

Despite her many important achievements, Clara Thompson never realized her full potential as a professional or as a person.

Brilliant Baptist Tomboy

Clara Mabel Thompson was born on 3 October 1893, in Providence, Rhode Island. Her father, Thomas F. Thompson, was a self-made man who worked himself up from salesman to the presidency of a pharmaceutical company, Blanding and Blanding (later McKesson and Robbins). Her mother, Clara Louise Medbery, was a very moralistic, religious woman, with a pronounced self-righteous bent. Clara preferred her father and was his obvious favorite.[24]

The Thompsons were an affluent family and Clara grew up in an extended family which included aunts, uncles, and grandparents in a more or less rural area. On the surface warm and serene and secure, the family was actually full of tension and friction—Thomas and his wife did not get along, partly because of her religious fanaticism.[24]

Clara was a tomboy who sided with her father in the family controversies and often came into conflict with her mother and Clara Medbery was not only strict, but she took on the role of disciplinarian in the family. Just after her twelfth birthday (in 1905), Clara was baptised. Her baptism was not exactly a joyful event; Clara had to be forced into the pool and later to be forced out.[24]

Clara was popular as a child and as a teenager (at least with girls; she was not interested in dating). Like many adolescents, she became very serious about her studies and her religion. At Classic High School, Providence, where she was "at the top of her class in every subject," she was active in basketball, was elected president of the Girls Debating Society, and engaged in hiking, swimming, and boating. She decided that she would become a medical missionary.[24, 25]

Loneliness and Liberation

Clara Thompson entered the Women's College of Brown University (later called Pembroke College) after graduating from high school in 1912. Following a pre-med course of studies, she continued to do brilliantly academically and was elected to Phi Beta Kappa her senior year. "Mabel," as her few college friends called her, was also a successful college debater. But her college years were not happy; she is described as lonely, frustrated, and "embittered" during this period.[24]

In addition to her science courses, Thompson took courses in philosophy, religion, and the social sciences. Her deeply-held religious beliefs were challenged; she began to discuss theological ideas with her friends and stopped attending church. Since she was living at home and commuting to school, her doubts and transgressions brought her into serious conflict with her mother.[24]

Thompson was becoming interested in psychology in her pre-med days. She spent one summer working as an aide at Danvers State Hospital in Massachusetts.[24] More significantly, she decided against becoming a missionary, a decision which resulted in her mother not speaking to her for twenty years.[25]

In her 1916 college yearbook, Clara Mabel Thompson in answer to questions put by the editors, reveals her emerging character and style:

Future Plans—"To murder people in the most refined way possible";

Chief Virtues—"supreme faith in myself";

Fads—"being pious and studious";

Ambitions—"to succeed in my fads and overcome my virtues."[24]

It has been widely held, particularly by Thompson's later detractors, that her excessive zeal and personal dedication to theories and professional organizations were a result of sexual frustration. She was once, in fact, accused of "mothering" an entire institute which she directed, because of the absence of "any romantic attachment."[24] This is an interesting theory; it is not, however, consistent with the facts. The truth is that Clara Thompson became involved in a number of very passionate, very intense love affairs (perhaps rivalling Margaret Mead, in this regard, in quantity, if not in quality). It would appear that Clara, who never married, was extremely discreet, since at the time when she was accused of "mothering" the William Alanson White Institute, she was "living in sin" with an Hungarian artist.[24]

Clara's first romance occurred when she was in college. There she met and became engaged to a man who was a major in the Army Medical Corps. His insistance that she give up her prospective career led to the end of the engagement.[24] As she did after most of her intense relationships, which resulted in a feeling of tragic loss for her, Thompson "carried the torch" for her college sweetheart for several years.[24]

Clara Thompson entered Johns Hopkins Medical School in 1916, her first experience in living away from home. Her decision to become a psychiatrist was influenced by Lucille Dooley, the psychologist–psychiatrist trained at Clark University, who was the first "real," (i.e., practicing) psychoanalyst Clara ever met. Dooley invited her to spend summers at St. Elizabeth's Hospital where Clara met two psychiatrists who were to become important to her later, William Alanson White and Joseph C. Thompson.[24]

Clara received the M.D. in 1920 and completed her psychiatric internship at Johns Hopkins, with an additional rotation at the New York Infirmary for Women and Children, by 1922. She was then accepted at the Phipps Clinic at Johns Hopkins for her residency.[24, 25]

Baltimore and Budapest

Clara Thompson completed her three-year residency at the Phipps Clinic, which was the personal fiefdom of Adolf Meyer, at that time the unchallenged leader of American psychiatry. Meyer was a theoretician and teacher and became a father substitute to Clara, who was, without question, his "favorite."[24, 25]

In 1923, Clara began her first analysis, with Joseph Thompson, but more significantly, she met Harry Stack Sullivan, a man with whom she maintained a close comraderie that lasted until his death in 1949.[24, 26] Harry Sullivan, however, was more than a friend, he became another "father" to Clara.

In 1924 Clara was given the honor of being put in charge of Meyer's own private patients and a year later became an instructor in psychiatry at the Medical School. Her analysis was not going well, however, perhaps because she was dating her analyst.[24] Clara decided to go to Europe to begin analysis with one of the "masters," a decision which was opposed by White and Meyer as well as Sullivan.[24, 26] Clara's insistence so enfuriated Meyer that he dismissed her from Phipps.[24]

Clara Thompson opened a private practice in Baltimore in 1925. Two years later, with Sullivan's encouragement, Thompson met Sandor Ferenczi, the disciple of Freud's who had had such a profound influence on Melanie Klein. Ferenczi was lecturing in New York and Sullivan was impressed with his new, more "flexible" approach to therapy (and possibly with the fact that Ferenczi, once Freud's favorite, was beginning to meet with formal disapproval because of his "innovations").[26] During the summers of 1928 and 1929 Clara Thompson studied in Budapest, under Ferenczi.[24]

Clara Thompson's one excursion outside psychoanalysis occurred during the academic year 1928–29, when she taught mental hygiene at the Institute of Euthenics at Vassar College.[24, 25]

Thompson's relationship to Sullivan was odd primarily because of the intensity of her hero-worship of him. She was only one year younger and much better trained than Sullivan—later, in fact, she analyzed *him*.[26] The only explanation for Clara's devotion, continuing loyalty, and idealization of Sullivan seems to lie in a need on her part for a father-figure whose favorite she can become.

In 1930 Thompson's natural father died. That same year Sullivan organized the Washington-Baltimore Psychoanalytic Society and Clara Thompson was elected its first president.[24] Thompson, however, left

Baltimore for Budapest to begin a two year analysis under Ferenczi, a decision that was urged on her by Sullivan and was to have an important influence on Clara's professional role as a dissident—and also provided another personal tragedy for her.

From 1931 to 1933 Clara enjoyed life in Budapest. In addition to her sessions with Ferenczi, she began an affair with an American businessman who was also an analysand of Ferenczi. This idyll and Clara's treatment were ended abruptly by Ferenczi's unexpected death.[24, 25, 26]

New York

When Clara returned to the United States, she moved to New York and in 1933 joined the New York Psychoanalytic Institute and Sullivan's Zodiac Club. (All the members had nicknames; she was called "cat," Karen Horney was "water buffalo").[24]

Clara also became Sullivan's analyst, providing him the only formal training he ever received. The analysis, which took three hundred hours, was terminated, according to Thompson, because "she had such awe of Sullivan's intellectual capacities that she could not effectively go on with it."[26]

Clara Thompson was a training analyst and lecturer at the New York Institute and was voted "best teacher" by the students at the Institute. Her friends included Fromm (who later performed Thompson's final analysis), Silverberg, Karen Horney (with whom she became increasingly close), and, of course, Sullivan. When in 1941 Horney was disqualified as a training analyst, Thompson was one of the five who resigned immediately from the Institute. She became a charter member of Horney's American Institute for Psychoanalysis and the American Association for the Advancement of Psychoanalysis, and served as the first vice-president of the latter.[24, 25]

Clara Thompson remained stubbornly opposed to arbitrary exclusiveness and, as usual, continued to reject any concessions on moral questions. When Horney showed signs of increasing dogmatism, and the disgraceful exclusion of its non-medical members was perpetrated by the American Institute for Psychoanalysis, Thompson, Fromm, Freida Fromm-Reichmann, and Janet and David Rioch joined Harry Stack Sullivan's William Alanson White Institute and the Washington School of Psychiatry.[24, 25]

In 1943 the battle over lay analysis led to Clara Thompson's decision to defect. This division was undoubtedly a serious blow to the Horneyan movement, which never achieved the influence and success it promised;

the defection, after all, deprived it of many of its most brilliant and prominent members.

The William Alanson White Foundation had been established in Washington in 1933, but Sullivan did not take control of the Institute and the School until the late thirties.[26] Clara might have joined her comrade earlier, but she was involved in an affair with a married Hungarian artist named Henry Major, with whom she had set up housekeeping in Provincetown (on Cape Cod, Massachusetts).[24] When a New York branch had been established, Thompson joined the Sullivan group.

The next few years were extremely satisfying for Thompson. The William Alanson White Institute flourished; her practice in Provincetown reflected her prominence as one of America's premier analysts; she had friends, security, comfort, and a lover. In 1946, Clara was made executive director of the New York Branch of the Washington School of Psychiatry.[24]

In 1948 Henry Major died, ending the ten-year romance. In 1949 Harry Stack Sullivan died of a brain hemorrhage. In 1950 Thompson's mother died and that year, partly because of what was referred to as Clara's dictatorial, over-zealous, domineering attitude (she was also called "bitchy"), the Washington School summarily closed the New York branch.[24]

Curiously, although Clara reacted strongly to this series of tragic losses, the last ten years of her life were the most successful and the most productive. Close to sixty years old, she organized a new society, the Academy of Psychoanalysis, which gave her a forum to express her ideas and an opportunity to teach. Her practice became very selective and even more successful. Finally, her writing, which had never been very prolific, increased considerably.

In 1956 Clara underwent cancer surgery and was noted to be suffering from depression. She died on 20 December 1958, at sixty-five years of age, of cirrhosis of the liver.[24]

Contributions

Clara Thompson wrote one of the most popular books on the history of psychoanalysis. In a sense, *Psychoanalysis: Evolution and Development* was her most enduring homage to her friend and mentor Harry Stack Sullivan. Published a year after his death, the book traces major theoretical ideas in a progression from Freud to Harry Stack Sullivan. The history is presented in a succinct, compact, easy-to-understand style.

Many of her articles deal with statements about the theoretical and therapeutic innovations of the "cultural" school or the William Alanson White Institute and particularly of the contributions of Sandor Ferenczi, Erich Fromm and, of course, Sullivan; in short, except for her contributions to the psychology of women, very few of her publications reveal the clarity of thought and originality that characterized her teaching.

Among the more important articles published by Thompson were contributions to the understanding of transference and the role of the therapist and a contribution concerning "identification with the enemy" as well as a 1931 paper on resistance to psychoanalytic uncovering due to the patient's playing the role of "dutiful child."

Fully one third of Thompson's published articles deal with the psychology of women. She was, before she died, planning to write a book on feminine psychology (her only other book, which she co-edited, was *An Outline of Psychoanalysis*, published in 1955). In this area, her most important contributions were "The Role of Women in This Culture" (1941), "Cultural Pressures in the Psychology of Women" (1942), "Penis Envy in Women" (1943), "Cultural Complications in the Sexual Life of Women" (1950), and "Toward a Psychology of Women" (1953). Since Thompson shared many of the theoretical ideas and a sociocultural orientation with Karen Horney, it is not surprising that Thompson's papers on femininity are markedly similar to Horney's.

Like Horney, Thompson emphasized the role of experiences that a girl has, shaped by her culture, in determining her personality as a woman. She was, however, both more biologically and more socially-oriented than Horney. She did not ignore biological-difference factors in her paper and she tried to relate personality development to changes in contemporary society and its institutions. Thompson's papers are, however, not as daring and do not provide the sweeping generalizations that Horney's radical and comprehensive theory does. Thompson wrote cautiously and tried to stick to available data and her work therefore seems somewhat trivial and dated—it lacks the universality that a major theoretical contribution requires.

Summary

Clara Thompson was a brilliant analyst and teacher and a leading figure of psychoanalysis in America in the forties. Her life story reveals an important segment of the history of psychoanalysis since she was actively engaged in all the battles of this stormy era.

Why did she fail to realize her promise and potential? We think it is because she needed men too much. Compulsively reliving the fantasy of the "favorite" child of a father-figure, casting herself in this role opposite Meyer, Ferenczi, and Sullivan, Thompson never established herself as an autonomous, completely independent thinker. She settled for comfort, security, and acceptence and was a most competent practitioner, but her personal needs apparently prevented her from becoming a more important figure in psychology.

MOTHER OF BEHAVIOR THERAPY
Mary Cover Jones (1896-   )

While I spent considerable time as consultant and helped plan the work, Mrs. Mary Cover Jones conducted all of the experiments and wrote up all of the results.

—J. B. Watson

In 1924 Mary Cover Jones published an article that revolutionized clinical psychology. Inspired by Watson, who was then the leader of the behaviorist movement, she demonstrated that a fear or phobia could be eliminated through the use of conditioning principles.[27] This study, which was not considered adequate for the requirements of dissertational research at Columbia, can be said to have initiated the innovation in psychological therapy that is now referred to as behavior modification.

How fortuitous some events are when reflected upon later. Who could have suspected that an innocent change of plans, the decision to attend a lecture instead of the theater, would so influence a young woman as to point the direction of her professional life? When Mary Cover let a friend pursuade her to attend that lecture given by John B. Watson, on a spring evening during her senior year at Vassar, it set the stage for the later development of one of America's most widely used forms of treatment. For the year was 1919 and Watson lectured on a study which he and Rosalie Raynor had recently completed on "conditioning" the fear of furry objects with a little boy named Albert. This lecture was the event which inspired the pioneering work in behavior theory and therapy which would occupy a major part of Mary Cover Jones's professional career.[28]

Never one to demand star billing, Jones has encouraged and supported colleagues and students throughout her career and has often shared authorship; a frequent collaborator was her husband, the late Harold E. Jones. Mary Cover Jones has been a practicing psychologist for sixty-one years and is now, at age eighty-four, serving as a consultant for Intergenerational

Studies at the University of California at Berkeley, where she has been professor emeritus for twenty years. Jones still teaches adolescent and child psychology in University of California extension courses and she is now actively involved in a research project on the personality correlates associated with alcoholism and gerontology.[29]

Mary Cover Jones is best known for her early study on the de-conditioning of fear (the case of Peter) and her studies of early- and late-maturing boys and girls. Specialists in child development praise her work in that area through the Berkeley longitudinal studies, although the Institute of Human Development has, in its fifty-two years of research, now expanded to include the study of the full life cycle. Jones herself is a recognized expert today in the field of gerontology.

Mary Cover Jones has made at least one momentous contribution to psychology of historical significance, her experiment on "de-conditioning" fear. She has also published six books and over seventy-five journal articles and chapters in books. Like the other women of psychology, Mary Cover Jones has not received the recognition her achievements deserve.

In a recent biography of Jones[29] it is noted that a study by Kaess and Bousefield listed Mary Cover Jones as "one of the twenty-six most often cited authors in introductory textbooks."[30] More recent research, however, does not at all agree with the conclusion that due recognition is being paid this extraordinary women. Mary Cover Jones does not appear on any of the lists of most cited references in textbooks or journal articles based upon surveys conducted during the seventies (cf. Chapter 1 in Volume 1 of this book). Interestingly, an informal survey of introductory psychology textbooks with a 1980 publication date which we conducted reveals that Mary Cover Jones is cited in twenty percent of the most recent books and that in every case it was a reference to her work with Paul Mussen on early- and late-maturing boys. Nowhere is her pioneer work in behavior therapy mentioned at all.

Development of a Behaviorist

Mary Cover was born on 1 September 1896, in Johnstown, Pennsylvania, a small city seventy miles east of Pittsburgh which was made famous by the disastrous Johnstown Flood of 1889. The town is a major bituminous coal mining center with a steel plant built during the 1850s.[31] Mary grew up in the city and graduated from Johnstown High School during its reconstruction period (two thousand persons perished in the flood). The city itself is highly industrialized, but it is surrounded by farms and by the Allegheny Mountains. Mary Cover left town to go to college in 1915, long before the next tragic flood in 1936. (Johnstown built a flood-control system in 1937.)

Mary Cover matriculated at Vassar at the time when Edna St. Vincent Millay, reluctant fellow student, was referring to the school as a "hell-hole" and Poughkeepsie as having an "Alice-in-Wonderland" atmosphere.[32] Students were required to take both Greek and Latin to graduate. Mary Cover failed freshman Latin, and, because of a "C" in a previous laboratory course, she was denied entrance into Margaret Floy Washburn's psychology seminar.[29] Nonetheless, she later considered Margaret Washburn to be a mentor.[31]

Mary Cover made friends with Rosalie Raynor, a classmate at Vassar. Feminism was fervent on college campuses; women were close to "getting the vote"; and it was the dawn of the Jazz Age and the Roaring Twenties. The first recorded student rebellion at a woman's college occurred in 1917, when Vassar students protested the administration's refusal to allow Millay to attend her own graduation ceremony.[32] Parietal restrictions were loosened somewhat and students at Vassar were allowed to leave campus unsupervised and go to New York City. If the restrictions had not been removed, Mary would not have been able to go to New York City to hear Watson lecture and might not have gone on to found behavior therapy. Mary Cover received her A.B. from Vassar.

In 1919 Mary entered Columbia University to become a psychologist, interested in infant development. This was the year that Watson's *Psychology from the Standpoint of a Behaviorist* was published and caused a stir at Columbia. Mary was conducting research on infant behavior and taking a history course off-campus at the New School for Social Research. A fellow Columbia graduate student, two years her senior, was also taking that course and he struck up a friendship. He was impressed that another psychology student was, like himself, taking a course in history. She was impressed that he treated her as an equal and lacked the chauvinistic chivalry usual for the day.[29]

Mary Cover married Harold Ellis Jones in 1920 in a ceremony conducted by Norman Thomas, the Socialist leader. The marriage lasted until 1960 when Harold died unexpectedly on a trip they were starting in Paris, partly to celebrate their respective retirements.[33] They had two daughters, Barbara, 1922, and Lesley, 1925. Mary Jones now has six grandchildren and four great-grandchildren.[31]

Harold Jones was planning a career in experimental psychology and was considered Woodworth's "prize pupil." It was Mary and her work with Peter (and also Watson's 1919 book) that got Harold interested in developmental psychology.[28, 33] Throughout their marriage Harold's career was given top priority and he became a far more prominent and productive psychologist than she. Mary, especially early in her career, when family obligations occupied her time and energy, played "second fiddle" and achieved far less than she might have. Interestingly one of the persons she was to meet at Columbia was Christine Ladd-Franklin, a woman whose history is most like her own—for both, marriage was a limiting factor in their careers.[31]

1920 was a momentous year. Women got the vote; Mary Cover got her M.A. and Harold and a job administering psychological tests at New York City's Children's Hospital. And John B. Watson got divorced and fired. The last event involved a huge public scandal and resulted in Watson's being excluded thenceforth from academia and, in fact, professional psychology altogether. Rosalie Raynor, who attained notoriety as the "other woman," married Watson shortly after the divorce. This bit of excitement had one benefit for Mary—her old friend Rosalie introduced her to Watson and he and Harold encouraged Mary to treat Peter for his phobia.[28]

Watson checked on the progress of the treatment program and various other aspects of the research every Saturday afternoon. Mary has noted that she "never assumed a first-name basis in talking of John B. Watson. Our relationship was more formal than not . . . I have never lost the feeling of awe that I had for Watson, the scientific innovator." She states further that the relationship always maintained a student-teacher nature, despite the fact that Watson was then the husband of her friend. What is most remarkable in Jones's statements concerning her respect and awe for Watson is that she made them fifty years later.[31]

Psychologist-Wife

While completing the courses for her Ph.D., Mary Cover Jones taught emotionally disturbed children in New York City public schools (from 1920 to 1921), lectured at Women's Medical College, Philadelphia (from 1921 to 1922), resumed her career as a mental tester with the Commonwealth Fund Preschool Survey (from 1921 to 1923). Mary Cover Jones's first publication, in 1921, was a study comparing three group intelligence tests administered to NYC children.[31] In 1923, Harold received his Ph.D. and joined the faculty of Columbia; Mary joined the staff at Columbia's Institute of Child Welfare as a research associate, her salary provided by research grants.[33] Mary remained with the Institute until 1927; her research on "de-conditioning" fear was conducted on her own time.

Because of the publication lag, Rosalie and John Watson's article about Albert, who was the subject in the original study which had "incited" Mary in 1919, was not published until 1921.[34] The follow-up study, on Mary's treatment of Peter, was described in Watson's *Behaviorism*—the book which made him world-famous—written for the mass audience and published in 1924.[27] The study of Peter was also published as an article by Mary Cover Jones that same year. In fact, most of Mary's publications for the following five years dealt with Peter and/or how fears are learned and can be unlearned. Jones had become an expert on children's fears. But this study did not satisfy the faculty at Columbia, where her doctoral committee rejected the deconditioning study, calling it unsuitable "because of the limited number of cases."[28]

Mary Cover Jones received her Ph.D. in 1926. She was then the mother of two small children and although she was determined to have a career as well as manage the household, it is clear that her relationship to Harold was paramount in her mind. Mary frequently made decisions which obviously "sacrificed" her career. We most definitely agree with Deana Logan, Mary Cover Jones's biographer, that her marriage hindered her career advancement.[29]

Some of the factors impeding progress in her career were self-imposed; for example, Mary Cover Jones "never worked full-time while her daughters were at home."[29] Some of the impediments were institutional, for example, rules against "nepotism." Mary Cover Jones could attain only low-status jobs at California because Harold was a professor there; she was there for twenty-five years before she was offered an *assistant* professorship, at age fifty-six, and that in the education department, which had lower status than psychology.[31, 33]

But the event that occurred next in the chronology, in 1927, when Mary Cover Jones left New York where she had lived for twelve years to live three thousand miles away at Berkeley, California, had less to do with her own conditioning, free-choice, or social and institutional factors, than it did to another source of gender discrimination in psychology, personal connection and relationship. Mary and Harold decided to move to California to further his career (it was to be years before Mary was to land a "real" job), and the highly advantageous position Harold was offered came about because of a friendship he had developed.

Harold Jones had a degree in experimental psychology and had taught the low-level, undergraduate survey courses that new psychology faculty members are usually stuck with. He had little direct experience with clinical research or developmental psychology. He had published, by then, nothing of real originality or merit; his most memorable articles for years were collaborative efforts with Mary on *her* research. Yet Harold had gotten to know the man who directed the Laura Spelman Rocke-feller Fund, which was then arranging the establishment of child develop-ment research centers throughout the country (interestingly, Harold met Lawrence Frank because of Mary's research) and *Harold*, not Mary, was invited to become the director of the Institute for Child Welfare at Berke-ley and *he* was offered a position as assistant professor on the faculty.[33] Although it is widely believed that Mary was offered a position at the Institute as well,[29, 33] her position as research associate was "casual," often without salary, and omitted from the curriculum vitae she kindly sent us (Mary does not feel her work at the Institute was real employment until 1949).[31]

Berkeley

Mary Cover Jones has lived in Berkeley, California, for fifty-three years, since 1927 (she almost relocated to a retirement community in Santa Barbara in 1976, but was bored after seven months). The topics she covered as a research psychologist in developmental psychology, which was primarily achieved at Harold's Institute, peculiarly enough, seems to follow the life cycle exactly. At Columbia Mary Cover Jones studied infant development; her first research at Berkeley was conducted at the nursery school she organized (now named the "Harold E. Jones Child Develop-ment Center"); she was tangentially involved with the child studies of the Institute of Human Development (Harold's "Institute for Child Welfare" changed its name when it expanded, via longitudinal studies, to cover older age groups); and in 1932 she and Harold organized the Institute's adolescent study, usually called the Oakland Growth Study. Mary Jones continues to "follow-up" the subjects in this last study—this is a real longi-tudinal study; they provided the data for her research on adulthood, alcoholism and gerontology.[28]

Of all her developmental psychological work, Jones's best-known articles deal with early- and late-maturing adolescents. The two often-cited papers showed a relationship between physical measurements of maturation, for example, bone age via X-ray of the wrist, and self-concept, confidence, and popularity. The better-known paper is that for boys (Mussen and Jones, 1957), probably because the results—early-maturing boys have more positive self-attitudes—are clearer than in the girls' study (Jones and Mussen, 1958). Both studies have been criticized, however, for lack of generalizability of results, especially those of the study of girls (incidentally, among the girls, the *late*-maturing subjects showed a slight tendency to be more confident and popular).[29]

For many years, Mary Cover Jones conducted respectable, sometimes important, research studies while associated with the Berkeley Institute. She usually worked part-time and was either paid out of grant funds or, after 1948, worked without salary.[31] During these years, when Harold's career was being nurtured and he became a full professor at the University, Mary also did a lot of volunteer work and public service work or took marginal jobs, such as teaching in adult education (California's euphemism for "night school") or in the University of California Extension Division (glorified night school).

In 1952 Mary Cover Jones was made an assistant professor in the department of education at the University of California at Berkeley. In 1955 she was advanced to associate professor and for one year (1959–1960) she was a full professor.[31] This appointment lasted only that academic year because Harold was, at sixty-five, retiring and Mary did also. They were both made emeritus and then left for an extended vacation abroad. Four days after arriving in Paris, on 7 June 1960, Harold Jones died of a heart attack.[33]

Mary was crushed by Harold's death. Her report of her reaction is similar to that of Helene Deutsch's over the loss of Felix: when Harold died, she lost a lover, friend, and colleague all at once.[29] She was able to cope with her grief in a mature and constructive manner; she came out of retirement.

In 1961 Mary joined her old friend Nevitt Sanford who had established the Institute for the Study of Human Problems at Stanford University. She began the long-range studies of the etiology of alcoholism during this four-year tenure at Stanford, using the subjects from the Oakland Growth Study. Articles concerning her findings have only recently been published and she continues to write and to work.[29]

Although many of her recent publications have been retrospectives or histories and Mary Cover Jones is frequently asked to address groups on topics such as Watson's theories and her own pioneering work on behavior therapy, topics befitting a woman over eighty, she continues to produce new articles and other publications on research and on her theoretical ideas related to alcoholism and gerontology. Mary Cover Jones may be emeritus, but she has not retired yet. Since 1969, she has been a consultant (unpaid) to the Intergenerational Studies at the Institute of Human Development, University of California at Berkeley.[31]

In 1960 Mary Cover Jones was president of Division 7, Developmental Psychology, American Psychological Association, and in 1968 she was honored with the G. Stanley Hall Award by Division 7. Because she lived for her husband and was so dedicated to (long-range) research and her family, it is no wonder that Mary has not received more accolades and honors. She did win one more award, however, and the citation of the 1969 honor from the Institute of Human Development, the award commemorating the fortieth anniversary of the Institute, is interesting. Mary Cover Jones was described as

1) a charming hostess,
2) her husband's helpmate, and
3) a distinguished scientist.[29]

THE FUNCTIONS OF WOMEN
Therese Friedman Benedek (1892-1977)

Therese Benedek, an Hungarian who made her major contributions to psychology while on the staff of the Chicago Institute of Psychoanalysis (from 1936 to 1970), is another woman who fits the generalizations made about the women born during this decade. She is versatile and competent, accepted by her peers, and contributed to the science of human behavior throughout a very long professional career. She was considered expert in several specialized areas—psychosomatic medicine, psychosexual development of women, sexual dysfunction, family dynamics, and depresssion—but she was not responsible for a general, comprehensive theory and, although she played a leadership role late in her career, was never truly *the* leader of any professional group or movement.

We sometimes facetiously remember her as the Therese without the "a" and the Benedek without the "c," always the person in a bibliography where you anticipate a typographical error: like Theodora M. Abel and Lauretta Bender and many of the women included in this chapter, Benedek appears in numerous bibliographies. She did not publish much; she was primarily a practicing psychoanalyst and a training analyst, but in each special area where she turned her interest, Benedek made at least one important contribution which is frequently cited as a reference in subsequent investigations on the topic.

Therese Benedek is famous for her work in the psychology of women, especially on the psychological and physiological factors of the sexual cycle, and her book, *Psychosexual Functions in Women*, 1952, based upon over fifteen years of study and observation, is the unchallenged classic in the field.

After fleeing Germany in 1936, Benedek came to Chicago and for twenty years worked under Franz Alexander at his Institute for Psychoanalysis. She shared Alexander's interest in psychosomatic medicine and became with him and Helen Flanders Dunbar one of the pioneers of this movement during the forties, although she remained the least known of the three. Therese Benedek was both therapist and scientist, one of the few psychoanalysts to be accepted into the New York Academy of Science.

Life

Therese was born in Eger, Hungary, on 8 November 1892. Eger was a small city at the foot of the Carpathian Mountains, fifty miles from Budapest. Her parents were Ignatius Friedmann and Charlotte Link Friedmann. Therese attended the Humanistic Gymnasium in Budapest, receiving the A.B. in 1911.[35]

She received the M.D. from the University of Budapest in 1916 and completed her internship at the Budapest City General Hospital (from 1916 to 1917) and a residency in pediatrics at the Epidemic Hospital in that city (from 1917 to 1918).[35, 36] She accepted a position as instructor at the Clinic for Pediatrics in Pozsony, Hungary (from 1918 to 1919), but this was terminated when she married Tibor Benedek on 18 May 1919, and the family moved to Germany.[35]

While in Germany, Therese completed a second residency, in psychiatry, at the psychiatric clinic of the University of Leipzig (from 1920 to 1925). She then was appointed training analyst at the German Psychoanalytic Society and was elected Chairman of the Psychoanalytic Study Group at Leipzig, and held both positions from 1925 to 1932. Therese and Tibor had two children, Thomas and Judy. Their birth caused a delay in her career as a prominent psychiatrist in Germany; the rise in power of the Nazis ended it.[35]

Chicago

Therese Benedek was one of the early refugees to find sanctuary in the United States. She accepted a position at the Chicago Institute where only two years before Karen Horney had resigned, unable to reconcile her differences with Alexander. But Therese was no rebel; her contributions to psychoanalytic theory, unlike those of Horney, were elaborations and refinement well within limits acceptable to the orthodoxy. Her research was especially acceptable, both to Alexander, who shared an interest in psychosomatics, and to the most traditional analysts, for her success in establishing relationships between biological variables and psychological etiological variables was consistent with a life-long interest of Freud himself.

Benedek became a supervising analyst and member of the research staff at Chicago and remained there for thirty-four years, including fourteen years after Alexander had gone to California. In 1969, she retired from the Institute and began a full-time private practice; she was then seventy-seven years old. Her collected works were published in 1973.[36]

Therese Benedek maintained her practice in Chicago until her death in 1977. In her later years she directed her efforts to formalizing psychoanalytic education; dynamics of family life and family therapy; and depression, the diagnostic category of greatest relevance to our times. Much of Benedek's best work was completed after her seventieth birthday.[36]

Work and Significance

Benedek wrote five important books and numerous articles and chapters in anthologies. Many of her most significant papers were published in 1973 as *Psychoanalytic Investigations: Selected Papers*. Her published books were *Insight and Personality Adjustment* (in 1946); *Psychosexual Functions in Women* (in 1952); (with J. Fleming) *Psychoanalytic Education* (in 1966); (with E. J. Anthony) *Parenthood: Its Psychology and Psychopathology* (in 1970); and (with E. J. Anthony) *Depression and Human Existence* (in 1975).

Benedek was an important teacher at an important Psychoanalytic Institute. Her main claim to fame, however, is her work on the reproductive cycle of women. Her research in this area, some of it now almost forty years old, remains valid and is a major contribution to the understanding of sexual function and dysfunction in women. With the greater interest being shown nowadays in the psychology of women, it is likely that Benedek's accomplishments in this area, indeed her full lifework, will become better known.

DEVELOPMENTAL PSYCHOLOGY'S DISTINGUISHED SCIENTIST
Nancy Bayley (1899-   )

For the enterprise, pertinacity, and insight with which she has studied human growth over long segments of the life cycle. . . . Her studies have enriched psychology with enduring contributions to

the measurement and meaning of intelligence, and she traced
important strands in the skein of factors involved in psychological
development. . . .

Citation, D.S.C. Award
American Psychological Association, 1966

In 1956, the American Psychological Association inaugurated an annual
award to three members "who have made distinguished theoretical or
empirical contributions to scientific psychology." In the first decade,
none of the Distinguished Scientific Contribution Award laureates was a
woman. Among the first thirty recipients of the most prestigious honor
this august professional organization has to bestow were the *husbands* of
Janet Taylor Spence, Phyllis Greenacre, Margaret Harlow, Eleanor J.
Gibson, Louise Barker, Ada G. Allport, Ruth B. Guilford, and Grace
Heider. But none of these women of psychology had been considered for
this signal honor, even when they had been major collaborators with their
husbands. In 1966, Nancy Bayley, who for more than forty years has been
associated with the Institute of Human Development at California, became
the first woman to be awarded the Distinguished Scientific Contribution
Award.[37, 38]

When Harold E. Jones assumed the directorship of the Institute of
Child Welfare in 1928, he hired Nancy Bayley to head a study of more
than sixty infants, later referred to as the Berkeley Growth Study. She was
responsible for developing instruments for the measurement of the physical and mental development of these infants and is most famous today for
observations of infants and young children and for the instruments she
created (the "Bayley Scales"). In 1938, Bayley was cited by the American
Educational Research Association after publishing the monograph, "Mental Growth During the First Three Years: A Developmental Study of
Sixty-one Children by Repeated Tests" (1933), which was called "an
outstanding contribution to educational research."[39] The tables which
accompanied Bayley's 1933 monograph have been reproduced regularly in
all textbooks which discuss infant development.

Life and Career

Nancy Bayley, daughter of Frederick W. Bayley and Prudence Cooper
Bayley, was born in The Dalles, Oregon, on 18 September 1899. She
attended public schools in Oregon and graduated from the University of
Washington with the B.S. in 1922. She also received the M.S. from Washington, in 1924.[39]

She then entered the State University of Iowa, apparently planning to prepare for a career as a psychology professor. She was teaching assistant at Iowa and received her Ph.D. in 1926, with a study of performance tests administered to three-, four-, and five-year-old children. She then moved on to the University of Wyoming, where the chair of the department was June Etta Downey, and for two years was an instructor of psychology.[38, 39]

As noted above, Nancy Bayley took a position at the Institute of Child Welfare, with the title of research associate, in 1928. She received immediate recognition for her studies of infants and young children and a majority of her papers and books throughout deal with the observations of these original subjects, since the Institute organized its research efforts into a series of longitudinal studies (i.e., subjects were assessed repeatedly over a long period of time—in Bayley's studies for close to forty years).[29, 33]

On 27 April 1929, Nancy married John R. Reid, who is usually identified as a philosopher and a professor, who sometimes taught in the psychiatric departments of medical schools.[39a] This has been a warm, campanionate, although childless, marriage of fifty-one years. She retained her maiden name professionally.[39, 39a]

Although Bayley's career is intimately tied to her research at California—she was at the Institute from 1928 to 1954 and returned to the Institute of Human Development (its new name) in 1964, she also taught courses, usually part-time, during summer session, or on a temporary appointment, at various schools during her professional life. These schools include Stanford, University of California. Stanford Medical School, the University of Maryland, and the University of Hawaii.[37, 38]

In 1954, Nancy Bayley went to Bethesda, Maryland, to assume the duties of chief of the section on Child Development, Laboratory of Psychology, National Institute of Mental Health. She worked in this capacity until 1964, with a year off in 1961 to return to the Institute of Human Development and administer the Harold E. Jones Child Study Center.[37]

Nancy Bayley returned to the Institute of Human Development in 1964 as a research psychologist. She was now able to complete the study of her "infants," who were now mature adults. She collected data until 1968, the year she was made Emerita Research Psychologist by the Institute. These follow-up observations led to a series of articles, including one entire issue (1964, No. 97) of the *Monographs of the Society for Research in Child Development*. During this period, from 1964 to 1968,

Bayley was in great demand as a research consultant, including four years as a consultant with the Sonoma (California) State Hospital.

Bayley, who is now retired and living in Carmel, California, has received much honor, well-deserved, for her work in child development and her longitudinal studies, but her research interests extended into several other related areas, as well. She developed and refined techniques for ascertaining skeletal age (physical maturity) through X-rays; conducted research on body build changes in adolescence; and studied crying and rectal temperatures of infants, maternal behavior, and the development of intelligence. Throughout her career she developed instruments to measure basic variables relevant to human development and studied correlations of these variables with adult personality traits; however she never originated a major theory of development.

Nancy Bayley published four books and several papers and monographs. Like so many of the women of psychology who were born during this decade, Bayley was an administrator of a limited project and was a successful leader within limited responsibility—but Harold Jones was the boss of the Institute.

Summary

Nancy Bayley's professional career resembles that of her friend and colleague, Mary Cover Jones. Bayley's prominence and recognition were even more related to the progress of the Institute at California than were Jones's; though her work was more restricted she was even more successful at it. Bayley did not have the encumberances of a "full-time" marriage, rules against nepotism, or a husband who was illustrious in her field.

Bayley was given the full opportunity to gain eminence in a restricted area of psychology and she made the most of it. She was affiliated with the Institute and the University of California when both were at the height of their power and prestige. Like both Harold and Mary Jones, Bayley was a power in the Western Psychological Association (WPA) and Division 7 of the American Psychological Association. She was president of WPA in 1953-54 and of Division 7 in 1953-54. In addition, Nancy Bayley was also president of Division 20 (Maturity and Old Age) in 1951-58 and of the Society for Research in Child Development, 1961-63.[37, 39]

In 1971, Division 7 conferred upon Bayley the G. Stanley Hall Award for her contributions to the field of child development. This award, the last Bayley has received, was named for the founder of American psychology who was a leading figure in child psychology; it had been conferred, in 1968, upon Mary Cover Jones.

INVESTIGATOR OF THE INDIVIDUATION PROCESS
Margaret Shoenberger Mahler (1897-   )

Best known for her pioneer work on childhood schizophrenia, Margaret Mahler has been a leading child analyst for more than fifty years. She has been a world-renowned authority on a form of psychosis which she "discovered" and named symbiotic psychosis, failure in the individuation process. Mahler's research and clinical observations of severely disturbed children led to significant contributions to the understanding, diagnosis, and treatment of psychotic children; many would call it the best and most original work ever done in this area.

Despite the excellence of her work on childhood psychosis, Mahler would prefer to be remembered as a general theoretician in the area of child psychology, since her later work, an extension of her work with children with severe ego defects, did much to elucidate the individuation process in all children.[40]

A precocious interest and an independent investigation of psychoanalysis, thought and practice, from one more Hungarian woman trained in Germany (cf. Melanie Klein and Thereses Benedek), led to the development of one of the most innovative and creative theoreticians in the history of psychoanalysis.[41] Mahler's work is seen as the epitome of the process of interaction of direct observation and theory building, which served to broaden psychoanalysis into a general psychology.[41]

Life and Career

Margaret Schoenberger was born on 10 May 1897, in Sopron (Oedenburg), Hungary, a small town on the border with Austria, west of Budapest and forty miles from Vienna. Her father was the chief medical officer of the County of Oedenburg, a general practitioner.[40]

Since there was no high school for women in the region, Margaret attended a gymnasium in Budapest. There she made friends with "young people associated with Sandor Ferenczi" and became acquainted with psychoanalysis.[40] Although she attended University of Budapest, her medical training and much of her pre-medical education took place in Germany, since "political circumstances" prevented her from completing her education in Hungary.[40] She attended the Universities of Munich, Heidelberg, and Jena, and received the M.D., magna cum laude, from the last in 1922.[40, 41]

Because she could not obtain a medical license in Germany and because she "all along planned to pursue training in psychoanalysis at its main fountainhead in Vienna," Margaret moved to Vienna, where her father had also received his medical training, and obtained a second M.D. and her license to practice.[40]

After completing her degree at Vienna (1923), she did her internship and residency in pediatrics at the University Children's Clinic at the Pediatric Hospital of von Pirquet. At the same time, she began training at the Vienna Psychoanalytic Institute, of which Helene Deutsch was director.

Mahler became a "disciple and close collaborator" of August Aichhorn, a pioneer in the area of juvenile delinquency, whose book *Wayward Youth* describing a psychoanalytic-oriented approach to treatment had made him a powerful figure in psychoanalytic circles. It was Aichhorn who suggested that Margaret learn the Rorschach technique.[40]

Not much is known of Mahler's life or career between 1925 and 1938. She was married to Paul Mahler, Ph.D., a childless marriage that lasted until his death. She reports that she founded and directed "the first psychoanalytic child guidance clinic in Vienna" and served as Rorschach consultant and teacher of the Rorschach method at the University of Vienna Clinic for Neurology and Psychiatry during this period.[40]

In 1938, the year that Austria fell to the Nazis, Mahler's first important paper was published. Appearing in a Swiss journal, the paper, which signaled a Rorschach project she was involved in, was titled "The Rorschach Test as an Auxiliary Method for the Understanding of the Psychology of Organically Brain Damaged." Her Rorschach project and her career in Vienna came to an abrupt end, however, when she and her husband Paul fled to London and in October 1938 to New York.[40]

In 1940 Mahler made her debut at the New York Psychoanalytic Society with the presentation of her paper, "Pseudoimbecility: A Magic Cap of Invisibility," which, she reports, "describes a mechanism of pseudo-stupidity paramount to a type of learning disability on an emotional basis."[40] Mahler did not join the defectors from the New York Society when Karen Horney and her followers left in 1941; she was honored several years later by Clara Thompson's Academy, but she was in general too busy to be involved in the political upheavals of the rebels of American psychiatry.

Mahler has been a highly influential and successful member of he psychoanalytic movement in America. She was involved in teaching, clinical practice, and research for the next thirty-five years, publishing

120 scientific papers.[40, 41] In addition to her private practice, she worked at the New York State Psychiatric Institute at Columbia University, where she reorganized the Children's Service, one of the highly influential women of psychology to be associated with that school.[41]

Mahler established the child analysis curriculum at the Philadelphia Psychoanalytic Institute and was responsible for many innovations in child analysis. It is interesting to note that there are similarities in the theories and treatment contributions between Mahler and Melanie Klein and both seem to owe a debt to Sandor Ferenczi, even if the influence is indirect. Of the two, Mahler has been more successful in remaining within the orthodox fold, despite the fact that Margaret's revisions were more radical, particularly in the area of psychotherapy. Mahler, however, was working initially with psychotic children and was firmly accepted before she applied her theories to universal human development, she had tried to integrate her conceptualizations with psychoanalytic ideas generally, and was not in direct competition with Anna Freud.

Since 1958, Margaret Mahler has been associated with the Albert Einstein College of Medicine, where she is currently Emeritus. Although most of her research and theoretical articles appeared prior to her semi-retirement in the late sixties and the best of her articles were published in *The Selected Papers of Margaret S. Mahler* in 1979, her two very important books appeared in print only recently.[41]

Contributions

Mahler accurately sees her work as falling into three successive areas of interest and research in terms of theory construction, clearly a process of evolution.[40] In the forties, she was interested in motility disturbances, particularly tics, in children. She had noted that several children who had motility disturbances later developed psychosis in adolescence.[40]

She then went on to discover and clearly define "symbiotic psychosis," a failure to differentiate from the mother that begins in the locomotive stage, when the child first learns to walk. Mahler's first major book, *On Human Symbiosis and the Vicissitudes of Individuation* (1969), describes several years of research on psychosis in children. She suggested that psychosis is caused by constitutional weakness and/or environmental conditions very early in life:

> The psychotic child's primary defect in being able to utilize (to perceive) the catalyzing mothering agent for homeostasis, is inborn,

constitutional, and very probably hereditary, or else acquired very early in the first days or weeks of extrauterine life.[42]

In the same book, she presents the details of a treatment program which provides a "corrective symbiotic experience" in which there is an attempt to "reestablish the symbiotic bond between mother and child."[42] The goals of this treatment are (a) to allow the child to establish his or her body image, (b) to develop object relations, and (c) to encourage the restoration of ego functions.

The third area involved Mahler's extension of her previous findings to explicate the process of individuation to "non-psychotics," comprising her "normative" research studies.[40] The details of this work, which generalize the coping mechanisms of psychotic children to universal processes of ego development, are included in *The Psychological Birth of the Human Infant*, published in 1975.[40]

Margaret Mahler is, next to Anna Freud, probably the most-honored female psychoanalyst. She has been honored, not once, but three times by the New York Psychoanalytic Society, in 1962, 1970, and 1975. In addition she received the Agnes Purcell McGavin Award of the American Psychiatric Association and the Freida Fromm-Reichmann Award of the American Academy of Psychoanalysis, both in 1970. Mahler received an honorary Sc.D. from the Medical College of Pennsylvania in 1971; that same year a volume of essays in honor of Mahler was published by International Universities Press (edited by McDevitt and Settlage). In 1979 the Wilfred C. Hulse Memorial Award of the New York Council on Child Psychiatry was awarded Mahler "in recognition of her outstanding contribution to the field on child psychiatry and the mental health of children." Her greatest honor, however, was bestowed by the Medical College of Pennsylvania jointly with the Philadelphia Psychoanalytic Society and Institute: since 1969, these groups have cosponsored the Annual Margaret S. Mahler Symposium.[40]

TEACHER
Ruth May Strang (1895–   )

One of the most prolific writers in psychology, Ruth Strang, pioneer in the school guidance movement and a teacher for sixty years, published thirty-six books, hundreds of journal articles and pamphlets, and a film series. All of this production was accomplished on her own time and at her own expense, while she taught courses full-time and during summers. She was one of the first specialists in the area of school personnel work, but was interested in all aspects of education. She never married and she never rested.

Life and Career

Ruth May Strang was born on 3 April 1895, in Chatham, New Jersey, the daughter of a farmer, Charles Garrett Strang, and Anna Bergen Strang. She had two brothers. Growing up in the Greater New York City area, Ruth attended Adelphi Academy in Brooklyn, where she was a member of the German club, the basketball team, and the walking club. After graduation in 1914, she attended Pratt Institute for two years, majoring in household sciences. She then worked as an assistant to an interior decorator. Her hobbies today include walking and interior decorating.[43]

She decided to be a teacher and embarked on a career that she has described as "unplanned," where she was to "develop my interests and abilities, and doors seem to open."[43] She taught home economics from 1917 to 1920 in New York public schools and then enrolled at Columbia University's Teachers College, where she received her B.S. in home economics in 1922 and the M.A. in 1924. She was a research assistant in nutrition, from 1923 to 1924, at Teachers College.[43]

Strang received the Ph.D. in education in 1926. Until 1929, when she received an appointment as assistant professor of education at Columbia, she had a series of temporary teaching positions and for several years taught psychology at Women's College in Greensboro, North Carolina, every summer. She advanced to associate professor in 1936 and full professor at Columbia in 1940.[43] Three of her most noteworthy books, published early in her career, were pioneering efforts in school personnel (guidance) work: *The Role of the Teacher in Personnel Work* (1932), *Counseling Technics in College and Secondary Schools* (1937), and *Educational Guidance: Its Principles and Practice* (1947). These books became instant classics and were revised repeatedly.

Strang wrote scores of pamphlets in psychology, primarily for the mass market, but also two very popular books, *Introduction to Child Study* (the best-received was the 4th revised edition of 1959) and *A Psychology of Adolescence* (1957). She has long had an interest in reading improvement and remediation and was involved in the preparation of teachers of reading and remediation specialists and has been active in associations for reading improvement. For several years she was director of the high school and college reading center at Columbia and in 1955 was president of the National Association for Remedial Teaching.[43] With others, she prepared four volumes of the series, *Teen-Age Tales*, published in 1954, 1955 and 1958. Her *Explorations in Reading Patterns* (1942), was another important contribution.

Late in her career Strang became interested in educating the gifted child and dealt with the issue in her characteristically energetic activist manner. She became active in relevant associations, quickly assumed leadership positions, and wrote for professional and lay audiences. She focused upon how parents (*Helping Your Gifted Child*, 1960) and teachers (*Guideposts for the Education of the Gifted*, 1958) might help the bright child cope with social and psychological obstacles to his or her development.[43]

In 1960, Ruth Strang reached the mandatory retirement age at Columbia and was made professor emeritus. As might be expected, she was not to retire. She joined the faculty at the University of Arizona, as professor of education and director of the Reading Development Center.[44] In 1966, at age seventy-one, Strang was still teaching, directing the Reading Center, and working on revisions of some of her more important books. Hard as it is to imagine, she became even more involved in professional organizations than she had been.[44]

Contributions

This remarkable woman has been indefatigable in her efforts and in each area of education in which she has been involved her achievements have been brilliant. Her research was original, respectable, and always problem-oriented. Her publications (and she produced them for many years at a ten per year rate) were "optimistic and idealistic in philosophy," but replete with "practical suggestions—useful for teachers."[44]

Although a humble, self-effacing woman, tall, conservative in politics and religious values, Ruth May Strang played a leadership role in educational psychology for close to forty years and was an active advocate and administrator in educational organizations. During the fifties and sixties, Strang was one of the "biggest names" in education, the consummate teacher.

IN THE SHADOW OF PILLSBURY
Martha Guernsey Colby (1899–1952)

Today the psychology department at the University of Michigan is one of the largest and most influential in the world. From 1852 to 1952 the department was very small and there were virtually no women on the psychology faculty. For many years the department was dominated by one man, W. B. Pillsbury, an early student of Titchener and a founder of American psychology. Martha Colby was his most loyal disciple.

Life

Martha Guernsey was born on 22 February 1899, in Montpelier, Idaho. She attended public schools in Ogden, Utah, and graduated from high school at fifteen years of age. She completed her freshman year at the University of Utah and her sophomore year at the University of Michigan. She then quit to spend one year as an elementary schoolteacher and music instructor in Ogden. She returned to Michigan and received her A.B. (1919), A.M. (1920) and Ph.D. (1922) in psychology. She was the second woman to earn a Ph.D. at the University of Michigan.[45]

Martha was married to a physicist who became a professor at the University of Michigan. In histories and formal papers dealing with this period, she is usually referred to as "Mrs." Colby and her devotion to her mentor Pillsbury is frequently noted.[45]

Pillsbury, a theoretician and an historian, was a power at Michigan and Martha practically worshipped him as a person and was a "daughter to him, but she did not care for his psychology."[45] Although he was seldom involved in research, he agreed to direct Colby's dissertation. In fact, though Pillsbury was known to be an unusually inept carpenter, he personally helped her build her apparatus.[45]

Martha Colby was on the staff of this small department from 1921 to 1950 and was never able to advance in rank. As an instructor she usually taught what were then the "low-prestige" courses, such as psychology of music, genetic psychology, and experimental child psychology. Pillsbury was *the* psychologist at Michigan and Colby was the *woman* psychologist there.

Despite the fact that her efforts, including her innovative research in child development, went relatively unnoticed and unrecognized at Michigan and elsewhere, Colby won several wards and honors as an American scientist and received many fellowships that allowed her to visit Europe.[45]

On one of her earlier jaunts overseas Colby went to Berlin to work with Köhler and Wertheimer, planning to immerse herself in the study of gestalt psychology. She found the gestaltists cold and impersonal and felt unwelcome, left abruptly for Vienna, and met and made close friends with Charlotte and Karl Bühler. She did research at the Institute of Psychology for the remainder of that year and returned several times thereafter. She was said "to love" the atmosphere in Vienna.[45]

In 1949, Colby's husband, who had worked with the Atomic Energy Commission, was pressured to come to Washington to work on the AEC full time. They were reluctant to move, especially Martha, who would have to give up her career. As her biographer Raphelson sardonically notes, when the decision was made, "Martha naturally had to resign."[45]

In 1952 the AEC sent the Colbys on a trip to Europe to inspect physics labs there. This was as much an extended vacation, at taxpayers' expense, as a crucial governmental necessity. While the couple were being driven through the mountains in Greece, their driver swerved to avoid hitting a goat and ran off the road. Colby's husband was injured severely but survived; Martha Colby was killed.[45]

Evaluation

Martha Colby received her Ph.D. when she was only twenty-three years old. Her entire professional career was spent in a university department, during its early and less prominent days, where she never received the prominence or prestige one so bright and talented might have been expected to receive. She had competence and skill at least equal to that that propelled several others, in different locations, to considerable eminence. At Michigan, as a woman in Pillsbury's shadow, Colby remained an instructor and an "unknown."

FIRST WOMAN OF PHILOSOPHY
Susanne Katherine Langer (1895–   )

A rather small, usually severely dressed "Germanic" looking woman, Susanne Langer today prefers to work in her "snug Colonial cottage in Old Lyme, Connecticut."[46] In her writing and philosophical development Susanne K. Langer has had immense influence on psychological thought. She is also one of the few women philosophers to gain recognition in this predominantly male-dominated academic bastion.

She is best remembered for her third book, *Philosophy in a New Key*, which has had a profound influence on psychology, especially significant to psycholinguists, and has been immensely popular with college students and intellectuals, since its publication in 1942. This single impressive publication made Langer a prominent figure in the field of aesthetics.[47]

Life

Susanne Katherine Knauth was one of five children (she had two brothers and two sisters) born to Antonio Knauth and Else M. Uhlich Knauth. Her father, a successful Leipzig-trained lawyer by profession, was also an avid and proficient pianist and cellist. He passed his love of music on to his daughter, providing her training on both instruments, and her mother taught her to appreciate and write poetry.[47]

Cultivated and financially secure, the Knauths lived on the West Side of Manhattan, in the midst of the city's German colony, where Susanne was born on 20 December 1895. A precocious child, Susanne absorbed the cultured values of the German community, developing refined interests in philosophy, music, scholarship, and the fine arts, on the one hand, and on the other, a deep love of nature, an interest nurtured during summers spent at Lake George, a resort town in upstate New York. Her childhood home life was one that included not only a deep appreciation for the arts, but strict discipline and an extended family atmosphere.[47]

Susanne was a frail child and much of her early education was at home, much of it self-directed—she chose, for example, Kant's *Critique of Pure Reason* to read when she was still a teenager. She attended a private school located near her home, the Veltin School, but had some early difficulty because she was not accustomed to using English, as German, primarily, was spoken at home.[46, 47]

An anecdote from her childhood involves frogs (Langer has continued to regard the animals with great affection). After reading a book about them when she was quite young, she astounded her family by delivering, ad lib, a forty-minute lecture on frogs.

She also reports an early interest in logic and language. At seven, on hearing this little riddle or song—

> Dornröschen und Schneewittchen,
> Die stizen auf den Thron,
> Und jede hat zur Seite
> Den schönsten Königssohn (see note for translation)[48]

she noted that most children, including her sisters, decided that there must be two princes, one for each girl. The seven-year-old Susanne insisted, however, that there can only be one handsom*est* prince.[46]

Susanne's father loathed bluestockings and therefore refused his daughters permission to attend college. Susanne had to wait until his death to pursue her advanced degrees. In 1920, she obtained the B.A. from Radcliffe and was elected to Phi Beta Kappa.

While at Radcliffe, Susanne met William L. Langer, a graduate student at Harvard. They married on 3 September 1921, and then spent a year at the University of Vienna. Unlike many of her companions in psychology who spent time in Vienna during this period and loved it. Susanne describes it as "not a very successful" experience.[47] She divorced William Langer (who became a history professor at Harvard) in 1942, after twenty years of marriage and two sons.

In 1924 Susanne received her M.A. from Radcliffe. This same year, this serious and erudite young philosopher published her first book, *The Cruise of the Little Dipper*, illustrated by Helen Sewell. Langer later described this book of fairy tales, probably Langer's best-selling work, as congruent with her philosophical ideas, since "myth is the primitive phase of metaphysical thought."[46]

Susanne then received her Ph.D.—in 1926—from Radcliffe, studying under Alfred North Whitehead and Henry Sheffer. While she was able to write a few articles and one book, *The Practice of Philosophy* (1930), early in her career, she was decidedly underemployed during her marriage. Like many other women, Susanne found it difficult to be simultaneously wife, mother, and professional. For one thing, William Langer's career came first—they spent one year, for example, at Clark University, 1926-27, and then had to relocate back to Cambridge when he was "called back" to join the faculty at Harvard. Susanne observed in 1960 that although she had had a close relationship with her sons and enjoys her grandchildren, it is doubtful that "two deeply preoccupied parents can create the ideal environment for a family of children."[46]

For fifteen years Langer was employed as a tutor in philosophy at Radcliffe and taught an occasional course at Wellesley or Smith. (Incidentally—although it was not the position that a person of Langer's ability and calibre usually stays with—a "tutor" is not a person who helps prepare for eligibility on the basketball team; it is rather a part-time instructorship, but it is a position most often held by graduate students.) In any event, when in 1942 Susanne Langer broke free of her husband, she also broke free as a philosopher, with the auspicious publication of *Philosophy in a New Key*.

This book was an instant success and established Langer's reputation as an important philosopher. She began her academic career in earnest, as a famous and widely respected thinker at age forty-seven. She was an assistant professor at the University of Delaware at Newark for one year, 1942-43, and then moved on to Columbia University where she was a lecturer in philosophy from 1945 to 1950. She was in great demand and lectured and gave courses at several schools including the New School for Social Research, Northwestern, Ohio University, and the Universities of Washington and Michigan.[47]

In 1954 Langer went to Connecticut College in New London and assumed the position of professor and chair of the Department of Philosophy, where she is now emeritus. Her various awards included a research grant from the Edgar Kaufman Charitable Trust (1956), the Radcliffe Alumnae Achievement Medal (1950), and several honorary degrees, including Litt.D.'s from Wilson College (1954), Wheaton College (1962), and Western College for Women (1962). In 1960 Susanne Langer was elected to the American Academy of Arts and Sciences.[46]

Langer continues to write, study, and play the cello, long after her retirement from an active career as America's premier female philosopher. Her work continues to be controversial and original. She is now eighty-five and living in Connecticut.

Work

Susanne Langer wrote six books and her many essays and lectures have been published in several compilations. Following 1942, most of the dust jackets of her books contain the legend "by the author of *Philosophy in a New Key*," for it was this single, most important contribution that determined her position of eminence in philosophy and psychology.

In *Philosophy in a New Key* Langer differentiated between discursive and non-discursive symbols. (Animals other than humans respond to "signs;" their inability to use discursive symbols, she suggests, is what separates them from us.) The former, the symbols used in discourse, are familiar to us and basic when we consider human intellect. Discursive symbols, however, Langer argued, are inferior in the realm of aesthetics and that the conception of "the ineffable also has its form of logic, its semantics, and its symbolistic schema."[47]

In opposition to the then currently held belief that (a) lanugage is the only means of articulating thought and (b) everything which is not speakable thought is feelings, Langer wrote:

> I . . . believe that in this physical, spacetime world of our experience there are things which do not fit the grammatical scheme of expression. But they are not necessarily blind, inconceivable, mystical affairs; they are simply matters which require to be conceived through some symbolistic schema other than discursive language. And to demonstrate the possibility of such a non-discursive pattern one needs only to review the logical requirements for any symbolic structure whatever. Language is by no means our only articulate product.[49]

Other books by Langer are *An Introduction to Symbolic Logic* (1937), *Feeling and Form; A Theory of Art* (1953), and *Problems of Art* (1957). None of these had the impact of her 1942 masterpiece.

EDUCATOR FOR SOCIAL ADJUSTMENT
Caroline Beaumont Zachry (1894-1945)

Caroline Zachry was psychology's spokesperson and advocate for all the issues we call "progressive education." She was convinced that the personality and social adjustment of the child were the most important functions of educational institutions. In a relatively brief career, during most of which she taught English and was affiliated with a state teachers college in New Jersey, Caroline Zachry was able, by dint of her tenacity and administrative ability, to become a highly influential and respected psychologist. Zachry has been, for example, called the "broadest, deepest influence" on Dr. Benjamin Spock.[50]

Life

Caroline Zachry was born on 20 April 1894, in New York City, to James Greer Zachry, an attorney, and Elise Clarkson Thompson Zachry. The family is an old, powerful, Southern aristocratic one. Her maternal grandfather, Hugh Smith Thompson, a South Carolina educator, served as assistant secretary of the Treasury under Grover Cleveland, and had been governor of South Carolina; her paternal grandfather, Charles Zachry, had been a brigadier general in the Conferderate Army.[50]

One of three children, Caroline was not a particularly good student. At the Spence School for Girls, which she attended from 1908 to 1914, she graduated at the bottom of her class.[50] She then took undergraduate classes at Teachers College, Columbia University, for ten years, from 1914 to 1924, until she received her A.B. at age thirty. She also received her A.M., 1925, and Ph.D., 1928, from Columbia.[51]

Career

Prior to joining the psychology department at what was to be renamed the New Jersey State Teachers College in Montclair in 1927, Zachry taught junior high school at Columbia's experimental school from 1922 to 1926 and the following year taught English at Montclair.[50] In 1927, a year before her Ph.D. was granted, she was appointed assistant professor of education and psychology and head of the Department of Psychology at Montclair.[51]

Zachry took postdoctoral courses at the New York School for Social Work and at Oxford University and studied for one year with Carl Jung. In 1930 she added the directorship of the Mental Hygiene Institute run by her department to her duties. That same year Zachry, who never married, adopted two children.[50]

She was very active in psychology and education organizations and those advocating progressive education. In addition to writing five books, Zachry published a large number of brief articles for journals of education, generally polemic articles in which she took the position that schools should be oriented towards promoting social adjustment and mental health. She felt that schools should be reorganized around principles derived from psychology.

From 1934 to 1939, Zachry directed a large scale study of adolescence for the Progressive Education Association. She became director of the Institute for the Study of Personality Development (which was renamed the "Caroline B. Zachry Institute of Human Development" after her death).[50] Caroline Zachry died of cancer on 22 February 1945. She was fifty years old.

At the time of their publication, three of her books were quite influential in the progressive education movement. The first of these, *Personality Adjustments of School Children* (1929), was an expansion of her Ph.D. dissertation; the others, written with collaborators, were *Reorganizing Secondary Education* (1939), and *Democracy and the Curriculum* (1939).

CHAIRPERSON
Lois Meek Stolz (1891-   )

For more than fifty years Lois Meek Stolz has been involved in organizations and on commissions, has consulted with governmental agencies, and has been a major figure in the founding, administration, and popularization of mental health and developmental programs for children. A developmental psychologist, Stolz is a much-loved woman and is professor emeritus at Stanford University.[52]

Life

Lois Meek was born on 19 October 1891, to Alexander Kennedy Meek and Fannie Virginia Price Meek. She attended Washington, D.C., schools, and graduated from Central High School in 1910 and Washington Normal

School in 1912. Lois then taught elementary school until 1916, when she became a supervisor in the Washington School system, a position she held until she received her A.B. from George Washington University in 1921.[53]

Lois then began her long association with Columbia University. She earned her M.A. in 1922 and the Ph.D. in 1925, at Teachers College.[52, 53] (Many women who later attained eminence in psychology were students at Columbia at the time.) It was also a time when a major influence on child psychology was the Laura Spelman Rockefeller Fund, which underwrote the development of institutes of "child welfare" (later "development") and encouraged professional training of women throughout the nation. Two special interests of Rockefeller charity were Columbia University and the American Association of University Women (AAUW). In 1924 Lois Meek became education secretary of AAUW and received a Spelman fellowship.[53]

Lois maintained a relationship with the Fund and AAUW for several years and began her career as an administrator and project director. Between 1926 and 1929 she chaired the first National Committee on Nursery Schools (later this group, which was also subsidized by the Rockefellers, was renamed the National Association for Nursery Education [NANE]). Once she got this group on its feet, she became its first president, serving from 1929 to 1931. At the same time Lois was also on several of President Hoover's National Commissions on Education.[53]

In 1929 Lois Meek got her first college faculty position. She was made a full professor of education at Columbia and associate director of the Institute of Child Development. One year later she was made director of the institute and six years later she was head of the Department of Child Development and Guidance; in both positions she influenced the training of a generation of child psychologists, a majority of them women.[53]

During this period she maintained her leadership role on committees, on boards of trustees, on editorial and advisory boards, and on a series of national commissions, by this time, under FDR. She was a charter member of the Society for Research in Child Development. In 1938 she was married to Herbert Rowell Stolz, who had preceded Harold Jones as Director of the Institute at the University of California at Berkeley.[53]

After one year as a research associate at the University of Chicago (1939-1940), the Stolzes moved to California and Lois joined the Joneses and Nancy Bayley at the Institute of Child Welfare at Berkeley. She began her association with the Institute, where she was a research associate, at the time of the publication of her most important book, *Your Child's Development and Guidance* (1940). This publication, which was given a *Parents' Magazine* award, made Lois a popular figure in America and many of her later publications were written for the lay public.[53]

During the period that she was at Berkeley (from 1940 to 1943) Lois Stolz worked on a longitudinal study of physical maturation of adolescent boys, a study which led to the book *Somatic Development of Adolescent Boys* (1951). This was wartime and Stolz was very actively involved in the war effort as well. In addition to serving as consultant to numerous groups, she was made an assistant to the Governor of California and helped found child services.[53]

Stolz joined the faculty in psychology at Stanford University in 1944 as an instructor; in 1947 she was advanced to professor. Her most important research, on the relationship between fathers and children born in their absence during World War II, was published, *Father-Relations of War-Born Children*, in 1954. She was made professor emeritus in 1957.[52, 53]

Lois Meek Stolz has won many awards, including the Distinguished Contribution to Psychology Award, 1967, and the G. Stanley Hall Award, Division 7, 1969, both from the American Psychological Association.

Lois is still active today. She lectures, usually on the psychology of women, serves on various fact-finding committees, boards of organizations, and as a consultant to *Notable American Women*, and continues to write.[53]

Work

Lois Meek Stolz has made important contributions to the research on child development and parent-child relations. A prolific writer, she has published two books for the popular press and four technical books, as well as thirty-three pamphlets and hundreds of articles for educational journals, magazines, and yearbooks.

Her major contributions, however, are in public service and professional organizations where, like Ruth May Strang and Caroline Zachry, she was mainly concerned with the education and welfare of children. What especially characterizes Stolz's contribution in this area and distinguishes her from the others similarly involved in administrative and organizational efforts, is that Stolz's contributions have been more often within the mainstream of psychology and have brought her into the high strata of national influence and circles of power.

ONE OF THE TERRIBLE TRIO
Thelma Gwinn Thurstone (1897–   )

Thelma Thurstone has been called one of the "terrible trio" of southern psychology. She, with Dorothy Adkins and Elizabeth Duffy, earned this epithet because of their positions of prestige and power at the University of North Carolina. This is somewhat ironic, for Thurstone did not arrive in Chapel Hill until she was fifty-five years old and most of her famous research was conducted in Chicago. She is also often referred to as "Louis Thurstone's wife," also ironic, since she was to gain prominence and a reputation as an autonomous psychologist after she was widowed from her more-famous husband. Thelma Thurstone has been the consummate mental tester and psychometrician for more than fifty years.

Life

Thelma Gwinn was born on 11 December 1897, in Hume, Missouri. She received the A.B., 1917, and the B.S., 1920, from the University of Missouri, in education. She then attended the Carnegie Institue of Technology, where she received the A.M. in psychology, 1923, and transferred to the University of Chicago.[54]

During the first year at Chicago, Thelma, who had been an instructor at Carnegie during the three years she spent there, was hired as a statistician by the city of Chicago. She also met Louis Leon Thurstone, a fellow graduate student, and in the summer of 1924 they were married. They had three children and enjoyed a long and happy marriage, working and travelling together. Thelma's career was eclipsed by her husband's and Thelma Thurstone sacrificed success and postponed fame in her own right until she was in her early fifties. Her husband was keenly aware of the sacrifice Thelma was making, often acknowledged his debt to her, and felt that she was unfairly deprived of recognition and a more productive career—in his words:

> Thelma has the outstanding achievement in our family in managing an active household at the same time that she was professionally active. She has been a partner in every research project in the Psychometric Laboratory. For many years she was in the laboratory daily, helping to plan the projects, supervising most of the test construction and participating especially in the psychological interpretation of results.[55]

After their wedding, the Thurstones returned to Chicago where Louis had been appointed an associate professor.[55] Thelma took a job with the American Council of Education as a mental tester and statistician; she remained associated with the group from 1924 to 1948.[54] In 1927 Thelma received her Ph.D. from the University of Chicago.

As noted above, Thelma Thurstone worked at her husband's laboratory, wrote articles and books with him, and successfully fulfilled the role of wife and mother, while she maintained a full-time job. She grew to be a formidable woman, fiercely independent, outspoken, and an outstanding administrator. In 1948 she and her husband travelled to Frankfort, Germany, where they were both appointed visiting professors at the University. This was one of several trips Thelma made overseas. Upon their return, Thelma accepted a position as director of the Division of Child Study of Chicago Public Schools, where she remained until the move to Chapel Hill, North Carolina in 1952.[55]

Thelma Thurstone was made a professor of education at the University of North Carolina and at her husband's death in 1955, director of the Psychometric Laboratory at Chapel Hill. She was replaced when she reached age sixty in 1957.[54] She has held many administrative positions there, and as late as 1970 Thurstone headed a research project and was an advisor to the Graham Child Development Center of the University of North Carolina.

Work

Thelma Thurstone is best known for her work on the development of the Primary Mental Abilities Battery, the primary source of fame for her husband. This project provided the first successful application of factor analysis to large-scale mental testing. Thelma, however much she was to contribute to this research and subsequent studies at Chicago, did not receive the recognition she deserved until much later. When Thelma Thurstone finally achieved prominence in psychology, she was in her middle fifties and the primary reason for her recognition was her ability to organize and direct an institute and laboratory.

Others

Like the other women included in this chapter, the women described below have gravitated towards positions as staff members of important clinics, hospitals, college faculties and research teams. In most cases these women each made one significant and notable contribution to psychology or several less prominent contributions. What they have in common primarily is that they were among the first generation of psychologists to be accepted into advanced training and into already existing positions of institutions. They had to struggle less to establish themselves than the earlier women of psychology but were less recognized for outstanding skill as psychological researchers than the women who followed them.

Rachel Stutsman Ball (1894–1980) is best known for her research in child development and test construction. She was born on 17 April 1894, in Greenfield, Indiana, the daughter of Lydia Winslow and Jesse O. Stutsman, who were the authors of *Curing the Criminal* (1926). Rachel received her A.B. in 1916 from the University of Missouri and the Ph.D. from the University of Chicago in 1928. In 1935 she married Albert P. Ball, an electrical engineer. From 1922 to 1937 she was on the staff at Merrill-Palmer Institute where she developed mental tests for infants and preschool children. Following several temporary and parttime teaching positions, Ball was appointed professor of psychology at Arizona State University– Tempe in 1947. She taught at Arizona State until 1964, when, at age seventy, she was made professor emeritus. In 1977, still active in clinical research and teaching, Ball was named Arizona Psychologist of the Year. Well-known in psychometrics, she is the author of *Mental Measurement of Preschool Children* (1931), *What of Youth Today?* (1935), and *Evaluation of Infant and Pre-school Mental Tests* (1939).[56]

Grete Lehner Bibring (1899–1977) was born in Vienna, Austria, on 11 January 1899. She received her M.D. from the University of Vienna in 1924 and was a training analyst both in Vienna, 1933–1938, and later in Boston, 1941–1976. For many years Bibring practiced and taught psychiatry and psychoanalysis at Harvard Medical School and at Beth Israel Hospital in Boston. From 1946 to 1955 Bibring was chief of psychiatry at Beth Israel and from 1965 to her death she was given the honored emeritus status at both Harvard and Beth Israel. She was awarded an honorary LL.D. by Brandeis Univesrity in 1968 and the Abram L. Sacliav Silver Medallion in 1971.[57]

Phyllis Blanchard (1895–   ) was born in Epping, New Hampshire, on 14 March 1895, and received her A.B. from the University of New Hampshire in 1917. She received her Ph.D. from Clark University in 1919. After working briefly in the New York Reformatory System and Bellevue Hospital, she joined her husband on the faculty (he was a chemistry professor) at the University of Pennsylvania, School of Medicine, after her marriage in 1925. Blanchard also began her long association with the

Philadelphia Child Guidance Clinic in 1925. Blanchard was unusually prolific for a clinical psychologist, producing an especially impressive number of books. Among her more interesting titles are *The Adolescent Girl* (1920), *Taboo and Genetics* (1920), *New Girls for Old* (1930), and *An Introduction to Mental Hygiene* (1930).[58]

Katharine May Banham (Bridges) (1897–   ) was born in Sheffield, England and received her D.Phil. in 1934 from the University of Montreal. Her most famous research was conducted in Montreal—after she had worked for several years in England—a study of emotional differentiation in infancy. Despite books and several articles, only one of her papers, "Emotional Development in Early Infancy" (1932), is well known and frequently cited. For several years Banham taught at Duke University and was on the staff of the Durham Child Guidance Clinic.[59]

Psyche Cattell (1893–   ) the daughter of James McKeen Cattell, is the developer of the *Cattell Developmental Scales*, an important contribution to the mental measurement of infants which extended the Binet "downward." She was born in Garrison, New York, on 2 August 1893, and obtained degrees from Cornell (A.M. in 1925) and Harvard (Ed.M. in 1925 and the Ed.D. in 1927).[60, 62] A prominent psychometrician early in her career, Cattell produced what appears to be a typographical error in bibliographies, since she created scales to measure physical maturation based upon "*d*ental age" in addition to scales of intelligence based upon "*m*ental age."[60] After working at Harvard for almost twenty years as a research and clinical psychologist, she relocated to Lancaster, Pennsylvania, the Cattell family homestead, where she opened a private practice (from 1939 to 1973); worked at the local mental health clinic and child guidance clinic (from 1939 to 1971); and was founder and director (from 1941 to 1974) of the Cattell School.[61]

Eleanor Touroff Glueck (1898–1972) was the outstanding authority in criminology and juvenile delinquency during the fifties in this country. She was born in Brooklyn, New York, on 12 April 1898, and attended Hunter College and Barnard, receiving her A.B. in English in 1919. After taking courses in sociology at the New School, she married Sheldon Glueck, an attorney who was taking courses in criminology at Harvard. Eleanor moved to Cambridge also. She and Sheldon collaborated in their famous research for fifty years, ending with her death at age seventy-four.

She was a classmate of Psyche Cattell and received the M.Ed. and the Ed.D. at Harvard. She taught, as did her husband, criminology at the Department of Social Ethics and at the Law School at Harvard for many years. She is the author of several books, but those on juvenile delinquency, written with her husband, are the best known. They include *Unraveling Juvenile Delinquency* (1950), *Delinquents in the Making* (1952), and *Physique and Delinquency* (1956). The major contribution of the Gluecks was a system for predicting delinquent behavior based upon physique variables and family disruption.[62]

Phyllis Greenacre (1894–) was a very important figure in the psychoanalysis of children during the forties and fifties, but is not well-known in psychology generally. Teacher, theoretician, and clinician, Greenacre is one of the most productive and most cited writers in her specialty. Greenacre was born in Chicago on 3 May 1894, and received her S.B. from the University of Chicago in 1913. She received the M.D. in 1916 from the Rush Medical College and joined the staff at the Phipps Clinic and the faculty of Johns Hopkins Medical School, from 1917 to 1927. In 1919 she married Curt Paul Richter, a psychologist at the Phipps Clinic, who later received the vaunted Distinguished Scientific Contribution Award of the American Psychological Association. She had two children, but the marriage later ended in divorce. Greenacre was on the faculty of Cornell University's Medical College, from 1935 to 1964, and was associated with the New York Psychoanalytic Institute as a faculty member, and from 1948 to 1950 as its president. She was a member of the New York Psychoanalytic Society, serving as president in 1956–57, and has been a member of the editorial board of the *Psychoanalytic Study of the Child* since its inception in 1945. She wrote numerous theoretical papers; particularly notable were those on sublimation in artists, transference, and fetishism. Her two most important books were *Trauma, Growth and Personality* (1952), and *Affective Disorders* (1953).[63]

Marguerite Hertz (1899–) is best known for her contributions to the scoring and interpretation of the Rorschach. She is a native New Yorker who migrated to Ohio in the middle twenties, and received her Ph.D. from Case Western Reserve University in 1931. Subsequently, she remained on the faculty at Case Western for thirty-four years. She made contributions in child development, psychopathology, and personality measurement.[64]

Helen Lois Koch (1895-1977) was a highly respected and very influential psychologist, who made several important contributions to the area of child development. She was on the faculty of the University of Chicago for thirty-one years and was made professor emeritus in 1960. Koch received her Ph.B. in 1918 and the Ph.D. in 1921 from Chicago and throughout her career was active in organizations devoted to child welfare and to the encouragement of research in child development. She is the author of *Twins and Twin Relations* (1965).[65]

Frieda Kiefer Merry (1897-   ) received her Ph.D. from Ohio State University in 1927. She is the coauthor of a comprehensive textbook on adolescent development. A clinical psychologist who was on the faculty of Morriss Harvey College in West Virginia for many years, Frieda Merry was one of the first psychologists to donate her personal papers to the Psychology Archives in Akron, Ohio.[66]

Emily Hartshorne Mudd (1898-   ) is best known for her work on the family and on marital therapy. She has writen prolifically for professional and popular journals. Mudd has always been at the University of Pennsylvania, from her position as research assistant in 1922 to her current status, since 1967, as professor emeritus of the School of Medicine. Mudd married in 1922 and had four children. She did not receive her M.S.W. until 1936 and her Ph.D. until 1950, both from Pennsylvania, but has emerged as a worldwide authority on marriage counseling in the past thirty years as well as an influential teacher at the School of Medicine. Among her titles, all of which she co-authored, are *The Practice of Marriage Counseling* (1951), *Man and Wife: A Sourcebook in Family Attitudes* (1957), and *Professional Growth for Clergymen Through Supervised Training in Marriage Counseling and Family Problems* (1970).[67]

Dorothy Rethlingshafer (1900-   ) was a competent teacher and researcher who contributed to comparative psychology, test construction, and motivational theory. Despite her many years of work as a psychologist and acceptance by her peers, Rethlingshafer never attained prominence and her career was marked by setbacks. She received her B.S. from Miami in 1920, the M.A. from Chicago in 1924, and the Ph.D. from North Carolina in 1938. For many years she was on the faculty at the University of Florida in Gainseville, underpaid and unable to attain status or rank, and when in 1966 she applied for full professor rank, Florida found that she "did not meet the criteria" and sent her a letter thanking her for "years of faithful service." Rethlingshafer published four books and twenty-five journal articles. Among her titles are *Motivation as Related to Personality* (1963), and *Principles of Comparative Psychology* (1961).[68]

Maria Rickers-Ovsiankina (1898–   ) has been an esteemed clinical psychologist and clinical researcher for the past fifty-two years. Since receiving her Ph.D. at the University of Giessen in 1928, she has been associated with several clinics, hospitals, and academic institutions, including Worcester State Hospital and the University of Connecticut. An acknowledged expert on the Rorschach, she was the editor of *Rorschach Psychology* in 1960. In addition to her well known contributions to the development of projective techniques and to personality assessment, she has gained recognition for her research in schizophrenia and the effects of brain injury.[69] Rickers-Ovsiankina has also been an accepted and respected member of the field theorist researchers who worked under Kurt Lewin, surely a very versatile psychologist.

Beth Lucy Wellman (1885– ??), who for years was a professor of child psychology at the prestigious and influential Iowa Child Welfare Station, State University of Iowa, is an educational and child developmental researcher best known for her articles on environmental stimulation, IQ, and achievement. Wellman received both her B.A. (1920) and Ph.D. (1925) from the State University of Iowa and, except for a brief stint at Columbia's Teachers College, where she worked and took post-doctoral courses, she spent more than fifty years at Iowa as a student and teacher. Wellman contributed many important research articles and several books, among the latter are *The Development of Motor Coordination in Young Children, Child Psychology,* and *A Study of Environmental Stimulation.* Wellman conducted research and wrote on several topics in child development, including language development, sex differences, and intelligence and its measurement. She influenced many other researchers and is "topical" today because of the implications of her findings for "compensatory education."[70]

Bluma Wulfomna Zeigarnik (1900–   ) was born in Prienai in Russia, close to the border with Poland, on 9 November 1900. She attended the University of Berlin and received the Ph.D. in 1927. That was the year also that her paper on the famous "Zeigarnik effect" was published, "Uber das Behalten von erledigten und unerledigten Handlungen" ("On the Retention of Completed and Uncompleted Tasks"). This very long article described her research and the finding that unfinished tasks are remembered longer than finished tasks. Her work is an often quoted proof of Gestalt principles. Zeigarnik returned to Russia in 1931 and has been associated with the Psychological Institute in Moscow.[71]

Notes to Chapter Two

(1)   Theodora M. Abel. Personal communication.
(2)   Gabaldon, J. Le Roy. "Patterns of an Age: The Psychological Writings of Theodora M. Abel." Unpublished doctoral dissertation. The Fielding Institute (1980). Graciously shared with us by the author.
(3)   "Abel, Theodora Mead" in *Who's Who of American Women* (1979).
(4)   Abel, Theodora M. "Washburn's Motor Theory: A Contribution to Functional Psychology." *American Journal of Psychology*, 1927, 39:91–105.
(5)   Abel, Theodora M. "Attitudes and the Galvanic Skin Reflex." *Journal of Experimental Psychology*, 1930, 13:47–60.
(6)   Kinder, Elaine F. "Oral History" (1966). Psychological Archives, University of Akron, Akron, Ohio.
(7)   Abel, Theodora Mead. *Psychological Testing in Cultural Contexts.* (1973) New Haven: College and University Press.
(8)   Abel, Theodora Mead & Metraux, Rhoda. *Culture and Psychotherapy.* (1974) New Haven: College and University Press.
(9)   Anna Freud is one of the women of psychology born during this decade whom the junior author has met—when he was 26 years old. (The senior author, Stevens, was not there; she was about to graduate from Rosemead High School at the time). Unfortunately, during the introduction and the speech Miss Anna made at Reiss-Davis Clinic in Los Angeles, she spoke in German and Gardner has no idea what she said. This meeting was far more important to Gardner than to Freud. (Incidentally he also had contact with Thelma Thurstone, Ruth Tolman, Charlotte Bühler and Rachel Ball, another fact which would have been seen as insignificant by the women involved).
(10)   Roazen, Paul. *Freud and His Followers.* (1974) New York: New American Library.
(11)   "Anna Freud" in *Current Biography* (1979).

(12) Pumpian-Mindlen, E. "Anna Freud b. 1895 and Erik H. Erickson b. 1902. Contributions to the Theory and Practice of Psychoanalysis and Psychotherapy." In Alexander, F., Eisenstein, S., and Grotjahn, M. (Eds.) *Psychoanalytic Pioneers.* (1966) New York: Basic Books.

(13) Freud, Anna. "A Short History of Child Analysis." *Psychoanalytic Study of the Child*, 1969, 21:7–14.

(14) Newman, Lottie, M. "Anna Freud." In Wolman, B.B. (Ed.) *International Encyclopedia of Psychiatry, Psychology, Psychoanalysis and Neurology.* (1977) New York: Van Nostrand Reinhold.

(15) Lustman, S. L. "The Scientific Leadership of Anna Freud." *American Psychoanalytic Association Journal*, 1967, 15(4):810–827.

(16) Freud's latest honorary cites her thus: ". . . seeing into the minds of children she has championed their needs and enhanced our understanding of the growth of human personality." She is called by Harvard "the world's leading psychoanalyst." *Harvard Gazette*, June 1980.

(17) "Lauretta Bender." In Knapp, Sally, E. *Women Doctors Today.* (1947) New York: Thomas Y. Crowell.

(18) Lauretta Bender. Personal communication.

(19) Bender, Lauretta. *Bellevue Studies in Child Psychiatry.* Springfield, Ill.: C. C. Thomas. Vol. 1. *Child Psychiatric Techniques* (1952); Vol. 2. *Aggression, Hostility, and Anxiety in Children* (1953); Vol. 3. *A Dynamic Psychopathology of Childhood* (1954); Vol. 4. *Psychopathology of Children with Organic Brain Disorders* (1955).

(20) Keith-Spiegel, Patricia. "Bühler, Charlotte." In Wolman, B. B. (Ed.). *International Encyclopedia of Psychiatry, Psychology, Psychoanalysis and Neurology.* (1977) New York: Van Nostrand Reinhold.

(21) Schenk-Danzinger, Lotte. "Fundamental Ideas and Theories in Charlotte Bühler's Life." *Journal of Humanistic Psychology*, 1963, 3:3–9.

(22) "Charlotte Bühler." *Who's Who in American Women*, 8th Ed.

(23) "Charlotte Bühler." *Revue de Psychologie Appliquee*, 1969, 19, (2) 141–147.

(24) Green, Maurice (Ed.) *Interpersonal Psychoanalysis. The Selected Papers of Clara Mabel Thompson.* (1964) New York: Basic Books.

(25) "Thompson, Clara, 1893–1958." In Wollman, B. B. (Ed.) *International Encyclopedia of Psychiatry, Psychology, Psychoanalysis and Neurology.* (1977) New York: Van Nostrand Reinhold.

(26) Chapman, A. H. *Harry Stack Sullivan: The Man and His Work.* (1976) New York: G. P. Putnam's Sons.

(27) Watson, J. B. *Behaviorism.* (1924) New York: People's Institute.

(28) Jones, Mary Cover. "A 1924 Pioneer Looks at Behavior Therapy." *Journal of Behavior Therapy and Experimental Psychiatry,* 1975, 6, 181–187.

(29) Logan, Deana Dorman. "Mary Cover Jones: Feminine as Asset." *Psychology of Women Quarterly*, Fall 1980, 5(1), 103–115.

(30) Kaess, W. A., & Bousfield, W. A. "The Use of Citations of Authorities in Textbooks of Introductory Psychology." *American Psychologist*, 1954, 9(4), 144–148.

(31) Mary Cover Jones. Personal Communication.

(32) Kendall, Elaine. *Peculiar Institutions: An Informal History of the Seven Sister Colleges.* (1975) New York: G. P. Putnam's Sons.

(33) Sanford, R. N., & Eichorn, Dorothy, & Honzik, Marjorie. "Harold Ellis Jones, 1894–1960." *Child Development*, 1960, 3, 593–603.

(34) Watson, J. B., & Watson, Rosalie Raynor. "Studies on Infant Psychology." *Scientific Monthly*, 1921, 13, 493–515.

(35) "Benedek, Therese (Friedmann)" in *Who's Who of American Women* (1956).

(36) "Benedek, Therese Friedman" in *Biographical Directory of the American Psychiatric Association* (1977).

(37) "Nancy Bayley" in *American Psychologist*, 1966, 21:1190–1194.

(38) "Bayley, Nancy" in *American Men and Women of Science*, 12th ed.

(39) "Bayley, Nancy (Mrs. John R. Reid)" in *Who's Who of American Women* (1956).

(39a) Nancy Bayley. Personal communication.

(40) Margaret Mahler. Personal communication.

(41) McDerutt, J. B. "Mahler, Margaret S." In Wolman, B. B. (Ed.). *The International Encyclopedia of Psychiatry, Psychology, Psychoanalysis and Neurology.* (1977) New York: Van Nostrand Reinhold.

(42) Mahler, Margaret, S., and Furer, M. *On Human Symbiosis and the Vicissitudes of Individuation.* (1968) New York: International Universities Press. Translated into French, German, Italian, and Spanish.

(43) "Strang, Ruth May" in *Current Biography* (1960).

(44) "Ruth May Strang." Mimeographed manuscript (1966). Psychological Archives, University of Akron, Akron, Ohio.

(45) Raphelon, A. C. Psychology at the University of Michigan, Vol. II. Unpublished mimeo. (1968). Psychological Archives, University of Akron, Akron, Ohio.

(46) Sargent, W. "Philosopher in a New Key." *New Yorker*. 3 December 1960, pp. 67–100.

(47) "Langer, Susanne K(atherina Knauth)" in *Current Biography* (1963).

(48) In English: "Sleeping Beauty and Snow White / They sit upon the throne / And each has at her side / The handsomest Prince."

(49) Langer, Susanne K. *Philosophy in a New Key: A Study in the Symbolism of Reason, Rite, and Art.* (1942) Cambridge: Harvard University Press.

(50) Graham, Patricia A. "Zachry, Caroline Beaumont." In James, T. et al., (Eds.). *American Notable Women: 1607–1950.* (1974) Cambridge: Harvard University Press.

(51) "Zachry, Caroline" in Murchinson, E. (Ed.). *Psychological Register.* (1935) Worcester, Mass.: Clark University Press.

(52) "Stolz, Lois Meek" in *American Men and Women of Science*, 13th ed.

(53) "Lois Meek Stoltz." Takanishi Record. Unpublished manuscript. Psychological Archives, University of Akron, Akron, Ohio.

(54) "Thurstone, Thelma Gwinn" in *American Men and Women of Science*, 12th ed.

(55) Thurstone, Louis L. "Autobiography." In Boring, E. G., Langfeld, H. S., Weiner, H., and Yerkes, R. M. (Eds.). *A History of Psychology in Autobiography, Vol. IV.* (1954) Worcester, Mass.: Clark University Press.

(56) Ball, Rachel Stutsman. *American Men and Women of Science*, 12th ed.

(58) "Blanchard Phyllis." In C. Murchinson. *Psychological Register.* (1939) Worcester, Mass.: Clark University Press.

(59) "Banham, Katharine May" in *American Psychological Association Directory* (1951).

(60) "Cattell, Psyche." In C. Murchinson. *Psychological Register.* (1939) Worcester, Mass.: Clark University Press.

(61) "Cattell, Psyche" in *Who's Who in the East* (1977–78).

(62) "Glueck, Eleanor T(ouroff)" in *Current Biography* (1957).

(63) "Greenacre, Phyllis" in *Who's Who of American Women* (1970).

(64) "Hertz, Marguerite R." in *American Men and Women of Science*, 12th ed.

(65) "Koch, Helen Lois" in *Who's Who* (1975).

(66) "Merry, Frieda Kiefer" in *American Women* (1939).

(67) "Mudd, Emily Hartshorne" in *American Men and Women of Science*, 12th ed.

(68) Dorothy Rethlingshafer. File at the Archives of Psychology, University of Akron, Akron Ohio.

(69) "Rickers-Ovsiankina, Maria Arsenjevna" in *American Men and Women of Science*, 13th ed.
(70) "Wellman, Beth Lucy" in *American Women* (1939).
(71) "Zeigarnik, Bluma." In C. Murchinson. *Psychological Register.* (1939) Worcester, Mass.: Clark University Press.

1953—a year of turmoil for the United States; a year of fruition for the Women of Psychology.

In **1953**, after three years of strife, the Korean War ended by truce.

In **1953**, Susanne Langer received mixed reviews for her book, *Feeling and Form: A Theory of Art*; in this year an earlier book, *An Introduction to Symbolic Logic*, came out in paperback. Langer, whose *The Cruise of the Little Dipper, and Other Fairy Tales* (1924) was actually her best-selling work, began her first permanent, full-time job—professor and chairman of the department of philosophy at Connecticut College. She was then 59 years old.

In **1953**, Anna Freud began her second year as director of the Hampstead Child-Therapy Course and Clinic.

In **1953**, RKO released *Tarzan and the She Devil*, with Lex Barker playing the title role for the fifth time.

In **1953**, Louise Bates Ames appeared weekly on live TV with a half hour show on WBZ-TV, Boston. The show was called "Child Behavior."

In **1953**, according to published surveys, college women were more interested in security and marriage and less interested in pursuing a career than at any other time in the history of higher education of women. A huge majority of women were majoring in psychology.

In **1953**, Joseph R. McCarthy, U.S. Senator (R-Wisconsin) accused the Eisenhower Administration of treason. He also made innuendoes—which turned out later to have unfortunate consequences—that the U.S. Army was not energetic enough in ferreting out communists.

In **1953**, Dwight D. Eisenhower, Republican, assumed the office of President of the United States. His vice-president was Richard M. Nixon.

In **1953**, Mexican women received the right to vote in all elections.

In **1953**, Dorothy Adkins was chairman of the psychology department at the University of North Carolina, Chapel Hill; Lauretta Bender was director of the Child Guidance Clinic at the N.Y. Infirmary; Augusta Bronner was co-director of Judge Baker Clinic, Boston; Anna Freud was director of the Hampstead Clinic; Louise Bates Ames was co-founder and director of Research at the Gesell Institute of Child Development; and Mamie Phipps Clark was Executive Director and co-founder of the Northside (N.Y.C.) Center for Child Development.

In 1953, Marilyn Monroe appeared in *Gentlemen Prefer Blondes*.

In 1953, Sir Edmund Hillary succeeded in reaching the summit of Mount Everest (he and a Sherpa guide were the first ever to reach the top).

In 1953, Theodora Abel, who was then fifty-four years old, was in the middle of her personal analysis. After a thirteen-year career as a professional psychologist, during much of which she had been mildly antipathetic toward psychoanalysis, the extremely versatile Dr. Abel had become a staff member of the Postgraduate Center, New York, and was working and training as a lay analyst.

In 1953, Joyce Bauer Brothers got her Ph.D. in experimental psychology from Columbia University. She began to read and memorize twenty volumes on boxing, a feat which was to bring her fame and fortune after appearances on "The $64,000 Question" in 1954.

In 1953, many prominent women of psychology were teaching at women's colleges. Among them were Magda Arnold (Radcliffe), Elizabeth Duffy (Woman's College, University of North Carolina), and Edna Heidbreder (Wellesley). During World War II and shortly thereafter, however, many women had been able to "move up" to co-ed universities from all-women schools, including Georgene Seward, Eleanor Gibson, Theodora Abel, Florence Kluckhohn, and Lois Murphy.

In 1953, the New York Yankees, then in their heyday, again defeated the Brooklyn Dodgers in the World Series. This was the fifth time these two teams represented their respective leagues in the "fall classic," with the same result each time.

In 1953, the U.S. government adopted a policy of "termination," by which Indians were to be made independent by ending federal support and protection of certain reservation Indians. Many unprepared Indians suffered economic hardships and cultural upheaval as a result of this policy.

In 1953, having published five theoretical articles in journals and books the year before, Melanie Klein was recognized as a major force in British psychoanalysis.

In 1953, most of the Academy Awards went to the film *From Here to Eternity*, including that for "best supporting actor" to Frank Sinatra.

In **1953**, Clara Thompson's "Toward a Psychology of Women" was published in *Pastoral Psychology.*

In **1953**, the Minneapolis Lakers, led by superstar George Mikan, defeated the New York Knickerbockers to win the National Basketball Championship.

In **1953**, Ruth May Strang was a professor of education at Columbia, where she had been educated herself and with which she had maintained a formal affiliation for forty years (she later retired from Columbia in 1960 at age sixty-five). In addition to her other assignments, Strang was editor of the *Journal of the National Association of Women Deans and Councelors* and, with others, was preparing a series of volumes of readings for teenagers.

In **1953**, Stella Chess was the psychiatrist at Northside Center for Child Development—the clinic which Mamie and Kenneth Clark had established in 1946.

In **1953**, Margaret and Harry Harlow had their second child, Jonathan. Joan Guilford became a mother that year as did Lois Hoffman, Virginia Johnson, and Jane Mercer.

In **1953**, Virginia Sexton returned to her Alma Mater, Hunter College, where she had received her B.A. in 1936, as an instructor. She also published "Psychology in Italy" that year.

3

The Researchers

In a sense the women of psychology born between 1901 and 1910 provide what might be called the "Golden Age of Theelinocentric Psychology." The battles for acceptance had been waged and won by their predecessors and there was no longer any doubt that some women could attain eminence in the science of human behavior. The women whom we have named "the researchers" were at least the equals of the males with whom they competed and, in many cases, better scientists than their spouses, a generalization that could not be applied to the women included in the previous chapter.

In indication of the success attained by the women of this group is that two of the five women elected president of the American Psychological Association were born during this decade, Anna Anastasi and Leona Tyler. The fact that the two ran the APA for consecutive terms and that the years were 1972 and 1973 is significant, as we shall explain later. For now, it is enough to observe that during their professional life the women included in this chapter saw first a resurgence of femininity, then World War II, and then a second resurgence of femininity.

The eminent women psychologists of the era had completed their education, even more frequently than before, at Columbia University, and had made the initial successes of their career when the war started. Typically these women made significant contributions and began to gain recognition during the war and immediately afterwards. In many cases, however, they were unable to compete with male peers who were returning from wartime service and this led to perhaps the worst incidents of discrimination against women of psychology in their brief history. Only the most brilliant, most competent, most productive women would gain wide recognition during the fifties and sixties.

The women included in this chapter were, in the main, experimentalists and scientific researchers, although clinical psychology, psychiatry, and child development remained the primary professional interest of a minority of them. This is not to say that public service and child psychology

81

were not still of primary importance to the large number of women who were entering the ranks of the still-young science; simply that those women who are the best known and most honored women psychologists of this period were the academicians and scientists. The women who now arrived on the scene and are included in this history are women who successfully competed against men (who often were their intellectual inferiors), on their own turf.

The women in this chapter were the intellectual descendants of Margaret Washburn, Leta Hollingworth, Florence Goodenough, and Christine Ladd-Franklin, whose students, in many cases, they were. They were dedicated to objective research, experimentation, and reductionistic science. Much of their research and all of their theoretical contributions were in four areas: (a) physiological psychology, particularly in the area of emotions (Magda Arnold, Helen Flanders Dunbar, Elizabeth Duffy are examples); (b) perception (Eleanor Gibson); (c) psychometrics (Anne Anastasi, Leona Tyler, Anne Roe, Marie Jahoda, and Audrey Shuey); and (d) the psychology of women (Florence Kluckhohn, Margaret Mead, and Georgene Seward). These are areas that had been dominated by men and are areas that their mentors had pioneered for the entrance of women.

Of course some of the women born during this period were to continue the traditional involvement in clinical, child, and social psychology. This chapter includes Grace Heider, Margaret Mead, Else Frenkel-Brunswik, Dorothea Leighton, and Tamara Dembo, who are renowned social psychologists; Lois Murphy, Louise Bates Ames, Pauline Sears, and Dorothea McCarthy, who made important contributions to child psychology; and important clinical psychologists, including Karen Machover, Molly Harrower, Eugenia Hanfmann and Hedda Bolgar. But even within the more traditional areas, these women were more sophisticated in their research and more self-confident in their scientific competence than women of any previous generation.

Like the women of the previous era, most of these women are still alive and working. Some of the most famous and innovative, for example, Helen Flanders Dunbar, Margaret Mead, and Else Frenkel-Brunswik, are deceased, but there is a current resurgence of interest in their work. Although these women have been contributing to the store of information concerning psychology for at least the past thirty-five years, there has elapsed only enough time for a partial critical evaluation of their work; to some extent one cannot get the "big picture" of a person's professional worth in so short a time.

RESEARCHER AS CELEBRITY
Louise Bates Ames (1908-   )

There are few literate Americans who have not heard of Louise Bates Ames. Her books have been bestsellers, for many years her syndicated newspaper column, "Child Behavior," provided advice to thousands of readers, and her work at Yale on child development led to TV series, films, and celebrity.

Although Ames's contributions to child development are extremely important, there has been much more to the work of this highly productive woman. She is a recognized expert on the Rorschach and the 1974 recipient of the Bruno Klopfer Distinguished Contribution Award of the Society of Personality Assessment, her normative research on the Rorschach responses of children, adolescents, and of the aged being the most authoritative work and the classic in the field.

In addition to her early famous research on motor development, Ames has studied and written articles on every aspect of child psychology, including laterality, bedwetting, parent-child relations, the meaning of the IQ, emotional needs of children and adolescence, the sociocultural context of child behavior, explaining death to children, reading, the concept of developmental lag, learning disabilities, and readiness for school.

Ames has conducted research on women of psychology—her findings provided evidence for the discrimination against women of the post-war period—and has written on the psychology of women. Like Mary Cover Jones, Nancy Bayley, Charlotte Bühler, and several other female psychologists involved in developmental psychology who, in their own advanced years, turned their attention to gerontology, Ames has become an expert on the elderly. The difference between her and the others is revealing: she was herself not old when she began to study the elderly and her research efforts have been more sophisticated, more scientific, and more psychometric than those of the others.

Looking at Louis Bates Ames's bibliography, one cannot but be overwhelmed. Her work extends to many more than one thousand entries and she is clearly one of the most prolific writers in the history of psychology, perhaps the most prolific. She has written twenty-two books, numerous newspaper columns, hundreds of technical articles, scores of features for such popular magazines as *Family Circle*, and has had several TV series of her own (dating back to 1952, which makes her a television pioneer as well). At one time she made a living producing films on child development at Yale. Like several other women who have corresponded with us in the collection of data for this book, Ames underestimates the stunning volume of her work.[1]

Except for Arnold Gesell, with whom she collaborated early in her career, her collaborators in research and co-authors in publications were usually women. In this long list are Harriet Fjeld, Janet Learned, Elizabeth Hellershert, Ruth Metraux, Marjean Kremer, Judith August, Betty Scott, and Louise's own daughter, Joan Ames Chase. But her main collaborator and her partner for more than forty years has been Frances L. Ilg, the pediatrician whom she met at Yale in 1933 and with whom she founded the Gesell Institute and who has co-authored more than five hundred works with Ames.

Louise Bates Ames has been one of the most publicized women of psychology and is a celebrity. She is in the company of Maria Montessori, Margaret Mead, Anna Freud, and Joyce Brothers in this respect. But unlike the other celebrity-women psychologists, Louise Bates Ames has continued to conduct important, original research, now for forty-seven years, in addition to her better-known role as developmental psychology's pre-eminent publicizer.

Ames is also considered one of Maine's "best known daughters." One of her two honorary degrees is the Sc.D. from the university of Maine in 1957 (the other, also the Sc.D., was granted by Wheaton College in 1967) and her alma mater later conferred upon her "an even greater honor," the University of Maine Alumni Career Award in 1974.[1, 2]

Life and Career

Louise Bates was born on 29 October 1908, in Portland, Maine. Her parents were Samuel Lewis Bates and Anne Earle Leach Bates. Louise attended the University of Maine and received the B.A. in 1930. That same year, on May 22, she married Smith Ames. This marriage lasted seven years, ending in divorce in 1937 following another milestone, the granting of her Ph.D. from Yale.[3, 4] This marriage was to produce one daughter. Louise today has three grandchildren and three great-grandchildren.[1]

She also received her M.A. from Maine, in 1933—her thesis was an impressive lengthy study of the development of motor coordination in infants— and began work on her doctorate at Yale. She joined the staff of the Yale Clinic of Child Development and worked there from 1933 to 1948.[1, 3, 4] Her duties initially were to serve as personal research assistant to the director, Dr. Arnold Gesell, and as the secretary at the Clinic.[1, 4]

She continued to work on the research she had begun at Maine, received her Ph.D., in experimental psychology (1936), and published her first major work, a fifty-one page monograph which appeared in *Genetic Psychological Monographs* (1937).

In 1938 Ames produced her first film, for Encyclopedia Films. When, in 1944, she added a full-time position as curator of Yale Films of Child Development, she had already developed a new method of making films of children's behavior surreptitiously and of objectively analyzing them.[4] She also taught at Yale Medical School during this period, first as an instructor and then as an assistant professor (from 1936 to 1950).[1, 2]

Ames produced a steady stream of publications also, usually, early in her career, with the staff of the Yale Clinic. She was one of the co-authors of the three world-famous books published by this group, *The First Five Years of Life* (1941), *Infant and Child in the Culture of Today* (1943), and *The Child From Five to Ten* (1946). Her studies during her Yale period were basic research studies on various child development topics of interest to Gesell. Ames's superior technical skill in experimental design and development of methods for objectively observing and analyzing behavioral data made her a valuable, if young, member of the staff.

When Gesell retired, Ames joined forces with Frances Ilg and Janet Learned to form the Gesell Institute of Child Development in New Haven, Connecticut, in 1950.[1, 4] Ilg was the first executive director and Ames was made director of research. The two are still actively involved with the Institute, thirty years later; each has assumed various duties and titles over the decades. Three months ago Ames called herself the "co-director" of the Institute.[1]

In July 1951, Ames and Ilg began their very popular syndicated newspaper column, "Child Behavior," appearing five days a week. This answer column ran for many years and led to their equally popular book, also titled *Child Behavior* (1955). They changed the name of the column to "Parents Ask" in 1962, which was coincidentally the title of another widely selling book they published together that year.[1, 2]

In 1952, to give an example of the incredible work schedule and productivity of this woman, Ames (et al.) published the monumental normative study of children's Rorschach responses and she also published three journal articles on three widely different topics. She and Ilg also had their daily column to get out. Louise Bates Ames then added her half hour, weekly TV show, called "Child Behavior."[3, 4]

To say that Louise Bates Ames, in the last twenty-five years of her career, was exclusively an editor, writer for popular magazines, and a publicizer and spokesperson for child development and related topics, is untrue. This "accusation" denigrates the importance of her research and scientific publications during this period and in fact she made several significant contributions to psychology during even her most frenetic days. It is also inaccurate to put Ames's contributions in the past tense. Today, at seventy-two, she is not retired; on the contrary, she remains active at the institute and is currently immersed in important research in gerontology.[1]

Contributions

Louise Bates Ames's immense body of literature, especially that for the popular market, and her celebrity status tend to conceal her primary professional identity, that of a highly competent, successful, and productive research psychologist. On the basis of her scientific investigations and technical writings alone, she would deserve a reputation as one of America's most eminent psychologists.

However, by virtue of her long and prolific writing career, Louise Bates Ames has achieved what few other women of psychology have: she has been a major influence on our culture. Much of her writing has been directed toward parents and her influence on childrearing practices in this country is impossible to measure. Earlier and no less importantly than Benjamin Spock, Ames advocated a sort of common-sense permissiveness in parenting (which she later toned down) and she has been an advocate for many issues in what is (relentlessly) called "progressive education." Not a flamboyant person, Ames appears to be what she really is—a calm, unemotional, scientifically-oriented person when she speaks out on issues; and she is most convincing because of it.

At first living in the shadow of Arnold Gesell, a problem of most of the women who had been associated with the Yale Clinic, Ames made her reputation as an independent research psychologist. She did not suffer from unfair competition from males, although her own research documented the presence of discriminatory practices against female psychologists, but she might have had she stayed at Yale. She, in effect, avoided the problems that many of the women suffered during the late forties and fifites, by becoming the unrivaled champion of popular psychology.

THE PRESIDENT WAS A DROPOUT
Anne Anastasi (1908–   )

In 1970 Anne Anastasi, who was a full professor and chairman of the psychology department at Fordham University, was elected president of

Above: Louise Bates Ames; *below*: Anne Anastasi (photograph by Tommy Weber, New York)

Anne Roe (photograph by Robert Townsend Photography, Tucson, Arizona)

the American Psychological Association. She was only the third woman in the history of this august organization to be so honored; the other two were pioneers of psychology Mary Whiton Calkins (in 1905) and Margaret Floy Washburn (in 1921). When Anastasi began her term of office in 1971, at the height of the current feminist agitation, it had been fifty years since a woman of psychology had been recognized as its leader. Interestingly, she was in her prime some twenty years earlier and at the time she was honored as first among her peers, she was close to obtaining emeritus status.

With origins and early educational experiences that would seem unlikely to produce a powerful figure in a science, Anastasi has been an authority in differential psychology, test construction, and statistics for many years. Three of her publications, for example, have become the most important, influential textbooks in their field. In a sense, Anastasi was a "child prodigy," since many of her significant research contributions and her most influential book were completed before she was thirty years of age.

Anastasi was still young also when she became the "expert" in scientific psychology, a role that is indicated by the large number of review articles, critiques, and summaries of research findings she has published in the past forty years. It is Anne Anastasi who is asked to write the chapter on individual differences or psychological testing, the substantive critique of a new scientific concept, or the erudite comment on a controversial issue or about a promising new test instrument, and it has been that way her entire professional life. Anastasi has been respected for her brilliance and incisive understanding by her colleagues ever since she entered graduate school at Columbia.

Life with Mamam and Mimi

Anne Anastasi was born in New York City on 19 December 1908. She never knew her father, who died of a stomach ailment when she was one year old, and, because of some sort of family feud, never met her paternal relatives.[5] She lived during her childhood with her grandmother ("Mamam") whom she describes as a "grande dame," her maternal uncle, "the dilettante," and her mother ("Mimi") who was the "realist—someone had to keep the family alive."[5, p.2]

With very few exceptions, the eminent women of psychology were precocious and bright and bookish as girls. This was true of Anne Anastasi as well. Her education, which was the responsibility of her grandmother, began very early and she was able to impress the adults with her intellectual accomplishments. She had no playmates, not even an imaginary companion, and never learned to roller-skate or ride a bicycle or skip rope.[5]

In her early years Anastasi's life most resembles that of Lillien Jane Martin and Ruth Fulton Benedict, who also were reared in a father-absent family. Like these others, Anastasi's mother had to earn a living and the daughter became competent in adult concerns, achieving a level of maturity and organization denied to "more fortunate" girls. Like Martin and Benedict incidentally, Anastasi had a perceptual defect, nearsightedness, which was not diagnosed until Anne was a freshman in college.[5] One important—and fortunate—difference, though, is that Anne Anastasi has been happily married for forty-seven years.[6]

It appears that, despite the fact that none of the adults of the Anastasi household was equipped to earn a livelihood, finances did not continue to be a life-and-death struggle. Anne's mother taught herself bookkeeping and after several jobs (and one futile and brief attempt to run a family piano manufacturing business), Mimi finally became office manager of *Il Progresso Italo-Americano*, one of New York's largest and most successful foreign newspapers. Before long the family moved to a middle-class neighborhood and things were not so desperate.[5]

Meanwhile Mamam had some peculiar ideas about education and child-rearing. Like her daughter, she felt that Anne must have an excellent education and be prepared to support herself. But she was concerned that her granddaughter might learn bad manners from public school children. Consequently, Anne did not attend school until she was nine years old.[5]

Dropping Out

After only several weeks of elementary school, Anne Anastasi dropped out of public school and returned to the private tutoring she had enjoyed at home (A Miss Ireland was her tutor). In 1918, she again tried public school and stayed with it long enough to graduate from elementary school at the top of her class. She also began to make friends.[5]

Anne then entered Evander Childs High School, New York City, which she described as old and overcrowded and, even in 1921, populated by remote and impersonal teachers and administrators. She found the school unattractive and uncomfortable and could tolerate it for only two months. She then dropped out again. To this day Anastasi has doubts that high school is necessary.[5, 7]

Anne and her family decided that she should go to college, so she was enrolled at Rhodes Preparatory School in New York City to prepare to take the College Entrance Examination Board exams. In June 1923, she passed the exams and was admitted to Barnard College.

Barnard and Columbia

Anastasi entered Barnard College at fifteen years of age, intending to major in mathematics with minors in physics and chemistry. Her first course in psychology was during her freshman year and, although taught by a woman in the philosophy department, provided "solid scientific fare" and was enjoyable.[5]

During her sophomore year, Anne had two experiences that influenced her decision to switch majors from math to psychology. The first was a course in developmental psychology taught by Harry Hollingworth. A generalist, Hollingworth impressed her with the breadth of psychology; he was then chairman of the department at Barnard and, she reports, a stimulating teacher. The second incident was her reading an article in statistics by Charles Spearman. This article convinced her that she could "enjoy the best of two possible worlds: I could remain faithful to my first love, mathematics, while pursuing psychology too."[5]

Anastasi took "extra" courses, some without credit; her intellectual curiosity and energy seemed unboundless. She convinced a reluctant Hollingworth to permit her to undertake an honors program during her junior year (these were not encouraged in psychology), a study on music preferences with Frederick H. Lund, an instructor at Barnard.[5]

In 1928 Anastasi received the A.B. degree, with an almost straight "A" average and was elected to Phi Beta Kappa. She received the Caroline Duror Graduate Memorial Fellowship and, that same year, her first publication, with Lund as senior author, appeared in the *American Journal of Psychology*.[5, 7]

Anastasi went next to Columbia, where she achieved a superb record. First, she was allowed to "skip" her M.A.—her honors research, which had been published, was accepted in lieu of a master's thesis. Secondly, she was able, by taking an overload of courses and working feverishly during the summer, to complete all her work for the Ph.D. in two years.[5] She received the Ph.D., under H. E. Garrett, in 1930, when she was twenty-one years old.

Perhaps more amazing than the rapidity with which Anastasi, public-school dropout, was to complete her formal education, is that she found time for extracurricular achievements as well. During the summer of 1929, for example, she worked as a research assistant to C. B. Davenport at Carnegie Institute of Washington (the project was housed at Cold Springs

Harbor, Long Island), where she developed a "culture-free" intelligence test. This was her first experience in large-scale project research and in test-construction. Later that summer, she was able to put to use Mamam's insistance that she become proficient in foreign languages, when she attended a high-powered genetics conference, serving as a French interpreter for the Cold Springs Harbor Group. Still later that summer, Anastasi attended the first International Congress of Psychology to be held in this country, at Yale. She was able to "hear and meet" such luminaries as Karl Lashley, James Cattell, Spearman, McDougall, Pieron, and Pavlov.[5, 7] During her second year of graduate school, she also renewed her association with Barnard College, joining the faculty there after returning from the Yale Congress, and began an even longer, new association with a fellow student, John Foley.[5]

Career and Marriage

Anne Anastasi was made an instructor at Barnard in 1930 (the Ph.D. was required) and reports that she was happy to get any position during the Depression. The same year an article based on her dissertation was published, "A Group Factor in Immediate Memory." She remained at Barnard until 1939, teaching the usual undergraduate courses, such as general, experimental, applied, and differential psychology. She continued to conduct her own highly respectable research and to write; her published work was not voluminous but was extremely influential and important, right from the beginning.[5, 7]

The type of woman she was when young can be inferred from her relationship to Garrett. In her dissertational work Anastasi was part of a group of students who were, at Garrett's direction, applying the "tetrad technique" to isolate group factors in data. Anastasi's analysis was successful, but she insisted that she has discovered *a* group factor in memory, not, as Garrett encouraged, *the* memory factor. She also was courageous enough to debate Garrett—who was an anomaly at Columbia, since he was the leading advocate of the inheritance of ability at the school most noted for its environmentalist orientation—on the question of nature vs. nurture.[5] Remember that at the time she was twenty years old and he was an authority on mental testing and individual differences and was also the chairman of her dissertation committee.

Anastasi shortly afterwards published, with H. E. Garrett as the senior author, a definitive article on the tetrad technique (1932). It was not until 1954 that Anne Anastasi published what is probably the best exposition of the nature-nurture controversy every produced by a psychologist; her brief article, "Heredity, Environment, and the Question 'How?'," has been reprinted in scores of anthologies as the most intelligent, clearest statement of the problem.

In 1931, during the summer, Anastasi again demonstrated her quest for an education through unconventional means, which characterizes her early life. She decided to rush off to the University of Minnesota to take a course with R. A. Fisher, whom many call "the Father of Statistics," on the then not yet accepted analysis of variance procedure. Fisher gave this course upon the invitation of the American Mathematical Society, which was meeting at Minnesota, and Anastasi, learning about it by chance, went to Minnesota, of course.[5]

On 26 July 1933, Anne Anastasi married John Porter Foley, Jr., who was also a Ph.D. and a fellow psychologist out of Columbia. In a real sense, she did not allow her marriage to interfere with her career. If anything, at least at the beginning, it was the other way around, since John taught, for several years, in Washington and Anne remained in New York, and they spent weekends together.[5]

Because of the anti-nepotism rules and Anastasi's unwillingness to accept a position with the Washington bureaucracy, Anastasi and Foley did not share a primary residence until 1944, when *he* moved back to New York.[5] Also in this case the wife's career rather obviously overshadowed the husband's. Foley has been her most frequent collaborator in research and publication; they did not have any children.

It is very symptomatic that with three exceptions, Anne Anastasi has been the senior author of all those publications that were collaborative efforts: her honors research article, the article with Garrett on the tetrad technique, and a 1968 article on testing for creativity in adolescent boys were the exceptions. It must be noted, as Anastasi indeed does,[5] that she also suffered gender discrimination, but, as in everything she was to deal with, she has managed to overcome discrimination also.

In 1939 Anastasi was appointed assistant professor, "Chairman"—and sole member—of the psychology department of Queens College of the City University of New York. She was able to recruit six faculty members, who, like her, had high hopes for this new department in this new college. She remained at Queens during the war years, but grew to dislike the school and despise its "administrative climate."[5] She and most of her faculty left in 1946.

In 1947 Anastasi was appointed associate professor of education at Fordham University. The undergraduate student body and the faculty of the liberal arts division was "exclusively male" at that time. She reports that for once gender discrimination worked in her favor: although all her previous teaching experience was at the undergraduate level, at Fordham she was only allowed to teach (the much more prestigious) graduate courses.[5] Anastasi was also a famous psychologist when this "discrimination" occurred; her 1937 textbook, *Differential Psychology*, was being widely used throughout the country.

In 1951 Anastasi was advanced to full professor and in 1968, despite her dislike of red tape and the onus of administration, she accepted the (rotating) chairpersonship of the department. She served her full six year term. In 1979, at age seventy-one, Anastasi was made professor emeritus at Fordham, retiring from teaching but still actively involved in the official duties of an elder statesperson and a "power" in the psychological establishment.[6]

Anastasi has been, in addition to one of America's most brilliant psychologists, one of its most powerful figures. She was president of the Division of General Psychology of the American Psychological Association (APA) (1956–57), president of the APA Division of Evaluation and Measurement (1965–66), and, of course, president of the APA itself (1971–72).

She has been awarded the following honorary degrees: University of Windsor, Litt.D. in 1967; Villanova University, Paed.D. in 1971; Cedar Crest College, Sc.D. in 1971; Fordham University, Sc.D. in 1979; and La Salle College, Sc.D. in 1979.[6]

Work

Anne Anastasi's best-known publications are her three textbooks, especially her first. They have been translated into several languages and are used throughout the world, repeatedly revised and kept up-to-date and topical. *Differential Psychology* first appeared in 1937. Usually referred to as "Anastasi and Foley" (he was the co-author of the 1949 and subsequent revisions), this book did much to formalize this area of interest in psychology; in fact, Anastasi renamed the topic. Prior to this book, the area was called "individual differences," but she chose a literal translation of William Stern's 1900 book title (from the German)[8] to broaden the area to include group differences as well as differences between members of a group.[5, 7]

Her two other influential textbooks are *Psychological Testing*, published first in 1954, and *Applied Psychology* (1964). As noted above, many of her publications have dealt with theoretical issues and concepts on a very wide variety of subjects relevant to psychology.

According to Anastasi, her major areas of research interest include: (a) the nature and identification of psychological traits; (b) the operation of environmental and experiential factors on psychological development; (c) test construction and evaluation; and (d) expression in art, particularly that of children and of the "insane."[5]

The last area is interesting. She and John Foley have long been interested in art and are avid museum devotees. Many of the fifteen or so collaborative publications of the two deal with their studies of art. One important finding of their controlled studies, not frequently cited and certainly controversial, is that the artistic productions of psychotics are not reflective of their pathology and, as a consequence, cannot be used for diagnostic purposes (despite these findings, they most definitely still are).[5]

In Anne Anastasi we have a woman who is both a brilliant scholar and a major political force in psychology, well-honored and recognized in both roles. She has always been controversial, courageous, scientificially conservative—and a little wild and devilish in her personality. This formidable woman who presided over psychology and did battle with Garrett and the hereditarians, was also the woman who dropped out of high school and rode the Penn Central from New York to Washington every other weekend to be with her husband (incidentally they're still married after forty-seven years, a fact which provides opposing evidence to the value of "togetherness" in early marriage.)

·

MOTHER OF HOLISTIC MEDICINE
Helen Flanders Dunbar (1902–1959)

The goal is not so much to find or manipulate a 'cause' as to discover a means of effective intervention. This is, after all, what concerns the physician more than historical explanations of causes which may be irrelevant to the changes desired.

—Helen Flanders Dunbar

In this period of enthusiasm for the holistic approach to medicine, it would be simple justice if the reputation and prominence of Helen Flanders Dunbar is restored, for this brilliant psychoanalyst was the leading advocate of this position during the forties and early fifties and she was then highly criticized for her ideas and work. The continuing poor estimation of her ideas may be due to ignorance, for, as her recent biographer notes, "Dunbar must rank among the century's most cited yet unread medical authors."[10]

Helen Flanders Dunbar has been a "name" in psychology for the past forty years, yet as a person she was a mysterious figure and her published work, although consistent with current philosophical conceptions of medicine, is not known to even those who share her prescient views. Most of her contemporaries do not remember her personally; most of our contemporaries, male and female, who are aware of the "name," do not know that it belonged to a woman, since she always referred to herself professionally as "Flanders Dunbar."

It is debatable whether Dunbar or Franz Alexander, her most vocal and persistent rival and critic, deserves to be called the "founder" of psychosomatic medicine. Since Alexander's published articles precede hers by a year or so, the honor probably belongs to him. But as Robert Powell has suggested, Dunbar's claim to primacy has considerable supporting evidence: she published a survey of literature on studies of psychosomatic disease, *Emotions and Bodily Changes* (1935), "which many consider to have launched the movement"; she published *Psychosomatic Diagnosis* (1943), "the field's first handbook"; she also wrote *Mind and Body: Psychosomatic Medicine* (1947), "the field's first bestseller"; she founded the American Psychosomatic Society and its journal *Psychosomatic Medicine*; and she conducted, from 1934 to 1938, the "first large-scale psychosomatic research program."[10]

The controversy and criticism surrounding Dunbar's approach to psychosomatic medicine were actually reflections of a broader theoretical and political battle within American psychiatry and, in a sense, were a continuation of the ancient "mind-body" problem that philosopher-psychologists had debated throughout the nineteenth century.

Until the late thirties, American psychiatry was led by Adolf Meyer and his colleagues and adherents, a group which later would include, loosely affiliated, Lauretta Bender and Flanders Dunbar among many others. The approach taken by these persons, usually called psychobiologists, was eclectic and holistic (or "organismic"). They all received some psychoanalytic training and indeed usually referred to themselves as "psychoanalysts," but they were in no way "controlled" by the Viennese orthodoxy.

Seen in this context, Dunbar's views must be considered as initially part of the mainstream of American psychiatry. She was, in fact, primarily a researcher and organizer in the movement, rather than a major general theoretician.[10] At the beginning Dunbar and the Meyer group represented the American orthodoxy and Alexander, whose theoretical views were more traditionally Freudian than were Freud's, was in the minority.

After 1938, when the onslaught of refugees from Europe, most of whom were orthodox Freudians, entered the ranks of American psychiatry, the majority became the minority. Alexander's specificity theory, which focused on the past and looked for etiologically significant unconscious mechanisms as the specific "cause" of psychosomatic disorder, was generally accepted as "right." Dunbar's advocacy of treating the patient as an "integrated whole" rather than as an isolated trait or symptom and her repudiation of the specificity theory (an early experience, say in feeding, would cause a particular gastric problem later in life) were seen as "wrong."

Dunbar's position which had, up to then, been seen as conventional, became unconventional. More recently the pendulum, in terms of the politics of medicine, seems to be swinging back to Dunbar's approach. In terms of the relationship of mind to body, her psychosomatic theory is very congruent with modern mainstream psychology. To separate mental processes from physical ones, for that is a necessary step in the development of an etiological theory which describes the interaction of one "force" on another, which is what Alexander taught, is a "dualistic" conception. Dunbar's position, in the emphasis upon the unitary nature of the totality of a person, has been the preferable solution to the mind-body problem in psychology in modern times.

Life and Career

Helen Flanders Dunbar was born in Chicago, Illinois, on 14 May 1902, to Francis William Dunbar and Edith Flanders Dunbar. Her father was a physicist and mathematician, whom she credits with inspiring her scientific orientation. As a young child, she was taught physics and calculus by her father. An indication of Helen's dedication to education and a major accomplishment in itself is the number of academic degrees she was to earn between the ages of twenty-one and twenty-eight: B.A., M.A., Ph.D., B.D., and M.D.[11, 12]

Throughout her life, Helen is said to have had a "fury" about work and accomplishment, while maintaining a "childlike spontaneity" and leaving her "personal affairs in confusion." She maintained her childhood love of horses and was an excellent horsewoman.[11]

After graduating from the Brearly School in New York City, Helen received the B.A. from Bryn Mawr College in 1923, with a dual major in literature and science. She then went to Columbia where she received the M.A. and Ph.D.; her dissertation led to her first publication, a book called

Symbolism in Medieval Thought. Simultaneously she attended Union Theological Seminary, where she earned the B.D. in 1927.[12]

The details of Dunbar's medical training are obscure. She spent one year, 1929–30, at the University of Vienna, where she obtained training in psychiatry and neurology and became acquainted with Felix Deutsch. She devoted part of that year to a training experience in Zurich as well. Dunbar received the M.D. from Yale University Medical School in 1930.[11, 12]

The problem in describing Dunbar's later education and early career is that both are extremely complicated, because she was involved in an incredible number of simultaneous activities. She was not only involved in completing the formal requirements for several advanced academic degrees, she was engaged in clinical research (Worcester, Mass., State Hospital, 1925) and a sub-internship (New Haven, 1928) while in medical school; she wrote a book; and even found time to marry twice and have a daughter, Marcia Winslow Dunbar-Soule.

When she married George Henry Soule in 1929, she retained her own name by law (and her daughter was given a hyphenated last name which includes Helen's maiden name). Soule appears in the history of psychiatry as the man who brought Wilhelm Reich, the very controversial psychoanalyst and author of *Character Analysis*, to America.[10] Nothing has been written about the fate of this first marriage, but it is known that in 1932 she married a man named Theodore Wolfe. Nothing at all has been written about this marriage.[12]

Consistent with the feverish pace of her career, Dunbar completed a residency at clinics of Columbia Medical College, particularly at Presbyterian Hospital, from 1930 to 1934. She also was an instructor at Columbia's Medical college, from 1931 to 1936, and in charge of psychosomatic research there from 1932 to 1949.[11, 12] It was in this last role at Columbia that Dunbar completed her now famous study: the "holistic evaluation of over 1,600 serial admission to Columbia-Presbyterian Hospital."[10]

This study, conducted between 1934 and 1938, established the relationship between "personality constellations" and psychosomatic disorder, resulting in a conception that is similar to Ruth Benedict's holistic "pattern" and to Gestalt-psychology theory. It is also the origin (along with contributions by Meyer and his colleagues) of the recent "personality-type" theories of psychosomatics, for example, the well-known "Type A-Type B" personality distinction in heart disease research.

This amazing career continued, with Dunbar adding on increasing amounts of time and energy to her clinical practice. She maintained offices in New York City and in South Kent, Connecticut, and was on the attending staff of several hospitals simultaneously. She found time somehow also to write four important books and, arguably, to "found" the psychosomatic movement.

In addition to her clinical work, which occupied her later career interests, Dunbar served as editor-in-chief of the journal she founded, *Psychosomatic Medicine*, for nine years, and from 1941 to 1949 as an instructor at the New York Psychoanalytic Institute (this was the period when the Institute was plagued by internal conflict and suffered famous defections).[11, 12]

Helen Flanders Dunbar was clearly a workaholic, seeing patients, working energetically for the several professional organizations of which she was a member, doing research, teaching, and writing. She died on 21 August 1959, at age fifty-seven. Her death occurring unexpectedly while she was in the country (where she usually wrote on weekends). Dunbar had just received a first press copy of her latest book, *Psychiatry in the Medical Specialties*[9] and was looking forward to her annual summer sojourn to an international congress, from the end of World War II on, her primary source of recreation.[11]

Contributions

Helen Flanders Dunbar is best known for her organizational work, which perhaps entitles her to be named "founder" of psychosomatic medicine, and for her monumental research. Equally important was her successful careers as an eclectic (psychobiologic) psychoanalyst and teacher. But her most significant contributions were to psychosomatic theory, which resulted from her original research efforts.

In 1948, Stanley Cobb distinguished three types of psychosomatic theories: psychoanalytic, physiological, psychobiologic.[13] Helen Flanders Dunbar was, of course, the epitome of the psychobiologist theorist, who developed much of the theoretical conceptions and conducted most of the research that support this approach.

Dunbar's theoretical position concerning personality was not entirely unique. Holistic theories have been presented for the past fifty years, never more influentially than the present time. When, however, Dunbar applied a holistic conception to psychosomatics, Alexander and Therese Benedek were proponents of a competing theory and the latter approach was to prevail.

Her thesis, that "the organism in its totality is as essential to an explanation of its elements as its elements are to an explanation of the organism," is similar to that of Meyer, William Alanson White, Draper and others, but opposite to the basic premise of the psychoanalytic theory of psychogenesis.

Dunbar taught that personality constellations and environmental conditions at the current moment, not historical experiences, were predictive of the development of certain diseases. The procedure was to observe patients carefully and analyze personality along four dimensions (the "panels" of personality presented by Draper): the anatomic, the physiological, the psychical, and the immological.[14] Dunbar and her followers successfully discovered correlations between personality configurations and certain diseases including gastric, cardiac, respiratory and other ailments.

In Helen Flanders Dunbar we have a woman who, like the other women included in this chapter, gained prominence and power during the late thirties and during the war. Unlike the others, however, her "demise" was as much a result of theoretical conflict as of political infighting. Her conceptualizations were repudiated by majority opinion in psychiatry, but they have never died; witness the resurgence of interest in holistic theories today. We are optimistic that Dunbar's major role in the history of psychology and of holistic medicine will be recognized and her reputation and prominence will be restored.

EMANCIPATED ANTHROPOLOGIST
Margaret Mead (1901-1978)

America's most popular and most highly respected cultural anthropologist, Margaret Mead was for thirty years the leading feminist-researcher as well. Her two most famous books, *Coming of Age in Samoa* and *Sex and Temperament in Three Primitive Societies*, have been major influences on our culture; her observation of cultural differences in sex roles did more to dispel the notion of "innate" sex differences in basic temperament traits than any other source of information.

In her later years, frequently called upon by the public media to comment on conditions in our contemporary American society, Margaret Mead became the most respected of the spokespersons involved in the feminist movement. As an old woman, Mead's pronouncements on family life, adolescents, marriage, and the role of women were fresh, youthful, wise, and outrageous.

In *Blackberry Winter*, an autobiography published in 1972, she wrote:

If we are to have a world in which men and women work together, then women must learn to give up pandering to male sensibilities, something at which they succeed so well, as long as it was a woman's primary role, as a wife, to keep her family intact, or as a mistress to comfort her lover.[15]

Margaret Mead was the "first" student of Ruth Benedict and became her biographer and very close friend. Although the two of them worked together and shared similar ideas about anthropology, they were almost opposites in temperament, life experiences, and in the details of the contributions each was to make to social science. For example, unlike Benedict, Margaret Mead was fun-loving, affable, and self-assured. A Columbia classmate of Mead described her to us as "sexy," an appellation hardly suiting Benedict (who has been called "sensitive," "moody," or even "gloomy"). Throughout her long life, Margaret Mead was a successful anthropologist, feminist, lover, wife, and mother. She was always comfortable with herself and never questioned the "rightness" of her interests or her choices.

Also unlike Benedict, who was primarily an integrator of data and a theoretician, Margaret Mead was primarily a researcher. In a sense, this "spoiled priest" of a psychologist[16] always remained to some degree "a psychologist" in her attempts to assure objectivity, careful measurement, and experimental research style. A large number of her publications indeed appear in psychology anthologies and her focus upon human development in her field studies might justify the label of "applied psychology" to much of her work. In any event, Mead, especially early in her career, was not an "armchair" anthropologist (as were many of those at Columbia during that time), but a very active data gatherer—Samoa, New Guinea, and Bali—who loved research.

Life and Education

Margaret's early life, while unconventional, was perfect for the development of a strong-willed, competent individual. She was born on 16 December 1901, to Edward Sherwood Mead, an economist by training and a professor at the University of Pennsylvania, and Emily Fogg Meade, a sociologist, in Philadelphia, Pennsylvania.[15]

Due to her father's preoccupation with finding the "right" investment which would make the family rich, Margaret and her family moved several times, sometimes several times in one year. This early lesson in adaptation (and she generally was successful in adjusting to novel situations) probably was responsible, in part, for Margaret's ease and enjoyment in doing field work.[16]

The eldest of five children, Margaret was able to benefit from the singular attention provided first children. Home life involved the intellectual exchange of ideas, with an inculcation of respect for research, for the questioning mind, and for never being content with the mundane.

> We were the kind of family who argued about historical facts and quotations at meals . . . my father regarded as the most valuable activity in the world 'the addition to the store of knowledge of exact facts' . . . actual facts, verified, indisputable, untampered with by imagination or veniality, were the most important thing in the world.[16]

Most interesting, in terms of Margaret's report of being identified with her father, is that when she was six years old, her mother, Emily Fogg Meade (apparently the rest of the family changed the spelling of the last name when Margaret was a child, but the mother used the original spelling in her professional identity), published a sociological study of Italian immigrants. Almost exactly twenty years later, Margaret also published a study of the children of Italian immigrants, based upon her master's thesis.[16]

Unlike those families where the first son reigns, in this family the eldest was not made to feel inferior nor displaced at the birth of her brother. Her nickname had been "the punk" and when her brother arrived, she became "the original punk."[15] She never doubted that women "have brains" or that she would have both a career and a successful marriage. She observed, "I knew that I had my father's mind and he had his mother's."[16] Her grandmother believed that males were more fragile than females, a theory that seemed to be confirmed by her brother's many illnesses, and her father believed that education was easier for girls to master and thus expected Margaret to excel academically.[16]

In her autobiographical writings, Margaret Mead observes that her early experiences prepared her specifically for a career in anthropology, but we would add that they also provided a background for her life-long interest in child development, socialization, and parent-child relationships.

Her mother, for example, taught her to maintain carefully recorded observation data by providing a model for her: she filled thirteen "fat" notebooks with details of Margaret's early life. The frequent family relocations also led to Margaret's first childhood "anthropological study," of counting-out rhymes and rules of juvenile games as they appeared in different versions in different locations. Margaret was also encouraged by her grandmother to study the development of her two younger sisters; this led to an early interest in the problem of strephosymbolia and to Mead's later involvement with the mixed-cerebral-dominance fad.[16]

In addition to the obvious influence of her social scientist parents, Margaret Mead was to be exposed to another most remarkable and brilliant member of the household, her grandmother. Margaret Ramsey was a suffragist, a college graduate, who had been a teacher and school principal. She was primarily responsible for Margaret Mead's education, since, until high school, the latter's exposure to public school was spotty at most.[15]

Margaret credits her grandmother for her strength of character and her "ease in being a woman." Like her grandmother, Mead became a feminist who, while rejecting sexual stereotypes, was convinced that an outstanding and clever woman could enjoy both a successful career and a happy personal life.

As a child, a career to Margaret meant to become a lawyer or a minister or a writer or a "minister's wife with six children."[15] She began to write when she was nine, began her first novel in 1915, and wrote plays and poems. Of her writing, except for her voluminous productivity in anthropology and related fields, only her poetry has been published.

College

One reason for Margaret's willingness to complete high school was her desire for social relationships with peers. She was especially eager to go to college where she expected to study "fascinating subjects" and to meet "brilliant students." She wanted to go to Wellesley, but her father rejected this idea. The ostensible reason was a serious financial reversal, which left the family "poor," but Margaret's engagement to Luther Cressman, a ministerial student, was probably the most cogent reason.[15]

In any event, Margaret's mother convinced her husband into a compromise and in 1919 she entered De Pauw University, a much less expensive choice and her father's school. The year she was to spend there was a disaster for Margaret, who was not interested in football, sororities, or dating, and she felt like a total outsider there.[16]

In 1920 Mead transferred to Barnard College, where like Anastasi she was influenced by Harry Hollingworth; his course in child development influenced her to add psychology as a second major. It was not until her senior year that she took her first course in anthropology, under Franz Boas, which was taught primarily by Ruth Benedict.[15] Her B.A., in 1923, was in psychology.

Career and Marriage

After graduating from college, Margaret announced her decision to marry Luther, a stable, solid man who she felt would make a good father to her children. Her father offered her a trip around the world if she would forget marriage, but the strong-willed Margaret married Luther Cressman (she had decided to "keep my own name" with Cressman's approval) and entered Columbia University to do her graduate work.[15]

Margaret had become disenchanted with psychology, which she found to be too much a laboratory science and too boring, but her master's degree in 1924 was in psychology. Her research involved administering group intelligence tests to Italian-American children and her thesis considered the effect of social factors in depressing scores on tests.[16]

Her friend Ruth Benedict helped convince her to work on a doctorate in anthropology and, despite the reluctance of her mentor, Boas, Margaret accepted a fellowship which enabled her to conduct a field trip to Polynesia. "Papa Franz" (the secret nickname for Boas invented by Benedict and Mead) was certainly paternal at this time; he did not at all like the idea of Margaret's going off alone to Polynesia. He preferred that she do a study of adolescent girls of the American Indians. Margaret's compromise with him was that she would investigate adolescent girls of Samoa.[15]

She looked forward eagerly to field work and this was always to be the most enjoyable aspect of her career as an ethnologist; it was a "vivid desire rather than a mere necessary part of a chosen career" for her.[17] In the preface to *Coming of Age in Samoa*, Mead explains the urgency she felt at this time for anthropological research: these primitive societies have only a limited time before they are changed through epidemic, discovery, and missionary effort, changes which would result in "blotting out forever the living record of what their way had once been."[17]

For the next several years Margaret Mead travelled to several exotic places, studying the people and producing, after each study, a memorable and well-received manuscript. Among her field studies were the Manus, 1929, the Arapesh and Mundugamor, 1931, and the Balinese, 1936. Her second very popular book, *Sex and Temperament in Three Primitive Societies*, was published in 1935.[18]

During the years of her most intensive work in the field, Mead notes, her only real home was at the National Museum in New York. For her entire career in anthropology, in fact, Mead's primary source of employment was at the museum: from 1926 to 1942, assistant curator; from 1942 to 1964, associate curator; and from 1964 to 1974, curator of ethnology.[15, 19]

The trip to Samoa had several important effects upon Margaret Mead. It established her reputation in anthropology and made her famous, it brought her the Ph.D. (Columbia, 1929), and it led indirectly to her divorce from Luther. Mead had realized that she and her husband had few common interests and because of a diagnosed gynecological problem, was told that she could not have children. But to make things worse for her marriage, on the way home from Samoa, she met Reo Fortune.[15]

Fortune was a New Zealand psychologist interested in the cross-cultural approach. He was also a somewhat wild, exciting, bohemian type, almost the opposite of the more solid but conventional man to whom she was married. After a lengthy "intellectual" affair with Reo, she divorced Luther and in 1929 married Fortune.[15] She and her second husband then went off and studied the Manus together.

She found in Fortune a partner in her research and with him was able to make contact with or to study primitive cultures which would, she believed, be too warlike or aggressive for a lone woman to encounter.[18] From 1931 to 1933 they collected data on the three societies in New Guinea which led to Mead's most popular book, *Sex and Temperament*. Early in the field work, while studying the Arapesh, Margaret met a young anthropologist named Gregory Bateson, who introduced her to the Tchambuli, a society that he had studied in which the institutionalized sex roles involved expected temperament traits that were the opposite of those of western cultures.[15, 18]

When Mead became acquainted with the Mundugamor, one of the three societies included in this study, she was revolted by the behavior of this group where both sexes were excessively aggressive, exploitative, and rejecting of their children. "I reacted so strongly against the set of the culture," she wrote, "that it was here that I decided that I would have a child no matter how many miscarriages it meant."[15] She had, however, long before decided that Fortune would make an awful father.

Complicating her personal life considerably, Margaret Mead had also fallen in love with the handsome, debonaire Bateson. In 1935, the same year that *Sex and Temperament* was published, she divorced Fortune. The next year, in Singapore, she was married to Gregory Bateson, interrupting briefly their study of Balinese mother-child relations. In 1939 she gave birth to a daughter, Mary Catherine Bateson.[15, 19]

With Gregory Bateson and many other social scientists, Margaret Mead was actively involved in the war-effort. Her book, *And Keep Your Powder Dry: An Anthropologist Looks at America* (1942), was her most ambitious project up to that time, since the subject matter was so broad. Most of her

publications subsequent to this book were also applications of anthropological (and psychological) methods and findings to an analysis of contemporary American culture.

After the war, she joined her close friend Ruth Benedict in her Culture
at a Distance project at Columbia. Upon Benedict's death, she and Rhoda
Metraux assumed leadership of the project and in 1953, the two of them
edited the book that described the method and achievements of the
project, *The Study of Culture at a Distance*.

Mead became a popular lecturer and taught courses at many different
schools including Vassar, Columbia, the University of Cincinnati, and
from 1968 to 1971 was chair of the social sciences division at Fordham
University.[19]

During the sixties and until her death, Margaret Mead was the acknowledged expert on the state of our society. She spoke and wrote on childrearing and socialization, on the generation gap, on marriage and family,
on the role of women, and on creativity and violence. She had well-
thought-out, incisive, and outspoken ideas on virtually all the institutions
of American life.[16]

Mead was an acknowledged leader of her discipline as well. She was
president of the American Anthropological Association in 1960, president
of the World Federation for Mental Health in 1956–57, president of the
Society for General Systems Research in 1972, and president of the
American Association for the Advancement of Science in 1973.[19, 20]

Mead wrote twenty-four books, almost all of them were bestsellers and
were reprinted several times. She co-authored or co-edited another eighteen books. She published scores of important articles in child development, psychology, sociology, and current events, as well as in anthropology.[16, 20] In 1978, shortly before her death on November 15, the
United Nations paid Margaret Mead a unique tribute: she was given a silver
medal as the "Planetary Citizen of the Year."

Summary

A friend of Margaret Mead's once said that she was "never quite forgiven"
by her peers "for communicating easily and widely. It's the sin of being
popular."[20] Mead was popular indeed. Her literary style made her reports
of her data and conclusions lively and interesting. For a majority of educated lay people, who have read her research reports, Margaret Mead *was*
American anthropology.

Mead was initially trained to be a psychologist and if she had had
greater exposure to social psychology at Columbia, might have remained a

psychologist. There is some justification to conclude that with her interest in personality theory, developmental psychology, and cultural patterning of temperament, motivation, and behavior, Mead was, in fact, primarily an applied psychologist in her productive career. Although she found the content of experimental psychology dreary and dull, she was always to maintain the objective and scientific research attitude that even Robert Woodworth would have respected.

Mead was a researcher and a scientist. Unlike Benedict, she is not the author of a general, integrative theory. The holistic, cultural relativistic, and functionalist theoretical orientations that underlie her best research efforts were correctly credited to Boas, to psychology, and most notably to Ruth Benedict.

Mead's influence on the psychology of women, in the sense of both the formal science and the internalized values of women, is incalculable. Mead's findings concerning the cultural arbitrariness of sex differences once thought to be "natural" and "biological" prepared a generation of women to assume "man's" occupations during World War II and thereafter. Like Leta Hollingworth before her, Margaret Mead conducted research which effectively dispelled sexual stereotypes and put to rest antiquated myths about the nature of women. Herself an emancipated woman, Mead is the person who most influenced the inception of the current world-wide feminist movement.

THE MAKING OF A RESEARCH PSYCHOLOGIST
Anne Roe (1904–   )

To Anne Roe . . . in recognition of her early and imaginative application of biographical study, personality assessment, and clinical evaluation of eminent and creative scientists in different fields.
Citation, Richardson Creativity Award 1968[21]

Anne Roe is best known for her famous research on the creative productivity of various groups of scientists. She has also been, for several decades, the acknowledged expert in the field of vocational choice and the psychological-personal meaning of work. Before her *Psychology of Occupations* in 1956, there was no in-depth treatment of the relationship between occupational choice and personality correlates.

Anne has been a much-honored psychologist whose research in a variety of fields and important books (six) and lengthy monographs (several) have provided significant contributions to the accumulated knowledge of psychology. Among her other distinctions: she is one of only a few women to be made Professor Emerita at Harvard University and probably the only psychologist to become a member of the Society of Vertebrate Paleon-tology.[22] Her biographer is her stepdaughter, one of four daughters of George Gaylord Simpson, whose mother she became in 1938.[23, 24]

Growing up in Denver, Colorado, Roe, who maintained her maiden name during two marriages, had expected to become a high school teacher. She did not anticipate becoming a full professor at Harvard, only the *ninth* woman to attain this rank in the first three hundred years of the history of this institution. Nor did she anticipate marrying her very close childhood friend, practically a brother to her, but she and George Gaylord Simpson have been happily married and partners for more than forty years, even suffering "his and her heart failures" together in 1964 and hospitalized together in Albuquerque.[24]

Life and Occupational Choice

Anne Roe was born in Denver, Colorado, on 20 August 1904, the second of four children, born into a family headed for financial disaster.[25] Her father's transfer company went bankrupt and he had to become a book-keeper. Her mother Edna, on the other hand, who was a superb role model for Anne, was successfully involved with the Parent-Teachers Association. Edna Roe became the Colorado field secretary and went on to become the national travelling secretary of the PTA.[23]

Anne's older brother Bob made friends with a neighborhood boy, George Simpson, when they were both four years old. The two remained life-long best friends and when the neighborhood teenagers organized a band, Anne was included because she was the best musician in the group. Anne was an active child and adolescent—she was primarily responsible for managing the household and caring for a younger brother and sister— but she was sickly much of her life. For several years Anne suffered from (undiagnosed) undulant fever.[24]

After graduation from Denver public schools, Anne entered the University of Denver with the "vague" intention of becoming a high school English teacher, a goal encouraged by her parents.[22, 23] A major impetus for a change in major in college was Dr. Thomas R. Garth, Professor of Education, who, she writes, "picked me out of a class in my junior year." Garth suggested that if Roe would accelerate her completion of the B.A., "he would take me on as graduate assistant for two years and then see to it that I got a job in Thorndike's office at Columbia Teachers College and become a psychologist."[22]

Anne received her B.A. in 1923 and her M.A. in 1925, both in psychology and education, from the University of Denver. She then moved on to

Columbia.[23, 25] At Columbia, where her interest in vocational choice began early with a study of dentistry, with Charles Brown, Roe was not as actively involved in research as one might expect. She also was not impressed with Teachers College, except for Woodworth, and her observations resemble those of Heidbreder.[22]

Roe's complaints about her Columbia experience are very curious. She found the place to be unfriendly. More than this, she specifically notes, "There was very little interaction between faculty and students or among students."[22] Almost all the other women of psychology who have commented upon Teachers College during that period have emphasized the comraderies and the close relationship with their professors.

The list of women who were graduate students around the time that Roe was at Columbia includes Anne Anastasi, Mary Cover Jones, Ruth Monroe, Lois Murphy, Georgene Seward, Theodora Abel, Margaret Mead, Elizabeth Duffy, and, of course, Edna Heidbreder. Of these women, only Heidbreder and Roe seemed to have missed out on the close friendships and the dating that prevailed. What has been so interesting to us is that so many eminent women psychologists were not only educated at Columbia, but were married to fellow students, often after his Ph.D. and before hers. Perhaps contributing to Anne Roe's feeling of being an outsider to this group was that at some time while she was at Columbia, she married a man who is described as "a former student of Terman's at Stanford University."[23]

The program at Columbia in psychology during the twenties and thirties has been criticized for being too practical applications-oriented and geared toward clinical psychology. The more philosophy/theory-oriented women like Heidbreder disparaged the emphasis upon mundane content and mental testing. Roe, however, writes that what was lacking, in this relatively impersonal setting, was adequate training in clinical psychology: she suggests that there was "no instruction in clinical psychology."[22]

While finishing her doctoral work ("A Study of the Accuracy of Perception of Visual Musical Stimuli"), Anne Roe worked on a research project investigating differences between normal and aphasic adults, 1931 to 1933, her graduate school interests being in both research psychology and clinical psychology. Roe, like many of the women included in this chapter, had a variety of professional interests, but was first and foremost a premier researcher.

Roe obtained her postdoctoral clinical training at Worcester State Hospital under David Shakow. This was a period when this hospital was developing an outstanding staff and a reputation as a training and research center that was as uniquely identifiable as that at Minnesota or at University of California or Yale. Roe and Worcester were suited for each other and she received "all" her clinical training there. Shakow was to remain a long time friend and professional influence on her.[22, 23]

After leaving Worcester, Roe entered a rather long period of "underemployment." She worked as a research psychologist on a WPA project (1935–36) and conducted "private research" in New York City on problem children and aphasic retraining.[22] Her publications, related to her studies of intelligence and aphasia, were sparse.

Anne Roe's poor health and her desire to fulfill the duties of marriage clearly interfered with her career achievements for several years. Elizabeth Simpson, who has written a biographical sketch of Roe, suggests that she was keenly aware of the expectations of the two roles, career and family, and that her emerging career activities were "grafted" upon the older role definitions.[23] Roe's life changed drastically when, in 1938, she married George Simpson, the paleontologist and evolutionist, who had been her childhood friend. For one thing, she "inherited" four daughters.[24]

Psychological Researcher

We have noted that women of psychology have often spent the early years of their marriage attempting to develop a career on a catch-as-catch-can basis while they relocate to accommodate their husband's career. Imagine the problem of establishing a professional identity with a husband who goes off on field trips to all sorts of wild places, all over the world. Anne succeeded, according to her husband's account, in becoming a "real" mother to her step-daughters. She also accompanied her husband on several paleontological expeditions and collaborated with him on a number of important publications.[24]

In 1938 Roe and Simpson, following a brief honeymoon, were in Venezuela doing biological research, where she learned to trap and skin animals. She published an article, "La Fauna de Mamiferos de Kamarta y Santa Elena" ("The Mammals of Kamarta and Santa Elena"), based upon her observations there, in 1939. *Quantitative Zoology* was also published that year. This collaborative effort, begun the year before their marriage, combined concepts and methodology of zoology and psychological statistics. It was a pioneering effort and turned out to be a highly influential work.[24]

One of the ways that Anne Roe would manage to continue her own individual career, albeit a slow-to-develop one, was to obtain a series of personal research grants and fellowships. These enabled her to conduct studies at her own pace and when she began to publish extensively in the 1950s and 1960s, her major publications were extensive, complete—almost monumental—works. Her articles, books, and monographs reveal none of the hasty, desperate, and sloppy quality that characterizes the work of many of her colleagues, hallmarks of the "publish or perish" imperative—for, until 1959, Anne Roe did not have an academic position as primary employment. Before then, she was a most "independent" researcher (quite literally), who had the time and the talent to conduct research as it pleased her and to write when and how she pleased—and it pleased her to be excellent.

During wartime and her husband's army duty, Roe was at Yale (again, because Simpson had been hired there). She conducted a survey of alcohol education in the public schools and from 1943 to 1946 was an assistant professor working at the Laboratory of Applied Physiology at Yale University. She maintained her relationship with David Shakow, and collaborated with him on some of her papers on alcoholism as she had in the area of intelligence and mental disorders.[22]

After the war, Roe finally became connected with Columbia University; George became a member of the faculty there. Except for stints in clinical research and training for VA Hospitals (1946–47 and 1955–57), each time as chief of service, Anne's most well-known employment before 1959 was as director of the Study of Scientists. This famous study, reports of which are still reprinted in anthologies and the results of which are still widely cited, was conducted between 1947 and 1951, financed by a grant from the National Institute of Mental Health awarded personally to Anne Roe.[22]

In 1959, George Simpson was invited to Harvard. Anne wrote to a friend, psychologist David McClelland, who had recently joined the faculty there, inquiring about job opportunities in Boston or Cambridge. Roe was surprised to be invited to join the faculty at Harvard's Graduate School of Education.[23] She brought a research grant and a research assistant with her. Hired as a Lecturer in Education, she was made a full professor in 1963, the same year she was made director of the Center for Careers at Harvard.[22] In 1967, Anne Roe became professor emeritus at Harvard. She and Simpson then moved to Arizona; they were both always most partial to the Southwest.[24]

Despite the fact that neither Roe nor Simpson have been in very good health—Roe, for example, had pneumonia several times in Cambridge and elsewhere and has had heart surgery—neither of them is retired. Anne is an (unpaid) lecturer in the psychology department at the University of

Arizona, Tucson, and George teaches part-time there in the Department of Geosciences.[24] For the past several years they have operated a tax-exempt foundation (the Simroe Foundation), to make their libraries and research facilities available to qualified students.[24]

Work

Anne Roe's research interests have been broad—they include intellectual functions in normal, aphasic, and mentally disordered adults; behavior of new-born infants; the status of foster children of alcoholic parents and the effects of foster-home rearing upon later personality development; the effects of alcohol; the personalities of artists and scientists; contributions to nature-vs.-nurture research; the psychology of occupations; behavior and evolution; the psychology of creativity; and relations between early experiences and career patterns.[22]

Roe's research on career choice and the personality characteristics of people in certain occupations has been her forte and her most important publications have been in this area: "Alcohol and Creative Work: Painters" (1946); "A Psychological Study of Eminent Psychologists and Anthropologists, and a Comparison with Biological and Physical Scientists" (1953); *The Making of a Scientist* (1953); *The Psychology of Occupations* (1956); "Early Determinants of Vocational Choice" (1937); and *The Origin of Interests* (1964). Roe is also credited with formulating the first comprehensive theory to explain the career choices people make.[22]

It must be remembered, when evaluating the scope of her work, that Anne Roe accompanied her husband on field trips for close to thirty years. We are in no position to evaluate the quality of her contributions to biology ourselves, but we are aware that two of her books, *Quantitative Zoology* (1939) and *Behavior and Evolution* (1958), both published with her husband, have been well-received.

Honors and Accolades

Among the professional honors bestowed upon Anne Roe are several honorary degrees; an M.A. from Harvard University in 1963, an L.H.D. from Lesley College in 1965, and the Sc.D. from Kenyon College in 1973. She was the recipient also of a Guggenheim Fellowship (1952–53), a Lifetime Career Award from the National Vocational Guidance Association (1967), the Harvard Graduate School of Education Association Award (1967), the Richardson Creativity Award of the American Psychological Association (1968) and the APA's Award for Distinguished Contributions to Clinical Psychology from the Clinical Division (1972), the University of

Denver Alumni Association Award (1972), and the Medal for Distinguished Service of Teachers College (1977). Along with serving on various committees and in consultation with organizations, Anne was elected president of the New England Psychological Association, in 1964-65.[22, 25]

The Problem of Identity

Like many of the women of psychology born in the decade 1901-1910, Anne Roe was able to achieve success in both career and marriage. Unlike most of the others, however, Roe placed her professional career second, was less directly competitive with men, and as a consequence, with voluntarily lower career ambitions, she felt the effects of gender discrimination less. Most of the slights Roe suffered directly, such as being excluded from a dining room at Harvard's Faculty Club, were personal and social.[23] Roe was willing to accept even the demeaning aspects of social and institutional discrimination, because she appreciated the rewards that family provided.

The fact that Roe never became an active feminist, did not revolt against the socially-determined definition of femininity, should not imply that she was unaware of the deterrents to achievement faced by the women of her generation. In articles, such as "Satisfactions in Work" (1962), "Women in Science" (1966), "Women and Work" (1966), and "Womanpower: How is it Different?," Roe explicated the problems facing females who sought careers during her lifetime. The problems, the social definitions, and the differential expectations (and differential rewards) were recognized by Anne Roe, but she "believed in the *transcendence* of culturally defined sex roles for both males and females."[23]

Roe's own research sheds light on one very important aspect of the psychologist-wife role's inhibition of occupational success. Many women of psychology, Roe included, have had to delay entrance into psychology or to engage in part-time pursuit of a career, because of the inequitable division of labor in household tasks related to traditional family life. One major finding of Roe's investigation of the attainment of distinction in creative endeavors (artistic and scientific) is the preeminent value of uninterrupted work.[23] The most eminent physicists, for example, are those, other factors being equal, who work hardest and longest.

For most women, extra-career demands upon time and energy serve the purpose of automatically excluding them from any eminence in their selected field. As noted above, Anne Roe herself was able to "transcend" this barrier by opting for excellence in her research and writings; she chose quality over quantity. In her scientific investigations at least, Roe has been able to work at her own pace, to assert her own control and autonomy, and to be her own very accomplished woman.

FROM POSSIBILITIES TO ACTUALITIES
Leona Elizabeth Tyler (1906-   )

Leona Tyler was the fourth woman to be elected president of the American Psychological Association (1972-73). Like Anne Anastasi, whom she succeeded, Tyler is an expert in the area of individual differences. She has conducted important research on interests and on the process of making personal choices and decisions, a topic which she pioneered and might be said to have "invented," and is the author of several infuential textbooks.

In all her work, Tyler has enjoyed the reputation of being extremely competent but not remarkable. As she is the first to admit, her success was a result of hard work, dedication, and persistence, rather than virtuoso performance. Tyler's attainment of prominence in psychology was a slow and gradual process. It was, ironically, not until she was president of the APA that Leona Tyler established herself as a major thinker in psychology, her Presidential Address, "Design for a Hopeful Psychology"[26] was perhaps her most brilliant theoretical contribution to psychology.

A product of rural middle-America and of clearly humble origins, Leona Tyler came to psychology somewhat later in life—at least in comparison to the other women included in this chapter. She was a precocious child and a brilliant student, who grew up to approach life with equanimity, contentment, and affability. She is one of the few women of psychology to report never having been the victim of sex discrimination: "The people who were important to me were not much concerned with psychological sex differences."[27]

In her published work, especially her textbooks, Leona Tyler resembles Anastasi. In her research, especially that on interests and vocational choice, of course, her areas are similar to those of Anne Roe. She shares a personal irony with Roe: both women are recognized for their elucidation of how a person arrives at significant choices in life, particularly occupational choices, and they both emphasize the volitional, deliberate, and conscious nature of such choices. Yet Roe and Tyler both note that the choices in their own personal life, including choice of career, were most often serendipitous and the product of external events.[23, 27]

Parallels to Anastasi and Roe are restricted, however, to her professional work. In her life experiences, personality and temperament, and style, Leona Tyler is very unlike either of her contemporaries. For one thing, she never married and psychology was more a monopolizing in-

Leona Elizabeth Tyler

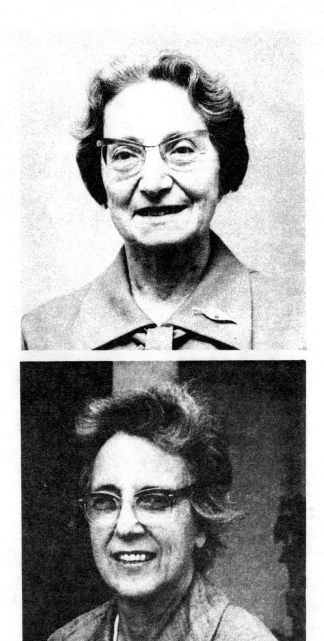

Above: Magda Blondiau Arnold; *below*: Lois Barclay Murphy

fluence in Tyler's life—in fact, she has called her autobiography "My Life as a Psychologist." If we were to select one person to represent Tyler's professional ancestor, it would have to be Margaret Washburn. Both she and Washburn were notably well-accepted by male colleagues, enjoyed friendships with men who were powerful figures in psychology, and were included in the inner sancta of psychology's establishment. The two also, of course, gradually acquired power within organized psychology themselves and rose to become presidents of the APA. More than this, however, both Washburn and Tyler saw as one of their functions to become what the latter calls an "interpreter" of psychology, that is, to produce textbooks which integrate large amounts of research findings and bring order to the enormous number of bits of data. In this regard, Tyler has been almost as outstandingly successful as Washburn.

Rural Foundations

Leona Tyler was born on 10 May 1906, in Chetek, Wisconsin, and spent the first six years of her life on a farm. Neither her father, Leon M. Tyler, nor her mother, Bessie Carver Tyler, was a college graduate, but it was expected that she would eventually go to college.[27]

The oldest of four children and the only girl, Tyler reports that there was a "considerable respect for intelligence" and that "being female has never made me feel inferior" in what she describes as a "lower-middle-class" family.[27] She learned to read and to play the piano when she was very young, a life-long love for music was instilled by her mother, a self-taught pianist.

Just prior to her entrance into school, the family moved to Minnesota, near the Mesabi Iron Range. The region was a rather backwoods area of northern Minnesota, but it was a "boom" period economically and, she reports, numerous cultural events and intellectual opportunities were available. Leona was considered ahead of her classmates when she began school and, precocious and bright, she completed the first six grades in three years. Tyler suggests that being three years younger than her subsequent classmates and her fundamentalistic Protestant background contributed to problems in "social development" later. She notes, for example, that her religious beliefs prohibited dancing, a problem for social adjustment in high school.[27]

At fifteen Leona entered the newly formed junior college in Virginia, Minnesota, where the family was residing. She intended to become a teacher. It had been long understood that she would get an education, but also that she would do it as cheaply as possible and would emerge with an employable profession.[27] In 1923, she transferred to the Unversity of Minnesota; since the family also relocated to St. Paul, it was not necessary for Leona to "leave home." At Minnesota she majored in English and trained to become an English teacher. She actually preferred chemistry, but could not afford to take the classes which were required to make up math deficiencies. Tyler reports that she was an "omnivorous" reader in college and the library was her "real spiritual home." She had also once had the notion of becoming a writer.[27]

When she was still only nineteen, she left the University with a B.A. and a teaching certificate. She got a job teaching English at a junior high school. Initially she thought that this might be temporary; her objectives in life were still unsettled and she considered science or writing as a career—not psychology; she found the field distinctly unappealing, because of some dull and uninspiring courses she had taken.[27]

Teacher

Leona Tyler taught junior high school English and mathematics for thirteen years. She became self-supporting and, in fact, was able to contribute to the family's financial resources, and helped pay for the education of her three younger brothers.

Although Tyler did not entertain notions of continuing her education during her teacher years, and certainly had no ambition to become a professional psychologist, she notes that her experiences in the classroom inspired interest in areas which did, in fact, become research concerns later. Her interest in individual differences, for example, was stimulated as she tried to improve writing skills and began to recognize the vast differences among students in any one classroom. A curiosity about occupational success and the complexity of its determinants was inspired by her recognition that there was more to teaching skill than intellectual ability, that the most intelligent teachers were not always the most skillful.[27]

Tyler suggests that her interest in motivation and behavior stems from her problems in "controlling" her classroom. It was somewhat of a surprise to read in her autobiography, "I was not then, and am not still, a person whom it is natural for others to obey without question."[27] This is surprising, not only because if one word can be used to describe the reaction of peers to Tyler, it would be "respect," but because when one of the authors met Tyler, several years later, in her capacity as a member of the APA Evaluation Committee, he was quite intimidated by her.

One preoccupation reported by Tyler seems somewhat out of character for her: in her twenties she was an active, dedicated pacifist. It is not suggested that we are surprised that Tyler was so staunchly against war, but rather that she had become fervently involved in any issue. She was hardly a wild young woman and seemed an unlikely candidate to be involved in a radical social movment. Yet World War II was very disillusioning to Tyler, who never understood the grotesque inhumanity of war.[27] Although still living "at home" with her family, Leona was becoming an adult, or at least an idealistic young person, and her feeling of self-assuredness and competence would develop belatedly, during her twenties.

In any event, Tyler notes that it was during this period that she developed social skills, made friends, and eventually developed self-confidence and leadership ability (that she herself was apparently slow to recognize). In a sense, it was while a teacher that she underwent some developmental changes associated with adolescence herself. Her decision to take graduate courses at Minnesota, to improve her teaching ability, can be seen in this light also, as part of a "growing-up" process.

Graduate School

The University of Minnesota was selected because it was inexpensive and did not require leaving home. It was, she notes, an excellent choice for a thirty-year-old junior high school teacher. The intellectual climate, she found to be open rather than doctrinaire (an opposing view is that of Edna Heidbreder, who had left Minnesota's faculty two years earlier and had found the behavioristic orthodoxy unbearable).

> What I enjoyed then (and still enjoy) is picking up ideas from diverse sources, and combining them in my own way. The absence of a dominant ideology and the attitude of tolerant skepticism that is the essence of 'dustbowl empiricism' encouraged this kind of activity. Each narrowing down that I have had to accept during the years since I left Minnesota has left me with a feeling of regret. Specialization is necessary for present-day psychologists, but we have lost something in the process.[27]

Tyler had "everything" to learn in psychology—she therefore proceeded to read everything. A major influence on Tyler at that time was Donald Paterson, her advisor, who encouraged her to attend school full-time and to enter the Ph.D. program.[27] Minnesota was an exciting setting in the late thirties, especially if you were interested in mathematics and science, were interested in research on vocational choices, and were interested in applied psychology and individual differences. Minnesota was then a world-leading center for psychometric research, vocational psychology, and research in developmental psychology, coincidentally exactly what Leona Tyler was seeking. As a clincher, Florence Goodenough was also there, at the Institute for Child Development

Tyler lists Goodenough, with whom she worked at Minnesota, as one of the most important influences on her career. Later, beginning with a 1959 edition (published after Goodenough's death), Leona Tyler was to update and revise her mentor's monumental *Developmental Psychology* several times, and the book is now usually referred to as "Goodenough and Tyler."

In Leona Tyler we also see another historic trend, that of research on the psychology of women, a research interest that was, to some degree, to occupy all the women of psychology born during the decade of 1901-1910. Since the women included in this chapter were primarily researchers in specialized areas, they studied women's issues in the context of their own unique research framework. This is especially true of Tyler, whose research on the interests of high school girls led to her thesis (M.S., 1939) and her doctoral dissertation (Ph.D., 1941).[27, 28]

In addition to Paterson and Goodenough, Leona names, as the most important person at Minnesota to her, Richard M. Elliott. "Mike" Elliott, who was also a friend of Goodenough, was the professor who introduced Tyler to the "basic issues" of psychology, those issues that she was to address more than twenty years later.[26] She describes Elliott as one of her closest, life-long friends.[27]

Psychometrics, Psychoanalysis, and Possibility Theory

In 1940 some months before her Ph.D. was actually "officially" granted, Leona Tyler accepted a position at the University of Oregon as an instructor in psychology. After two years, she was made an assistant professor and in 1947, an associate professor. Tyler attained the rank of full professor in 1955, a position maintained until, at age 65, she was made emeritus professor of psychology, in 1971. From 1965 to 1971 she served as dean of the Graduate School.[27] In other words, when Tyler finally left home, she found a new home in Eugene, Oregon.

Because Oregon was still a small school then, Tyler was able to use the wide range of exposure she experienced at Minnesota. She was to teach practically the entire gamut of psychology courses: general psychology, experimental psychology, individual differences, testing, counseling, abnormal psychology, child psychology, adolescent psychology, educational psychology, and social psychology. As she observed, her reading and coursework had prepared her in clinical psychology and general psychology, as well as in statistics and test construction.[27]

Tyler also initiated the counselling service at Oregon and during her tenure there, would spend anywhere from one third to one fourth of her time involved at the center. Her clinical work was as eclectic as her theoretical understanding of motivation, including behaviorism, psychoanalysis, psychometrics, Rogers, Piaget, and cognitive theory.[27]

Her first research activities had been concerned with the development of an interest inventory. As she progressed in this area, she came to realize that interest at a given point in time is probably not as meaningful as the changes in interests over time. There were, of course, no instruments which would fit this process and subsequently over the years Tyler, with the help of Norman Sundberg and several graduate students, developed the needed tests and the process.

Tyler later came to believe that the interest inventories and tests we usually use focus on the wrong areas, that is, on disinterest and abnormality, rather than interest and normal adaptation. She hypothesized that "what makes one person different psychologically from everybody else is what he choses from the offering life presents to him and the kinds of constructs he uses to organize his experience."[27] Based on this innovative approach to individual differences, actually in anticipation of the more current multidimensional scaling techniques for obtaining an idea of an individual's cognitive structure, Tyler invented the Choice Pattern Technique, a process by which an "individual could report not just what they liked and disliked but the concepts underlying such responses."[27]

The result of this research approach has been the development of a theory that Tyler and Sundberg have called the Possibility Theory. This theory, in process, has been reported in Tyler's two books, *The Work of the Counselor* (1969), and *Clinical Psychology* (1973). In essence hers is a tripartate theory: "The most basic tenent is that development entails the transformation of a tremendously large number of *possibilities* into a limited number of *actualities*." Second, "a living organism is spontaneously *active*." Third, "an organism is *finite*; its time is limited. Thus selection from among action possibilities is required of the individual."[27]

Basic Issues

In her memorable Presidential Address to the APA, "Design for a Hopeful Psychology," 1973,[26] Leona Tyler dealt with many of the basic issues facing psychology. Unlike most such addresses, Tyler's produced a brilliant, original, and concise essay, possibly her best work.

With suggestions for merging the disparate elements of psychology as profession and as body of thought—scientific vs. humanitarian, determinism vs. free will, basic vs. applied research, and technology vs. human values—Tyler also presents a blueprint and a reconceptualization for psychology based upon her general theory of the psychology of choice.

In discussing some of the problematic and "ethical" issues facing contemporary psychology, Tyler suggests that scientific and technological accuracy do not need to ignore social and human values. For example, instead of devising or using a test to classify a person or to assess the person's ability to succeed in a given situation, "it is possible to begin with the assumption that the purpose of a test is to analyze what each person who takes it has to offer, so that a suitable place can be found for him."[26]

Tyler's preference in the determinism vs. free choice is to opt for the assumption that "an individual has at least limited freedom to choose his own course of action. . . . The most important distinction is between the concepts of possibility and actually, *what might be* versus *what is*."[26]

Textbooks

Leona Tyler's major occupation has been teacher and most of her publications have been textbooks. Although they all have the qualities of clarity and comprehensiveness, two of them, *The Psychology of Human Differences* (1947) and *Clinical Psychology: An Introduction to Research and Practice* (with N.D. Sunderberg, 1962), are standard textbooks, almost classics, and are constantly revised.

She recognizes that professors have an obligation to be "interpreters," to present research findings in "usable form," since research information has proliferated so drastically in psychology. To this end Tyler has produced six excellent textbooks.[27]

A Job Needed to be Done

Had anyone predicted at the beginning of my career that I would one day be President of the American Psychological Association, I would have viewed such a prediction as sheer fantasy.

—Leona Tyler, 1978

Tyler insists that she is unaware of the process by which she became a member of the bureaucratic structure of organized psychology or more especially how she attained power. She had been active in organizations and was always willing to volunteer for committees or assume official duties, if, as she put it, she saw that a job "needed to be done." But she did not perceive herself as the leader.[27]

In many of the professional organizations, Tyler would eventually attain "secretarial" status and was comfortable with the required duties. Within a few years, however, both the Western Psychological Association and Division 17, Counselling Psychology, of the APA elected Tyler as their president. In 1971 Leona was elected president of the American Psychological Association, her term of office ran from 1972-73.

For most of its history the APA has correlated eminence with longevity; most of its presidents have emeritus status when elected. In the case of Tyler, the election actually changed her "image" in psychology. Where she had been a competent "journeyman," she has become one of American psychology's most erudite thinkers.

TOKEN WOMAN
Eleanor Jack Gibson (1910-   )

Not a woman to mince words, Eleanor Gibson, who has won numerous awards and honors very late in her career, has had the courage to describe the impediments to success in psychology which the women of her generation had to face. Writing in Volume 7 of *A History of Psychology in Autobiography* (being selected to contribute is itself considered a great honor), Gibson wonders if the recognition she has received—coming as it did at the height of America's and psychology's most fervent feminist activism—constitutes her becoming a "token" woman. "Better," she writes, "to have a token woman in these things than none at all."[29]

Eleanor Gibson might well ask, "What does a woman need to succeed in a profession that seems to have evolved chiefly for men?"[29] After years of "second-class citizenship" in her own career, Gibson, one of the most talented experimental psychologists of this era, was not honored by her profession until she attained professorial rank at Cornell in 1966.[29] Along the way, she suffered all the aspects of gender discrimination, injustice, and institutional impediments that women of psychology have had to face: anti-nepotism rules, relocations for husband's career, low-status positions, under-employment, and part-time employment, among others.

Eleanor Gibson was to obtain three honors that are truly memorable. She became the first woman to attain the rank of full professor (but half-time) at Cornell and was elected into the Society of Experimental Psychology, which once specifically *excluded* women; as late as 1976-77 she was the only female member.[29] Most significantly, Gibson was one of the three recipients of the 1968 Distinguished Scientific Contribution Award of the American Psychological Association, only the second woman to be so honored. The citation read:

> For distinguished development of perceptual learning and perceptual development. . . . [Eleanor Jack Gibson has] advanced our understanding of depth perception in infants and young organisms. . . . [Her] analysis and experimental study of the discriminatory and decoding aspects, as well as semantic and syntactical features of reading have indicated what must be learned.[30]

Eleanor Gibson is best known for her studies in collaboration with Richard Walk, on the visual cliff, in the late fifties. Part of their research on "innate" perceptual processes, the innovative procedure and spectacular results of this one series of experiments are very frequently cited in psychology textbooks. Gibson, however, has also been involved in other significant research in psychology for almost fifty years. To her credit, after Gibson had official honors heaped upon her, she decided to speak out publicly on the inequitable treatment that women of psychology, especially psychologist-wives, have had to suffer.[29]

A Dull Life

Eleanor Jack was born on 7 December 1910, in Peoria, Illinois, possibly the best place in America to enjoy what she describes as a boring, mundane, "middle-class respectability."[29, 31] She is, in fact, one of the few women of psychology to have had an "ordinary" early life and her experiences prior to college were much more similar than those of the others to women in general. She describes, for example, the demeaning practice of hiding her "A"–average grades from boys. Can you imagine Calkins or Martin or Mead or Anastasi or Hollingworth "playing dumb" in order to be popular with boys? Of course, none of the others grew up in Peoria.

Although Eleanor reports that she did not know that she was a bright child and she was not particularly encouraged to achieve academically, she was expected by tradition to attend Smith College.[29] At seventeen this provincial, protected, midwestern girl moved to Northampton, Massachusetts, where she was to spend eighteen extraordinarily happy years.[29]

Eleanor Gibson attended college during the last gasps of the Jazz Age and during Prohibition and the Depression, events which drastically affected Smith College, but seem to have had little impact on her.[29, 32] Elaine Kendall has noted that this was a period of upheaval in women's

The Researchers 121

colleges, upheaval of traditional values and in many cases, the dropping-out from college forced by financial disaster at home.[32]

Eleanor, however, found the atmosphere heady with intellectual and cultural opportunity, a place where women were recognized and rewarded for brilliance. She was not much of a scholar during her first two years, because "it was too important to absorb all the other wonderful and pre-viously unattainable things: symphony concerts, mountains in the distance to be climbed, courses and books about things I had never heard of and proms and houseparties at nearby men's colleges."[29]

Eleanor reports not "finding" psychology until the close of her sopho-more year, aided in this discovey by Margaret Curti. Curti, who had received her Ph.D. at Chicago, under the guidance of Harvey Carr, was one of the first to investigate the effects of wearing laterally displacing prisms, and was offering a course in animal psychology. What enticed Eleanor into psychology was the process of experimental research and she decided on this basis to switch from a major in French to a major in psychology.

She took one course also in psychological testing at Smith, with Hanna Faterson, a first-hand experience with children as subjects. Eleanor was interested in conducting research on the psychology of learning and for this purpose children were as adequate as *Rattus albinus*; "I thought," she writes, "I would like to work with children almost as much as rats." She, however, absolutely did not want to become an administrator of clinical tests.[29]

Smith College became a temporary home and a cultural refuge for a remarkable band of psychologists when Kurt Koffka, the world famous Gestalt psychologist, was made "professor-at-large" there. Among Koffka's "retinue of foreigners" who were to spend some time at Smith were Alexander Mintz, Eugenia Hanfmann, Tamara Dembo, Fritz Heider, and Molly Harrower.[29] Koffka's arrival was important because it turned Smith College, which was already developing a reputation for providing high academic standards, into a respectable center for psychological research and training.

At the end of her junior year, Eleanor Jack met a young faculty mem-ber, James J. Gibson, at a rained-out garden party. The next day she rushed out and enrolled in his advanced psychology course. "It was a wonderful course," she reports, "and I fell in love with experimental psychology and with the instructor."[29] Indeed Eleanor and her classmates were to develop a considerable level of competence as experimental re-searchers and their newly established clique produced some publishable studies during their senior year. Eleanor, for example, along with her lab partner, Gertrude Raffel, and her instructor, J. J. Gibson, published their work "Bilateral Transfer of the Conditioned Response in the Human Subject," in 1932 in the *Journal of Experimental Psychology*. Eleanor received the B.A. in 1931.

She decided to work for her master's degree at Smith and to help defray expenses during the mid-Depression year of 1931–32, became a T.A. for the Introduction to Psychology course. She took graduate courses with James Gibson and he became her thesis advisor. In September of 1932, he also became her husband. They have been married for forty-eight years and are the parents of a son (1940) and a daughter (1943).

J. J. and E. J. Gibson have seldom collaborated on research, although they have often worked, independently of each other, on similar topics. They frequently hold opposing theoretical ideas and working together has been stressful, according to both of them. Despite this, a milestone in both their careers was a brief article they co-authored on perceptual learning, published in *Psychological Review* in 1955. Eleanor was his T.A. for a course in Social Psychology just after their honeymoon and despite the problems of having your husband as a boss and thesis advisor, Eleanor received her M.A. in psychology from Smith, in 1933.[29]

Career and Frustration

Since Smith College had no anti-nepotism policy, it was possible for Eleanor to join her husband on the faculty, as an instructor. She reports that her course load, committee assignments, and advisees occupied a great deal of her time and precluded original research. Her bibliography for these early years includes articles primarily reporting the master's thesis research of her advisees.[29, 30] In 1940, the year she gave birth to her first child, Gibson was made an assistant professor at Smith.[29]

For one year (1935), Eleanor Gibson was a Ph.D. candidate at Yale. Many of the greats of psychology were then on the faculty at Yale in either the department of psychology or the Institute of Human Relations. Of the older generation giants and powers in psychology there—Clark Hull, Arnold Gesell, and Robert Yerkes—Eleanor chose the most unaccessible, Yerkes. When she approached him with the request to do her dissertational research under him, Yerkes's reply was "I have no women in my laboratory" and E. J. Gibson was shown the door.[29]

It was during the year at Yale that Eleanor, who had been insulated at a women's college, came face-to-face with the institutionalized and the more subtle discrimination against women practiced by her profession. Much later she was to recognize that she had already suffered gender-determined barriers to her becoming a prominent psychologist: (a) the chances of her being accepted by a major university, with ascribed prestige and where research is encouraged, were remote; (b) since her husband's career had priority and his salary was needed for survival, she could travel to New Haven only during his sabbatical year (she received a tiny scholarship and gave up her own meager salary); and (c) she felt she could handle any two of the three—teaching, research, and family, but unable to find time and energy for all three, she was likely to ignore the research.[29]

Yale's psychology department was to become most renowned a few years after Eleanor's year of residency, but she and James made friends with many of the "young" faculty (several of their contemporaries were already acquaintances of James through his membership in the "Psychological Round Table," an exclusive fraternity that was a cross between a learned society and Animal House, that specifically excluded women from membership). Among the scores of psychologists the Gibsons met in New Haven who eventually became prominent were Helen Thompson Woolley, Frances Ilg, Louise Bates Ames, Henry Nissen, Leonard Doob, Mark May, John Dollard, Molly and Hobart Mowrer, Irvin Child, Carl Hovland, and Elliot Rodnick.[29]

Eleanor felt that her acceptance in New Haven was more social than professional and that Yale "tolerated" women graduate students, rather than welcomed them. The female faculty members, of course, Ilg, Ames, and Woolley, all worked for Gesell.[29]

Eleanor and Clark Hull, who was the dean of learning theorists and the mentor of Yale's "younger faculty," corresponded by mail throughout the direction of her dissertational research for two years. Her stay at Yale was restricted to one year "for both marital and financial reasons." During that year, Eleanor attended seminars, passed examinations in two foreign languages and her "prelims" (qualifying examinations for the Ph.D.); in short, all the work for her doctorate save the dissertation.[29]

Although she does not say very much about her relationship to Hull, it is clear that she had much affection for the man, who, she reports, resembled her father. Admitting to a father-daughter fondness, Eleanor describes him as an elderly man, but according to our calculations he was then in his early fifties. James did not share Eleanor's enthusiasm for Hull's psychology, but the two of them often did not see "eye-to-eye" on theoretical issues. Eleanor received her Ph.D. from Yale in 1938. Her study on the conditioning principles (generalization and differentiation) applied to verbal behavior was the source of her one publication for each year—1939, 1940, 1941 and 1942. She did not publish again until 1952.

War Bride

*If I had ever had any doubts about the desirability of an academic
career and the joy of research as opposed to a life of feminine socializing, community service, and Women's clubs, they were thoroughly
dispelled. The boredom of it became awful. . . .*[29]

When World War II began, the Gibsons were at Smith. James soon joined
the Air Force as a psychologist and Eleanor abandoned her career to live
with him in Texas. She gave birth to a second child and became involved in
wartime "work" which she found "unsatisfying." Although she associated
mainly with other wives of psychologists, in Texas and later in California,
the boredom and inane routine of full-time wifing were more than she
could bear. Eleanor Gibson's "consciousness" was raised.

After the war the Gibsons returned to Smith; Eleanor felt that she had
returned to paradise and was somewhat relieved that they took her back
(he was tenured; she was not). But Smith had changed and was too low-
keyed for the Gibsons. James had also received a contract from the Navy
to conduct research on perception, and teaching at Smith left little time
for research. James accepted a position at Cornell and Eleanor and the
family went along. It was 1949.

Cornell

Eleanor Gibson came to Cornell as a research associate without pay, a
position which she maintained until 1966, when she became a full professor there. For much of the time Eleanor had "freedom" to do research
but no institutional support and Cornell did not, at first, give her the
opportunity to seek outside monies to set up a laboratory, hire assistants,
and pay for supplies and equipment.[29]

For two years she worked at Howard Liddell's Behavior Farm, where
"experimental neurosis" was studied. Gibson was interested in the implications for learning theory of the phenomenon induced and wrote an article
on her interpretation of what was going on when the subject goats were
becoming "neurotic" ("The Role of Shock in Reinforcement," 1952).
Gibson describes the Liddell "neurosis" research as "humbug."[29]

In her second year, Gibson began an ambitious project on mother-child
relationships in goats. Unfortunately this experiment was ruined when
some of her experimental animals were "given away during a weekend
absence of mine."[29] So much for Gibson's status at Cornell at that time.

For the next few years she turned to a study of perceptual learning and
began to develop a reputation for her experimental research. Among her

collaborators was her husband—she worked for him for two years. In addition, Eleanor began to work on a comprehensive theory of perceptual learning and perceptual development.[29, 30]

In the mid-fifties Richard Walk joined the faculty at Cornell, sharing Gibson's interest in perceptual development. The two collaborated on a series of studies involving early learning in rats. Serendipitously, Gibson, who had an aversion to cliffs since a trauma at the Grand Canyon as a child, and Walk, who had trained parachutists in the army, found the "visual cliff" perceptual phenomenon, in an elegantly designed experiment which made them both famous.[29]

Although Gibson was highly productive between 1956 and 1966, her theory and book on perception did not appear until 1969. The most important source of delay was that she had become thoroughly immersed in a new but related field, the psychology of reading. It must be noted that, unlike many of the more prominent women of psychology, Gibson was not a prolific writer. Most of her journal articles are quite brief and they are few in number. She has published two books, *Principles of Perceptual Learning and Development* (1969) and *The Psychology of Reading* (1975).

When in 1966 James Gibson was made a Career Professor by the National Institute of Mental Health, Cornell University, which no longer needed to pay his salary, made his wife a full professor. This was after the had worked as a research associate for sixteen years and was fifty-six years old and one of America's best-known experimental psychologists and the acknowledged expert on perceptual learning. In 1972, Gibson was given an endowed chair, the Susan Linn Sage Professorship, the first woman given a chair by Cornell.[29]

Accolades

Nothing succeeds like success.
—Eleanor J. Gibson, 1976

"After sixteen years of second-class citizenship," Gibson writes, "the honors, once the ice was broken and I had attained the dignity of a professorship, came one upon another."[29] She was elected to the Society of Experimental Psychologists, the National Academy of Sciences, the National Academy of Education, and the American Academy of Arts and Sciences. She was elected president of the Eastern Psychological Association (1967-68) and was invited to give a lecture tour for Sigma Xi, the national honor society for science. Her book on perceptual learning won the 1969 Century Psychology Prize.[29, 31]

There was more. Smith gave her the honorary degree, D.Sc., in 1972, and Rutgers also presented her with a D.Sc., in 1973. She was made an honorary member of the British Psychological Association and was the recipient of G. Stanley Hall Medal and the Howard Crosby Warren Medal by the American Psychological Association. Yale conferred the Wilbur Cross Medal. The APA, finally, provided her with its most prestigious award, the Award for Distinguished Scientific Contributions.[29, 31]

Perhaps the most satisfying reward to Gibson that resulted from her stupifying prominence was that she was finally able to get her laboratory. In 1975, at Cornell, she was able to set up a full-fledged facility for the study of "invariants" in infants. In a sense, the career of one of American psychology's finest researchers has now just begun.

UNACKNOWLEDGED GENIUS
Magda Blondiau Arnold (1903–   )

Of the women of psychology who are included in this chapter, none is more brilliant, more accomplished a researcher, or *less*-known than Magda Arnold. She has, for more than thirty years, made important contributions to experimental, clinical, and physiological psychology and to personality and motivation theory. Known primarily to physiological psychologists and motivational theorists today, Arnold's achievements have never received the public exposure that they deserve.

Like many of the women born during the decade 1901–1910, Arnold was a scientist who addressed the basic philosophical issues of psychology, especially the "mind-body" problem. Her most famous work was the formulation of an innovative, comprehensive theory of emotion, a monistic theory which anticipated, by several years, currently accepted cognitive theories of emotion.[33] An example of Arnold's integrative approach to conceptualization is her oft-cited definition of emotion, which she describes as "a strong appetitive tendency toward or away from something appraised as good or bad for the person here and now that urges to appropriate action and is accompanied (but not initiated) by physiological changes"[34]

In her theoretical formulations, Magda Arnold was extremely successful in integrating biological, behavioral, and cognitive data. Her neglect by psychology is shameful, but the loss is not merely one to Arnold's prominence. Since her genius in integrating data and developing concepts was much needed during the post-war era, the real loss was to psychology.

Born and reared in a region of Austria that is now part of Czecho-slovakia, Magda Arnold came to Canada when she was twenty-five years old and did not become an American citizen until 1954.[35] Arnold entered the ranks of academic psychology relatively late in life—she did not even receive her bachelor's degree until she was thirty-six. When she was granted some recognition—elected president of the American Catholic Psychological Association—Arnold was an elderly woman, divorced and the mother of three grown daughters.[35, 36]

Why have Arnold's achievements been pretty much ignored by psychology's main body? One important factor is that she taught at women's colleges or at Catholic institutions, rather than at universities that were centers of psychological research and/or training. Another is that Magda's first important papers were not produced until after World War II; the postwar period was not favorable for a promising female psychologist. Arnold was not able to compete for eminence in psychology against younger men, less competent than she.

Life and Career

Magda was born on 22 December 1903, in Mahr-Trubau, Austria. Her parents were Rudolf Barta and Marie Blondiau Barta.[36] Magda married Robert K. Arnold on 23 January 1926, and two years later they moved to Toronto, Canada. They spent the next nineteen years in that city and had three daughters, Eveleyn Joan, Margaret Anne, and Catherine Mary.[35]

As noted above, she did not receive her B.A., from the University of Toronto, until 1939. She did, however, make up for lost time. She entered graduate school at Toronto, took courses in experimental psychology (her major) as well as clinical and physiological psychology, and received her M.A. in 1940 with a study of tension ("A Study of Tension in Relation to Breakdown," published in 1942 in the *Journal of General Psychology*).[35] She went on to obtain the Ph.D. in experimental psychology in 1942, with a study of "experimental neurosis," and joined the faculty at Toronto as a lecturer.[35]

Magda separated from her husband shortly after she received her doctorate. Although she was not advanced in rank at Toronto, she published three journal articles while she was a lecturer there; one of them, "Physiological Differentiation of Emotional States" (1945), was the nucleus of her theory of emotion.[37] Teaching until 1947, Arnold was also, 1946–47, director of Research and Training at Sunnybrook Hospital (Veterans' Affairs Department).[35]

In 1947, accepting a position as visiting lecturer at Wellesley College, Madga and her daughters moved to the United States. A year later, she was made an associate professor and head of the psychology department at Bryn Mawr College; her meteoric rise in academia due to her teaching skill as much as to the recognized excellence of her research. She stayed at Bryn Mawr for only two years, and obtained her divorce there in 1949.[35] In 1950 Arnold became a full professor of psychology and head of the psychology department at Barat College of the Sacred Heart in Lake Forest, Illinois.[36]

In 1952, following a symposium on personality for Catholic psychologists held at Barat (Magda Arnold edited and prepared the papers submitted for publication), she accepted a position at Loyola University, Chicago. In just a few years she had advanced from beginning level academic positions to full professorship at a major university. Her research became more varied, including studies of suggestability and hypnosis; a personalistic technique with the Thematic Apperception Test; a test for screening candidates for religious orders; and one on saccharin as a positive reinforcer.[35]

In 1954, the book derived from the Barat Symposium, *The Human Person: An Approach to an Integral Theory of Personality*, was published, and in 1960 Arnold's monumental, two-volume *Emotion and Personality* was published.[34, 36] In 1961 Arnold was made director of the Behavioral Laboratory and in 1965, until she left in 1972, director of the Experimental Division of Loyola University.[35, 36]

Magda Arnold was president of the American Catholic Psychological Association, 1957–58, the same academic year that she was a Guggenheim Fellow. In 1962–63, she taught at Munich as a Fulbright Research Professor. Her papers became somewhat more philosophical and theoretical in orientation after 1960, as she became accepted as a spokesperson on theories of emotion, neurophysiology, and perception, particularly in Catholic circles, and was invited to write articles for several encyclopedias and chapters for anthologies. Between 1960 and 1970 she published four of her six books.[35]

In 1972 Arnold left Chicago and—like many of her colleagues who in their old age relocate to the "sun belt"—moved to Alabama. She did not retire yet; she accepted a position at Spring Hill College, professor of psychology and chair of the Division of Social Sciences, which she held from 1972 to 1975. Although she is now formally retired, Arnold is in the process of completing another book, *Memory and the Brain*.[35]

Honors

While at Toronto, as a student, Magda Arnold received the Gold Medal in Psychology, 1939, and the award as a David Dunlop Scholar, 1940. She has two honorary degrees, the L.L.D. in 1959 from St. Mary's College, California, and the L.H.D. in 1972 from Loyola University, Chicago.[35, 36]

She has also been a Helen Putnam Fellow in Advanced Research, Radcliffe College, 1952-54; Guggenheim Fellow, 1957-58; Fulbright Research Professor, 1962-63; and taught at Xavier University as a Reilly Distinguished Professor for one semester in 1969-70.[35]

The extent of Magda Arnold's neglect by psychology is reflected by the honors she has never received. This important researcher and theoretician has never been formally recognized by psychology at all. She has never received any of the many awards, honorific titles, or elected positions, for example, that the American Psychological Association has bestowed on scores of less worthy male psychologists.

CHARISMATIC AND IMAGINATIVE SOCIAL PSYCHOLOGIST
Else Frenkel-Brunswik (1908-1958)

Else Frenkel-Brunswik is best known for her research on prejudice and on the concept of "intolerance of ambiguity." The major milestone of her career was the famous book, *The Authoritarian Personality* (1950), in which she and her collaborators at U.C. Berkeley, T. W. Adorno, Daniel J. Levinson, and R. Nervitt Sanford, described their postwar studies of prejudice.

> The most critical result of the present study, as it seems to the authors, is the demonstration of close correspondence in the type of approach and outlook a subject is likely to have in a great variety of areas, ranging from the most intimate features of family and sex adjustment through relationships to other people in general, to religion, and to social and political philosophy. Thus a basically hierarchical, authoritarian, exploitative parent child-relationship is apt to carry over into a power-oriented, exploitively dependent attitude toward one's sex partner and one's God and may well culminate in a political philosophy and social outlook which has no room for anything but a desperate clinging to what appears to be strong and a disdainful rejection of whatever is relegated to the bottom.[38]

Although Frenkel-Brunswik's brilliant and monumental studies of antisemitism and prejudice brought her deserved fame, there is much greater breadth to her work. She conducted studies in child development; projective testing, particularly with the Thematic Apperception Test; perception experiments; and the learning process in general.

As early as 1950, she and her colleagues made the following sophisticated observations of self-concept and attitudes toward women:

> Prejudiced persons' conception of the sex roles is likewise highly conventionalized. The prejudiced man tends to think of himself as active, determined, energetic, independent, rough and successful in the competitive struggle. . . . The role of the woman, as seen by the prejudiced man, is one of passivity and subservience. She is an object of solicitude on the part of the man . . . of his wife he tends to require the conventional prerequisites of a good housewife . . .
>
> Unprejudiced men, on the other hand, tend to look primarily for companionship, friendship, and sensuality in their relations to the other sex. They are able openly to take and give nurturance and succorance in their relations with women. . . . Passivity and softness is thus an accepted part of the ego-ideal of the unprejudiced man, who at the same time is often more capable of giving real protection and support in return. . . .[38]

Frenkel-Brunswik had been one of the group at the University of Vienna who studied and worked under the Bühlers (Charlotte and Karl), and had been on the staff of the Institute of Psychology. She conducted research there with Charlotte Bühler and Edith Weisskopf, both of whom later enjoyed long and successful careers in the United States. Many of her colleagues in Vienna became important figures in social psychology, psychoanalysis, and child development. When she herself emigrated to the United States (to California), she became associated with the Institute of Child Welfare, where she worked with Mary Cover Jones and Nancy Bayley.

Else Frenkel-Brunswik's goal, from her earliest research, was to develop integrative personality theories, with contributions from psychoanalysis; social psychology; longitudinal child development studies; the experimental laboratory; and eclectic behavioristic observations. At her death, she had achieved a great deal in terms of assessment techniques and the development of objective measures of concepts, but her body of work was still in the segmental stage. She died prematurely before she was able to develop the integrative theory she had sought to create.

Frenkel-Brunswik has been called a dedicated teacher with "charismatic femininity" and a "founding figure" in the establishment of new fields of personality psychology by her colleague and biographer, Daniel Levinson.[39] A few years later, in the foreword to her published "selected papers," Gardner Murphy noted that she was "loved by all who knew her."[40] She was, most significantly, among the first psychologists, of either gender, to successfully merge a scientific orientation (Else was, with her husband, one of the earliest advocates of "logical positivism") with a program of research on very abstract concepts in which social-political issues were addressed.

Austria and the Vienna Salon

Else Frenkel was born to Polish-Jewish parents in Lemberg, part of the Austro-Hungarian Empire, on 18 August 1908. Very little is known of the early life of Frenkel and some of the sources do not agree on the dates when some of the agreed-to facts occurred.[39, 41] We shall consistently emphasize the data as presented by Levinson, the one source who knew Frenkel personally.

Frenkel received her Ph.D. in psychology at Vienna, under Karl Bühler as dissertation advisor, when she was only twenty-two years old. Her dissertation was published in 1931 in a *Zeitschrift fur Psychologie* article called "Atomismus und Mechanismus in der Assoziationspsychologie" ("Atomism and Mechanism in Association-Psychology"). This work was a rapprochement between associationism and the newer concepts of Gestalt psychology.[39]

Else joined the faculty at Vienna as a lecturer and researcher, including involvement with the Institute of Psychology, which was directed by Charlotte Bühler, with whom she collaborated on a series of studies. These were part of a longitudinal study in which several members of the Institute participated; consistent with Bühler's life-long interest in how a life is organized around long-term goals and adaptation, these studies combined several theoretical positions. They also combined data from different sources, phenomenological data, behavioral data and measurements from different assessment methods. Else, whose subsequent research was greatly influenced by her early work at the Institute, was at that time a highly respected scientifically-oriented experimental psychologist who was also interested in clinical psychology (mental testing and psychoanalysis.)[39, 40]

Else and her friend and colleague, Egon Brunswik, who was another member of the Bühler salon, were in close contact with a third group located in Vienna, a group of philosophers called the "logical positivists." This group, headed by Moritz Schlick, Otto Neurath, Philipp Frank, and Rudolph Carnap, organized in 1927, taught that the language of science must reduce terms to the communal language of physics. For psychology and other essentially observational sciences as well, terms must be reduced to the operations used to observe and measure them, to avoid confusion and metaphysics. This dictum led to the movement in science's being called "operationism." Else Frenkel and Egon Brunswik, who were the primary experimentalists of the Vienna "salon," brought this message into the group.

The procedure by which abstract concepts could now be quantified and said to be "operationally defined" made the Institute's work possible and scientifically respectable, because this band of generalists was involved in research on broad, abstract psychological, socio-cultural and political phenomena.

It is interesting that Egon, who had been a Hungarian engineer before receiving his Ph.D. in 1927 under Karl Bühler, never collaborated with Else Frenkel in an independent study. When he returned from California, on a Rockefeller Fellowship at the invitation of E. C. Tolman, one of America's leading learning theorists and himself a former engineer, Egon and Else Frenkel married. A few months after the wedding the Nazi *Anschluss* of 1938 took place and Else and Egon fled to Berkeley, California, where he had been offered an assistant professorship at the University of California.

The two were to develop divergent careers and did not publish together. They seemed to be totally in agreement on theoretical issues, often investigating broadly similar topics from different viewpoints. The marriage lasted until Egon's death in 1955, a death which was to have tragic consequences for Else.

It was in 1937 also that Else, who published relatively little in her career, had her first of two books published. *Wunsch und Pflicht im Aufbau des menschlichen Lebens* (*Wish and Obligation in the Course of Human Life*), was co-authored by Edith Weisskopf.

California

Else Frenkel-Brunswik became affiliated with the Institute of Child Welfare at Berkeley, but this is only one of the several simultaneous "careers" she enjoyed. This energetic young woman also worked at the Institute of Industrial Relations, and was a research psychologist and psychotherapist at Cowell Memorial Hospital.[42] She also began to write a series of extremely important journal articles and monographs. One paper, "Psychoanalysis and Personality Research," which appeared in the *Journal of Abnormal and Social Psychology* in 1940, was prepared from an influential speech she had given at a symposium. In this paper she outlines her plan for a global theory of personality based upon psychoanalysis, phenomenological psychology, and behaviorism. Frenkel-Brunswik was one of the first to recognize and emphasize the common elements of these three approaches.[39]

In 1942 Else Frenkel-Brunswik was made a professor in the psychology department at the University of California. She was also named co-recipient (with the anthropologist Kroeber) of a Social Science Research Council Fellowship for work in sociology and anthropology.[39, 42] That same year her important monograph "Motivation and Behavior" was published in *Genetic Psychological Monographs*. This paper presented a model for personality research, at various levels, and a methodology for studying clinical influences in combination with behavioral measures. Here Frenkel-Brunswik anticipated the social perception studies of the 1950s and, by objectifying clinical ratings and developing techniques to increase their explicitness and reliability, did much to make clinical research "legitimate" in the eyes of academician-scientist psychologists.[39]

In 1943, she joined Sanford and Levinson in their research on authoritarianism. Although this was a group effort, much like that at Vienna, Frenkel-Brunswik was responsible for the semistructured interviewing of subjects and the development of the ethnocentrism and authoritarianism (F) scales.[41] One of the concepts which Else was to isolate and measure, intolerance of ambiguity, became a topic of subsequent research. More basic than authoritarianism, the ability to deal with ambiguity, she had discovered, is relatively lacking in prejudiced individuals. Other researchers have confirmed tolerance vs. intolerance of ambiguity as a basic personality and perceptual factor; persons who are open-minded in attitudes and creative in temperament are, for example, relatively high in the ability to tolerate ambiguity.

In her work, Frenkel-Brunswik found that intolerance of ambiguity is associated with (a) a tendency toward oversimplification in perception, (b) deep uneasiness about ambiguity and lack of order in personal relations, (c) a proclivity to engage in moralistic, all-good or all-bad value judgments, and (d) an inability to acknowledge ambivalence.[39]

In 1950 Else was a visiting lecturer at the Institute for Social Research at the University of Oslo, the school where her mentors, the Bühlers, had taught on their escape from Austria. In 1954–1955 she was a fellow at the Center for the Advanced Study in the Behavioral Sciences.[42] Most of her publications at this time were integrative theoretical papers dealing with psychoanalysis and scientific research findings.[39, 40]

Else Frenkel-Brunswik's career, in a real sense, came to an end with her husband's death. Her writing and research stopped abruptly and there is evidence that her loneliness turned to despondency. On 31 March 1958, three years after Egon's death, Else committed suicide, in Berkeley, California. She was almost fifty years old.[41]

THE EFFORT TO UNDERSTAND PEOPLE
Lois Barclay Murphy (1902–   )

What is psychology then? For me, it is the effort to understand people–at any ages by every means possible. And as for child development, this means watching, listening to, playing and working with children, doing experiments when they are fair and helpful.
                                                            —Lois Murphy, 1978

For close to fifty years, Lois Barclay Murphy has been a leading researcher in social psychology and child development. In many respects, Murphy, who has been America's best-known investigator of normal children, has been a true pioneer in psychology: in 1938, for example, in an article with Ruth Horowitz, she was the first to use the term "projective methods," which has become the generic term for an entire class of assessment techniques. She is also credited with being among the first to study sympathy in young children; coping mechanisms; the concepts of vulnerability and resilience; and normal child development using a multi-disciplinary approach.[43]

In a review of her 1976 book which is based upon a longitudinal study of children in Topeka, Kansas, Robert White says of her:

> To my mind, Lois Murphy has no peer as an observer of children. In the amazing way that Freud detected unconscious motives and primitive defenses in adult free associations, Murphy discerns in children the constant effort to cope and to understand, even when this takes the form of strategic retreat, holding back, seeking help, keeping to one's own pace, and safeguarding a feeling of initiative.[44]

In her long and productive career, Lois Murphy has developed many research and assessment techniques for the study of normal child development. She has also authored, co-authored, or edited sixteen books and has produced hundreds of journal articles. Her most important publications have been *Experimental Social Psychology* (1931, 1937), *Personality in Young Children*, (2 vols.) (1956), *The Widening World of Childhood* (1962), and *Vulnerability, Coping and Growth* (1976). A recent widow, Lois Murphy lives in Washington, D.C., and at seventy-nine is completing *three* new books for publication.[43]

Early Life

Having written an autobiography and figuring prominently in the published autobiography of her late husband, Gardner Murphy, one would not expect many mysteries to remain in Lois Murphy's background. There is, however, one peculiar and unexplainable mystery: the year of her birth. She reckons her birthdate as 23 March 1901,[43] but *Who's Who in Science* gives 1902 and *American Men and Women of Science* gives 1903 as the year of her birth.[46]

In any event it is established that she was born in Lisbon, Iowa, the eldest of five children born to Wade Barclay and May Hartley Barclay. Her father left the traditional family occupation, farming, and became a Methodist preacher, and eventually became the National Secretary of Religious Education for the Methodist Church.[45]

Lois's mother was a teacher, also of Iowa stock, who had grown up in California. Her parents, she reports, met on the debating team of the University of Iowa. Many of her female relatives on the maternal side were educated and accomplished persons "so I was brought up from the beginning with the assumption that a woman would be expected to be intelligent and to have ideas . . . a woman was expected to do something worthwhile, and particularly as a Barclay to be pioneering and creative."[45]

Like many of the women of psychology, Lois had dreams of pursuing some sort of artistic career: a dancer, an artist, and then a poet. She was dissuaded from a career in the arts by her mother, who felt that she had not "genius" enough.[45] Her decision to choose a career working with children was an early one, arising out of a concern for neglected, "bad" and little children.[45]

This concern was fostered by two incidents; one was the visits to Chicago's Halsted Street (1907–09) with her father, as he visited other churches. In this area of town, Lois was first introduced to the squalor and primitive conditions in which the poor lived.

Secondly, her interest in child development was encouraged when, as the eldest of five children, and with her mother ill, she was given the charge of the youngest. She reports developing an almost arrogant confidence in handling infants and young children.[45]

In describing her early and high school years, Lois consistently acknowledged the wonderful teachers she had, all of whom were women (the wonderful ones, that is). In elementary school, she remembers thinking that her parents were smarter than her teachers but in high school, there were some challenges, especially those induced by the language teachers. Since languages came easily to her, Lois had considered becoming a language teacher.[45]

All through school Lois remembers thinking that "a woman teacher should be a woman as well as a teacher; a woman has no business giving up her warmth, intuition, and sensitivity to people by caging herself in some cognitive system."[45]

"Lois Barclay is not College Material"

Lois entered Vassar in 1919, selecting this college as much for its architecture and landscaping as for its intellectual tradition. She loved college, did not think much of the psychology taught there, and groped for a major that interested her. She reports a humorous incident that occurred in her freshman French class, a class in which the dull teacher bored her and her prep-school classmates intimidated her. One day she found a slip of paper near the desk of this teacher on which was written the woefully erroneous judgment: "Lois Barclay is not college material."[45]

It will be recalled that another young woman who would become a world-famous psychologist, Mary Cover Jones, was completing her undergraduate work at Vassar at this time. Unlike Jones, however, Lois was completely turned off by the behaviorist orientation there and especially disliked the ideas of J. B. Watson, whom she felt clearly "did not understand children at all."[45] Both her parents had studied psychology and at an early age, she reports, she was exposed to the ideas of John Dewey, William James, G. W. H. Patrick, and Carl Seashore. Psychology at Vassar she found to be very different; it was especially at variance with the work of Sigmund Freud, which she was then reading. She vowed to keep her distance form psychology and psychologists. She decided to major in comparative religions.[45]

This was also the era when many Vassar women were more interested in preparing for marriage and motherhood than for a profession. The interest in psychology, especially child psychology, among the students there has been related to its role in providing information for intelligent child-rearing.[32] Lois felt that most of the faculty reinforced the idea that a merging of a career and family was not likely and she reports being teased by the prediction that she and her classmates would abandon their intellectual pretensions, marry, and become "dummies."[45]

One exception, oddly, was Margaret Floy Washburn, the formidable leader of psychology, who was the head of the department of psychology at Vassar. Lois reports being impressed with having a teacher who was then president of the American Psychological Association and describes Washburn as "rather aloof and articulate, a very interesting lecturer with a real concern for the students."[45] Washburn told the students, "It's *important* for you to get married and have a good family life" and encouraged them to integrate a career with a successful marriage.[45]

Lois made several enduring friendships while at Vassar; the most notable and closest was with Ruth Munroe. Munroe, who became a psychologist and is the author of *Schools of Psychoanalytic Thought* (1955), was not only a classmate at Vassar and Columbia and Lois's roommate in New York, but was the person who introduced her to Gardner Murphy.[45]

Lois received her A.B. from Vassar in 1923 and entered graduate school at Union Theological Seminary.[46] It is interesting that Helen Flanders Dunbar, who graduated from Bryn Mawr also that year, went to Union as well and then to Columbia for her Ph.D. As we noted earlier, the hyper-energetic Dunbar, however, worked on several advanced degrees simultaneously and by the time Lois was finishing her degree at Columbia, Dunbar had earned the M.A., B.D., Ph.D., and M.D. There is no record of Lois and Flanders ever having met.

At Union Theological Seminary, Lois was influenced by Jules Bewer, Foakes-Jackson and Moffatt. These people did not merely spout ideologies or abstract concepts, rather they related the totality of humanness and human experience. "I was impressed with the importance of understanding inner experience of human beings at any stage."[45]

Combining Marriage and a Career

While she was a student at Union Theological Seminary, Lois's roommate brought home a young Columbia faculty member to meet her. Gardner Murphy, who was to become one of America's most beloved and powerful psychologists, was the kind of psychologist Lois Barclay admired—a social psychologist interested in philosophy, personality theory, history, political issues, and psychic phenomena.[45] They were married on 27 November 1926.[46]

Both Lois Murphy and Gardner have written of their romantic courtship and their loving and long marriage, involving mutual respect and an extraordinary amount of shared interests. They collaborated infrequently, however, although Gardner was co-author of her first book in 1931 and co-editor of her *Asian Psychology* (1968), and *Western Psychology: From the Greeks to William James* (1969).[44] This marriage produced also two children, a son Alpen ("Al") and a daughter Margaret ("Midge"); it thrived for more than fifty-two years, ending with Gardner's death in 1979.

In 1928, Lois B. Murphy received her B.D. from Union Theological Seminary and joined the faculty at Sarah Lawrence College. She remained there for twenty-four years, first teaching comparative religion and then psychology.[43, 46] One of the reasons Lois switched fields and entered Columbia's Teachers College to pursue the Ph.D. was that her speciality in religion required field work, much as that required in anthropology, and she did not want to leave her new husband.[45]

Lois Murphy's experiences at Columbia University were somewhat colored by the fact that she was married to one of the professors. Many of her classmates were getting married to each other (Anne Anastasi to John Foley, Georgene Hoffman to John Seward, Ruth Munroe to John Levy, etc.) and in their communications to us several woman have included the Murphys in the list of their graduate school friends. Lois specifically reports socializing with Margaret Mead.[45] In 1937 she received the Ph.D. from Columbia, the same year that the revised edition of *Experimental Social Psychology* (with G. Murphy and T. Newcomb) and her pioneering effort, *Social Behavior and the Child Personality: An Exploratory Study of Some Roots of Sympathy*, were published.[43]

The faculty at Sarah Lawrence College was very actively involved in research, particularly in child psychology. Much of Lois Murphy's early studies were conducted there, at the Nursery School to which she served as an advisor from 1937 to 1952. Several of her articles and two of her books stem from research at Sarah Lawrence.[46] A specialist in the assessment of children, Lois was the originator of new diagnostic techniques and became an expert on the use of the Rorschach test with young children; she taught clinical psychology at City College of New York, from 1947 to 1951, and lectured at Bank Street College of Education, from 1937 to 1941, while a full-time instructor and researcher at Sarah Lawrence.[43, 46]

In 1952, Lois and Gardner moved to Topeka, Kansas, to work at the Menninger Clinic and Foundation, she as director of Developmental Studies and he as director of Research. Lois had long been interested in psychoanalysis and had, in fact, been a lecturer at the William Alanson White Institute and the Chicago Institute of Psychoanalysis.[46] Now she took her formal training at the Topeka Psychoanalytic Institute and earned a Certificate in 1960.[43] The Murphys left Topeka to come to Washington, D.C. in 1967.

Lois Murphy has been a consultant to the Institute of Child Development and Mental Health in Amehdabad, India (1950–60), and to the Infant Rearing Study at Children's Hospital in Washington (1967–69)— since 1970 she has been serving the staff at Children's Hospital as an "academic advisor."[43] Of special concern to Lois has been Operation Headstart: from 1968 to 1974 she was a consultant to HEW on this program and she wrote ten booklets for Headstart.[43]

Typical of the women included in this chapter, Lois Murphy has been not so much a theoretician as an "observer," a "describer," and an "explainer." In her quest to understand normal child behavior, she has provided new observational techniques that are both innovative and concerned about the welfare of child subjects. Because of her humane attitude, she has disdained artificial laboratory experiments in favor of naturalistic observations.

While with the Menninger Foundation, for example, Lois and her colleagues were interested in studying how children growing up in a relatively stable community confront "everyday demands and stresses":

> The more global problem of how a child mobilizes and uses his resources as they are modified by the outcomes of learning processes, that is, how he puts his resources to work to meet his needs and to get along in the environment.[47]

To accomplish this purpose, rather than induce stress artificially, Murphy made observations of children as they reacted to real life stressors, such as John Kennedy's assassination, as well as to the demands of a developmental study—conducted by Sibylle Escalona and Mary Leitch— for which they were subjects.[47]

Lois Murphy was never really concerned with statistical significance or minute bits of information. She was interested in a global configuration of what "normal behavior" was.

> My deepest commitment is to an empirical approach which avoids formalization of experiments until after the terrain has been surveyed. . . . I feel very cautious about elaborate statistical procedures carried out by highly trained novices unacquainted with the nature of the facts with which they are dealing.[45]

In her quest for understanding of human behavior, Lois Murphy, innovative researcher and expert on child assessment, teacher, author, and child advocate, has done more than anyone of her generation to enhance our understanding of normal child development.

FEMINIST
Georgene Hoffman Seward (1902-   )

While we recognize a double standard in sexual behavior, we fail to realize that the difference in social sex roles goes so far as to constitute a major cultural cleavage . . . there is enough evidence from other cultures as well as from our own to indicate that men and

> *women do live in different worlds, or at least different subworlds . . .*
> *the distribution of rewards between the sexes is not equal, but con-*
> *sistently more favorable to men. Women, although in the statisti-*
> *cal majority, have the lower prestige status of an underprivileged*
> *minority . . .*
>
> *A vicious cycle is set up by the differential treatment of women.*
> *Prevented from displaying their capabilities, their only recourse is to*
> *exploit the situation by playing up the dependent role forced upon*
> *them. Out of this accommodative pattern a feminine stereotype*
> *emerged, according to which women are assumed to be 'emotional,'*
> *'undisciplined,' 'vain,' 'childish,' 'disorganized,' 'weak,' but withall,*
> *'charming.' Once the stereotype is set up, women are apt to be*
> *viewed collectively in terms of it rather than as individuals. . . .*
>
> —Georgene Seward

These words, which sound so contemporary, were actually written by Seward in 1956.[48] She has been speaking out as a militant feminist, has written five books and several articles on the psychology of women, and has conducted research on issues relevant to women, for more than forty years. It would be gratifying, especially since Georgene is our personal friend, to report that her words pricked the conscience of her colleagues and stirred up heated debate. It would be gratifying, but it would not be true. The fact is that until recently Georgene was effectively ignored by psychology. It is only in the past ten years that Georgene Seward has become recognized as an important psychologist, the darling of the militants.

Georgene Seward has been a professor and is a clinical psychologist who has always taken cognizance of sociocultural factors in the development of personality. She has consistently expressed ideas that were decades ahead of the time: for example, sympathetic to psychoanalytic theory, Seward reconceptualized Freud in terms of social realities; she was one of the first to suggest that women should be treated by female psychotherapists; and she has emphasized the role of social variables in the treatment process and in the etiology of neurosis. Above all, she notes, she has spent her long career investigating "sex behavior and sex roles."[49]

It is practically inevitable that women of psychology will address feminist issues at some time in their career. Georgene's involvement in empirical research is in the tradition of Leta Stetter Hollingworth and Helen Thompson Woolley; her theoretical ideas are in line with Karen Horney and Clara Thompson; her emphasis on cultural factors in sex role differences is, of course, consistent with the findings of her friend and former classmate at Columbia, Margaret Mead.

Life

Georgene Janet Hoffman was born on 21 January 1902, in Washington, D.C., daughter of Carl Henry Hoffman and Georgene Geddes Hoffman.[50, 51] With her conventional middle-class upbringing, it was not until Georgene had lived in New York that her socially and politically liberal values were established, along with her appreciation for cultural diversity.[49]

Her undergraduate work was completed at Barnard College, which, along with Columbia, Georgene describes as a "wonderfully exciting place to study."[48] Her college career was itself spectacular—she completed the requirements for the A.B. in three years, was elected to Phi Beta Kappa, and in her senior year, 1923, published her first article, "An Experiment in Self-estimation," in the *Journal of Abnormal and Social Psychology*.[50, 51]

She began her training in clinical psychology at Columbia's Teachers College, taking courses in experimental and social psychology as well. She describes a friendly, closeknit group of students; her friends included Elizabeth Duffy, Ruth Munroe, Margaret Mead, Lois Murphy, John Levy, and John Seward. There was much flirting and dating and friendly competition among the women over who was the "sexiest."[49] It was obviously not all play and no work since Georgene worked part-time while taking courses in that demanding department: first as reader (a sort of low-level teaching assistant; this was, in fact, to be your junior author's position much later, to Georgene Seward herself) at Columbia, 1923-24 and 1928-29; psychologist at the Neurological Institute, 1925-1927; and assistant psychologist, Children's Court, 1926. In 1926 Georgene became a Registered Examiner in Mental Defect by the State of New York.[51] She received her M.A. in 1924.

Marriage and Maturity

Georgene Hoffman and John Perry Seward, a brilliant student who was to become a prominent experimental psychologist and learning theorist, were married on 7 September 1927. They are still married, John's quiet, scholarly manner a perfect foil for the flamboyant out-spokenness of his wife. They have had two children, Barbara (now deceased), who was born on 5 September 1928, and Joan, born on 5 September 1934. The Sewards live in Los Angeles, and have recently collaborated on a book *Sex Differences: Mental and Temperamental*.[49]

Following her marriage, Georgene became closer to faculty members at Columbia; their friends included Robert Woodworth, Leta and Harry

Hollingworth, Otto Klineberg, and Lois and Gardner Murphy.[49] She received her Ph.D. in 1928 with a dissertation titled "Recognition Time as a Measure of Confidence."[51] She then accepted her first teaching position, at Hunter College, as an instructor.

After a year at Hunter, Georgene Seward returned to Barnard College, where she was to teach for seven years (from 1930 to 1937). During this entire period she did not advance in rank, but remained an instructor. Being passed over for advancement and promotion, often in preference for younger, less experienced, less competent men, was to plague Georgene during the remainder of her career.[49]

In 1937, Georgene Seward moved to Connecticut College, where she was appointed assistant professor. Shortly afterward there was an influx of psychologist and psychiatrist refugees from Nazi-occupied Europe and she made close friends with many of them, including Alfred Adler, Max Wertheimer, Charlotte and Karl Bühler, Wolfgang Köhler, Eva and Kurt Goldstein, Fritz Weiss, and Heinz Hartmann.[49] Herself a staunch anti-fascist, an avowed socialist, in fact, Seward, who is an outstandingly empathic, generous and loyal woman, developed a new cause: she became an acknowledged Hebrewphile (at least that is what she calls herself; she defines it as a gentile who can say that "all my best friends are Jewish"). Her feelings were eloquently expressed later, when in 1961 Seward read a paper at an International Congress in Vienna on the temperamental and intellectual attributes of Jews which made them excellent and compassionate psychoanalysts.[49]

Again, after eight years at Connecticut College, Georgene was not advanced in rank. She taught at Simmons College in Boston (from 1945 to 1946) as an assistant professor and when the Sewards moved to California, he at UCLA and she at the University of Southern California, Georgene was hired as an assistant professor. They arrived in Los Angeles about the time that her important (but ignored) book, *Sex and the Social Order*, was published.

Although Georgene Seward was finally given rank at Southern California—associate professor in 1949 and professor in 1958—it should be noted that she had been teaching full-time for twenty years before she obtained the rank of associate and almost thirty before she was made a professor.[50] On a faculty where she was often the only woman in the psychology department, Georgene taught courses in social psychology and clinical child psychology. Many of her students have become prominent psychologists and all of them remain loyal to this very generous and courageous woman. We all suffered when, shortly after obtaining professorial rank, Georgene was once again passed over, as head of the clinical program at USC. In 1971 she was made professor emeritus.

Five of Seward's books have dealt with feminism or related issues: *Sex and the Social Order* (1946), *Psychotherapy and Culture Conflict* (1956, 1972), *Clinical Studies in Culture Conflict* (1958), and (with J. P. Seward) *Sex Differences: Mental and Temperamental* (1980). Her sixth book, co-edited with her husband, *Current Psychological Issues* (1958), was a testimonial to their beloved mentor, Robert Woodworth, and coincided with a national meeting to honor him, which they and many of his students and colleagues had organized. This happy affair had tragic consequences for the Sewards, for while they were at this meeting their older daughter died of an accidental overdose of barbiturates.

Georgene and John Seward have always been fighters for a cause. Politically liberal, John was one of the UCLA dissidents who refused to sign a loyalty oath during the McCarthy era. The Sewards are not always on the same side on theoretical issues. When behaviorism took total control over academic psychology at their respective universities, for example, John was pleased and Georgene was appalled, since she felt that S-R theory was sterile and oversimplified. One of the many areas where the Sewards are in agreement and one to which they are dedicated is the cause of feminism, because they have always been involved in the struggle for social justice.

And it is simply justice that Georgene Seward's reputation is now being resurrected and she is at long last obtaining fame and prestige. Most young and militant female psychologists are becoming acquainted with Seward and her work. Twenty years ago almost no one (except, of course, her students and friends) knew her. In 1980 Seward's ideas do not seem so radical; in 1950 they were dynamite.

AN UNORTHODOX AND DISTINGUISHED
CLINICAL PSYCHOLOGIST
Molly R. Harrower (1906–   )

Life, you will lose a lover when I die!
For whom have you encouraged more; have I
Not always claimed
A thousand burning favors from you,
Proud, untamed and exquisite enchantress?

You say I should not love you, in my face
You have flung hardships, shown me to my place

> *For my bold daring;*
> *Yet as you spurn me, with the other hand*
> *You cast the colored splendors of the land*
> *For my own keeping; sun and wind and youth*
> *You give me in each kiss. Ah! Life, in truth*
> *You will have lost a lover when I die. . . .*
> *But while I live, leave me this ecstasy.*

—Molly Harrower, 1946

Best known for the development of the Group Rorschach Test in 1942, Molly Harrower, professor emeritus at the University of Florida, accomplished and published poet, and the first person to be granted the Ph.D. in psychology from Smith College (1934), is a remarkable woman whose life experiences have been exciting, varied, and more than a trifle odd.

She is one of the few women to be asked to write an autobiography for *The Psychologists*[52] and is the 1980 recipient of the Distinguished Clinical Psychologist Award of the American Psychological Association;[53] this to a woman who wrote, in a 1948 article entitled "The Evolution of a Clinical Psychologist," that there is no real discipline of clinical psychology, because there is no uniformity in the training of clinicians, only an area of shared interest.

In her fifty-two years as a psychologist, Molly Harrower has published twenty books, over one hundred articles and/or chapters in books, and has created several assessment instruments. She has worked for both the Canadian and United States governments, been in private practice, travelled extensively and now enjoys the Florida sun. Long recognized as a leading clinical psychologist, honored for her innovative contributions to diagnosis and treatment procedures, Harrower's early career was in experimental and Gestalt psychology and she has a long, illustrious career as a clinical researcher.

She was a woman who once flunked out of finishing school, a Scot who was born in South Africa, and a lecturer at the University of London without benefit of an academic degree of her own. When she received her first degree, it was the Ph.D. degree in experimental psychology, she had already published two books of poems (one for children), had taught dancing and art, and had been an accomplice in a criminal scam of C. K. Ogden.[52]

Early Life

Molly Harrower was born on 25 January 1906, in Johannesburg, South Africa, where her parents, James Harrower and Ina May White Harrower, were on business.[54, 55] After leaving South Africa, the family settled in a rural area outside of London, where Molly was reared in a traditional middle-class British style.

Molly describes her privileged English upbringing as very different from the typical American style in two important respects: (a) the child's primary caretaker is the nanny and (b) at age ten for girls (seven for boys) the child is sent to boarding school. While this approach to childrearing seems somewhat cruel, compared to the American middle class "cult-of-the-child" approach, Britishers consider a child handicapped later in life if the values associated with these experiences are not internalized.[52]

Molly reports that her central values as an adult are a direct reflection of early childrearing practices. Values such as fair play, being able to give and take affection, and self sufficiency, were firmly established while she was still young.[52]

The first instance of Molly Harrower's unorthodox life plan occurred after she had completed Godolphin School in Salisbury in 1924.[54] Women, at that time, were not expected to go on to college. Molly had her coming-out party and went off to finishing school to be made into a proper lady. This lasted only three months. Next she went to stay with a Swiss family where she could learn French. This family's daughters had hopes of becoming missionaries and since Molly did not, after one year and "reasonably good French," she returned home.[52]

Throughout her preparation for a career, according to Harrower's account, there was a great deal of "pulling of strings" and sometimes outright fraud as the resourceful young woman and her benefactors met obstacles by side-stepping them. The first such incident was going to college.

Harrower entered Bedford College of the University of London in 1926 with the help of the principal, who was a family friend. This was necessary since she had failed to take the entrance exams. She majored in journalism briefly, but became interested in psychology after taking a course with Beatrice Edgell, who had been a student of Kulpe.[52] Molly gave up her aspirations for a writing career (but subsequently published three books which were collections of her poetry) for a major in psychology.

Since Molly still had not taken any entrance examinations, special permission was required and obtained for her to work toward an Academic Diploma in psychology, a three-year program. Family financial reverses precipitated an early withdrawal from this program, however, but instead of finding work, Molly obtained a four-month scholarship to study the arts in the south of France. It was there that the twenty-two-year-old Harrower, blissfully enjoying painting and dancing lessons, met C. K. Ogden and became his assistant—or accomplice.[52]

Ogden, who was a world-renowned linguist, semanticist, and scholar, is generally described as an "eccentric." Wild man is more like it. He apparently delighted in perpetrating elaborate hoaxes and "conning" people, including his own powerful friends. In the summer of 1928 he hired Molly Harrower as a co-conspirator in a scheme to defraud purchasers of libraries—Ogden was the middle-man of some of their acquisitions. Harrower's "job" was to recopy the catalog for the purchaser, making certain deletions in the list of books.[52]

When Harrower informed him that she wished to terminate their "partnership" and wanted to emigrate to America, Ogden wrote to his good friend Kurt Koffka, one of the leaders of the world-wide Gestalt psychology movement. Koffka had recently been made research professor at Smith College and was developing a coterie of followers, primarily fawning undergraduate women.[29] James J. Gibson was an affectionate admirer of Koffka then; Eleanor J. Gibson was not.[29] Perversely Ogden not only highly recommended the almost uneducated Molly Harrower to be Koffka's secretary and assistant, but deliberately misrepresented Molly as the translator of Piaget's latest book. This deception led to Harrower's position at Smith College and directly to her successful career in psychology.[52]

Northampton and Montreal

Part of the group around Koffka at Smith known as "the foreigners," Harrower was given the title "Research Associate of the Research Laboratory."[54] In addition to making up for academic deficiencies, she began what was to be twenty years of estimable research and writing. In fact, while practically a total neophyte in psychology, Harrower wrote a series of important technical articles that explicated Gestaltist principles: in 1928, 1929, 1932, and 1936.

For the year 1931 Harrower taught at Wells College as an instructor and in 1933 she was a senior lecturer in psychology at Bedford College, replacing Victoria Hazlett, who was killed in a laboratory accident.[54, 55] All this before she received a single academic degree!

Although Smith College had conferred a few Ph.D. degrees before, Molly Harrower received the first in psychology. For this extraordinary event, an extraordinary examining committee was convened: Edwin G. Boring of Harvard, Arnold Gesell of Yale, George Humphreys of Queens

University of Canada, Kurt Koffka and other members of the Smith faculty.[52]

Her first job as a Ph.D. was director of students at New Jersey College for Women, a position which she held from 1934 to 1937. Harrower continued to write technical articles and her first book in psychology. Her interest turned to "psychological effects of surgical operations" and she was able to obtain a fellowship from the Rockefeller Foundation to work at the Montreal Neurological Institute.[52, 55]

Before leaving for Montreal, where she would become the first psychologist to be assigned to a general hospital, Harrower consulted with Kurt Goldstein, who "tutored" her on medical protocol and procedures. She also met through him, Bruno Klopfer, one of America's most prominent experts on the Rorschach test, and became interested in projective tests.[52, 53]

At Montreal, Harrower became involved in the diagnosis and treatment of neurologically impaired patients. She was now a clinician. As was true of all other aspects of her career, she quickly became a recognized expert in the area of brain lesions and is credited with being one of the first psychologists to utilize the Rorschach for diagnosis of patients with brain injuries. Although she was at the Neurological Institute for only four years, from 1937 to 1941, she and her colleagues wrote several important papers on this specialized area. One of her colleagues was Dr. Theodore Erickson.

According to Harrower, her experience in Montreal enabled her to (a) become comfortable with the Rorschach, (b) "cement my two psychological lives, the more scientifically precise and the more intuitive," and (c) convert the Rorschach, usually a one-to-one instrument, into a 'group procedure.'"[52]

Fame and Frustration

In 1938 Molly married Theodore Erickson, her colleague at the Montreal Institute (to eliminate confusion, Harrower was referred to as Harrower-Erickson between 1938 and 1945, the year the marriage ended in divorce). When Canada became involved in World War II, they decided to move to the United States, where Theodore had received a faculty position at the University of Wisconsin.[52] Discriminatory practices, which had been covert before, now struck Harrower directly, in the form of the anti-nepotism rule. She reports that, despite the fact that she was an important and well-known psychologist, when she applied to the university, she was told, "Sorry, no academic positions for wives."[52]

Harrower was able to obtain a grant from the Macy Foundation. Although she was given the title research associate of the Department of Neuropsychiatry by the University of Wisconsin, she spent the war years conducting research on her group form of the Rorschach and other innovative projective techniques she developed.[52] So, unlike most of the women psychologists who had established a reputation prior to the war and made gigantic steps forward in their career when there was a shortage of men, Molly Harrower's meteoric career advancement actually went into limbo during this period.

After the war, Harrower became a consultant to the Army (1947-49), the Air Force (1948-1951), and the State Department (1947-50); her services consisted primarily in selection of candidates for each agency—she had become the premier personality assessor. In 1945, Molly divorced Theodore Erickson.[53, 54, 55]

Between 1945 and 1964 Harrower was in private practice in New York, dividing her day between diagnosis, therapy, research, and consultations. One of the more famous people she saw during this time was Juan Batista's daughter, Lisa. On completion of her therapy

> Batista had two . . . guards deliver to me a three-way mirror with the most enormous flagon of perfume probably ever bottled. These were appropriate presents, he felt, to a lady doctor who also showed some feminine charm.[52]

During this period, for four years (from 1952 to 1955) she was also research director of the Child's Court of Manhattan. In this work she evaluated juvenile offenders and reported to the Judge.[52]

In 1955, Harrower remarried, this time more happily, to Mortimer Lahm, a businessman. They remained married until he died in 1967. She then moved to Gainesville, Florida and worked as a professor in the College of Health Related Professions of the University of Florida until her retirement and attainment of professor emeritus status in 1971.

While Molly Harrower was engaging in her clinical work, direct service, and research, she held, from 1953 on, simultaneous teaching appointments at several institutions. She was a visiting lecturer at the University of Texas, Department of Psychiatry, (1957); she was associate professor (1957-59) and professor (1959-64) at Temple University's Medical School in Philadelphia. She was very active in professional groups and in 1944 was elected president of the Society for Personality Assessment. She has received two of the most prestigious honors of her peers, the Distinguished Contributions Award of the Society for Personality Assessment in 1972 and the Distinguished Clinical Psychologist Award of the APA in 1980.[55]

Molly Harrower has had several notably successful careers in psychology: experimentalist, clinical researcher, premier personality assessor, expert on neurological impairment, teacher, writer, and clinician. She is, finally, perhaps the most popular and well-liked woman of psychology among women psychologists of her generation.

PSYCHOLOGIST IN THE PUBLIC INTEREST
Marie Jahoda (1907–   )

In a distinguished career in Austria, the United States, and England, Marie Jahoda has brought high psychological competence to bear on many significant human problems. . . . Through her work, we know more about psychological aspects of unemployment, prejudice and race relations, work satisfaction, mental health, and social forecasting. . . .

> Citation, Award for Distinguished
> Contributions to Psychology in the
> Public Interest, 1979

Best known for her work on prejudice and anti-Semitism and a classic textbook in statistics and research design, *Research Methods in Social Relations* (with Morton Deutsch and Stuart Cook) (1951), Marie Jahoda was a member of the Vienna "salon," presided over by the Bühlers. Like the others in this group, particularly her friend Else Frenkel, Marie Jahoda has been interested in broad social and political issues. Throughout her long career, she has demonstrated unusual personal courage and integrity.

Life and Career

Marie was born 26 January 1907, in Vienna, Austria. Part of the heady intellectual and political atmosphere at the University of Vienna, Jahoda was imbued with the spirit of scientific research and its application to social issues. Before she was thirty, she had published three important articles. She received her Ph.D. in 1932.[56]

Following her education, Marie accepted a position as assistant director of research for the Social Research Institute in Vienna (from 1932 to 1936).[56] Her first interest in the social conditions of prewar Vienna was in the area of the psychological implications of unemployment.[57] During this time, Marie was also a political activist. During the pre-Hitler regime of Kurt von Schuschnigg, Marie was jailed along with others who were protesting the oppressive political atmosphere.[57]

Since she was an avowed political liberal and an outspoken opponent of fascism, it was necessary for Jahoda to leave Austria. In 1937 she emigrated to England, was a research associate at Bristol University for one year, a research fellow at Cambridge University for two years, and worked for the Ministry of Information for one year.[56] After two years with the National Institute of Social and Economic Research (from 1943 to 1945), Marie emigrated to the United States. During these war years, she was involved in research on worker satisfaction and on consumer motivation.

Jahoda worked for the American Jewish Committee, New York City, as a research associate, from 1945 to 1948. This Committee was involved in underwriting research on anti-Semitism and prejudice, including the study at California which made her friend Else Frenkel-Brunswik famous. Jahoda also published an important book on this topic, *Anti-Semitism and Emotional Disorder* (with Nathan Ackerman) in 1949.[56]

Jahoda was a research associate at Columbia University for one year (1948–49) and then moved on to New York University, where she was the associate director of the Research Center for Human Relations (from 1949 to the mid-sixties).[57]

During the McCarthy era, Jahoda was, as might be expected, appalled by the atmosphere of political oppression and intellectual and social conformity. Again she spoke out; her articles, "Security Measures and Freedom of Thought" (1952) and "Psychological Issues in Civil Liberties" (1956), re-established her reputation as the leading libertarian social scientist in this country. Her monumental *Research Methods in Social Relations* established her credentials as a scientist. In 1955 Marie published "Psychological Problems of Women in Different Social Roles," an important statement on this feminist issue.[56]

Marie returned to England, where she was appointed professor of social psychology at the University of Sussex. She remained there until her retirement.[56] In addition to being honored in 1979 by the American Psychological Association, Marie Jahoda received honorary degrees from the University of Sussex and the University of Leicester.[56]

Contributions

Marie Jahoda has been involved in social research for over forty-five years. In all that time, she has maintained a consistent liberal attitude, leading the battles for civil rights and against repression and social injustice. She has written nine books and numerous journal articles. Her most important books have been *Anti-Semitism and Emotional Disorder* (1949), *Research Methods in Social Relations* (1951), *Studies in the Scope and Methods of the Authoritarian Personality* (1954), *The Impact of Literature: A Psychological Discussion of Some Assumptions of the Censorship Debate* (1954), the *Quality of Education Offered to Majority and Minority Children* (1956), *Current Concepts of Positive Mental Health* (1958), and *Freud and the Dilemmas of Psychology* (1977).

THE LANGUAGE OF CHILDREN
Dorothea Agnes McCarthy (1906–1974)

The developer of the McCarthy Scales of Children's Ability, a series of eighteen tests of the motor and mental abilities of children aged two-and-a-half to eight-and-a-half, Dorothea McCarthy was a leading clinical child psychologist and researcher in child development. Trained at the Institute of Child Welfare at Minnesota under Florence Goodenough, McCarthy joined the faculty at Fordham University as an associate professor of educational psychology when she was only twenty-six years old and already a world-known expert in child development. She remained on the faculty for thirty-nine years, until, with her retirement in 1971, she was made professor emeritus. She is best known for her extensive early research on language development in children.

Life and Career

Dorothea Agnes McCarthy was born on 4 March 1906, the daughter of Francis D. McCarthy and Mary Malloy McCarthy, in Minneapolis, Minnesota. Dorothea first attended the College of St. Catherine, a small women's college, between 1921 and 1922; she entered when she was only fifteen years old. Dorothea then moved to the University of Minnesota and received her A.B. in 1925 and her Ph.D. in 1928, when she was only twenty-two years old, the age at which most are only receiving their baccalaureate.[58, 59]

While a graduate student, she was a recipient of a Laura Spelman Rockefeller Fellowship and worked as an assistant at the Institute for Child Welfare (from 1926 to 1928), under Florence Goodenough. Her dissertation was completed under Karl Lashley, the great physiological psychologist; it was published as a journal article, with Lashley, titled 'The Survival of the Maze Habit After Cerebellar Injuries." Upon completion of her degree, she received a National Research Council Fellowship, which provided her resources to complete her classic studies of language development.[58, 59]

When she left Minnesota, it was for California, where for one year, 1929-30, she worked as a clinical psychologist with the California Bureau of Juvenile Research. For two years thereafter, McCarthy was an associate professor and director of the nursery school at the University of Georgia, from 1930 to 1932. During this period she published her most important papers on language development.[58, 59]

In 1932 McCarthy moved to Fordham University. She and Robert T. Rock married on 9 June 1934; Dorothea retained her maiden name. They had one daughter, Catherine A. Rock. In 1941 McCarthy joined the faculty of the Graduate School at Fordham, since women were not permitted to teach undergraduates, when Dorothea transferred to the Psychology Department. In 1948 she was advanced to full professor of psychology, a position she maintained until 1971, when, at sixty-five, she retired. In 1942 she took on the added responsibilities of director of Fordham's Child Guidance Clinic.[58] McCarthy died in 1974, only two years after her only book was published.

Work

Teacher and clinician, Dorothea McCarthy had a monopoly on the area of language development for more than twenty years. Although her publications were sparse, her writing on language development was extremely impressive and influential. Her most-often cited paper, "The Language Development of the Preschool Child," was published in 1930 (she was only twenty-four years old!) as a monograph by the University of Minnesota Press. McCarthy wrote the chapter on language development in both Murchison's famous *Handbook of Child Development* (1931), and Carmichael's equally famous *Manual of Child Development* (1946). Her one book, *Manual for the McCarthy Scales of Children's Ability*, published in 1972, was the culmination of more than thirty years of research on these widely used instruments, her crowning achievement.

SOUTHERN PSYCHOLOGIST
Elizabeth Duffy (1904-1970)

One of the "terrible trio" of leading women psychologists of the South, as acknowledged by her election to the presidency of the Southern Society for Philosophy and Psychology (1949-50) and the North Carolina Psychological Association (1954-55),[60, 61] "Polly" Duffy was once considered a potential leader of American psychology, but she was "lost" in Greensboro. Her original, general theory of motivation, which had been discussed in a series of journal articles over many years, was finally published in a book, *Activation and Behavior*, in 1962.[60]

Polly Duffy was one of the most popular of the Columbia graduate students, although she was part of that group for only one year before her Ph.D. and one year postdoctorally. In her forty years as a college teacher, in fact, her primary influence was personal and direct. Except for one national elected office—president of Division 1, General Psychology, of the APA, Duffy's prestige was local or at best regional, best known among her many students, colleagues, and friends.

For most of her career, Polly taught undergraduate courses in women's colleges, at two colleges with relatively high academic standards and research interests. But despite her early promise as a brilliant theoretician and researcher, Duffy never realized her full potential; she never became one of the leaders of American psychology nor attracted the wide following that, with her competence, personal achievements, and attributes of character, one might have predicted. Early in her career, in fact, she complained to a fellow psychologist that she felt unappreciated by the administrators at the University of North Carolina. She noted, at that time, "It seems to me that intellectual interests are really despised, even in most colleges."[62]

Life and Career

Elizabeth was born 6 May 1904, to Dr. Francis Duffy and Lida Patterson Duffy, in New Bern, North Carolina. Elizabeth attended the North Carolina College for Women (from 1921 to 1925) where she received her A.B. in 1925 and was elected to Phi Beta Kappa (this college is now the University of North Carolina at Greensboro).[61]

Polly then went to New York to attend graduate school, at Columbia University's Teachers College. She received the M.A. in 1926 in experimental psychology, from Columbia. She then transferred to Johns Hopkins, where she was a National Research Scholar, and received the Ph.D. in 1928. On 13 August 1928, she was married to Dr. John T. Baker, and then returned to Columbia to study on a National Research Fellowship.[61]

In 1929 Duffy joined Lois Barclay Murphy, one of her Columbia friends, on the faculty of Sarah Lawrence College, in the Division of Social Sciences. She was to remain there until 1937, when after several important articles and a divorce, she returned to her alma mater as a full professor of psychology.[60, 61]

Polly taught at Women's College from 1937 to 1969 and became a beloved fixture in North Carolina psychology. On 27 August 1938, she married Dr. John E. Bridgers, professor of English at Women's College. They were married for twenty-eight years, until his death in 1966, and had one daughter, Betsy Elizabeth Bridgers. Socially she was known as Elizabeth Bridgers, but professionally and to her oldest friends she was always Polly Duffy.[60] On 19 December 1970, she died of Hodgkin's disease.

Contributions

Polly Duffy's literary out-put was rather meager. There were only twenty-five articles and a single book.[60] Duffy's activation theory was anticipated eagerly by psychologists who knew her work, for several years. It is a general theory which integrates experimental and physiological data, subsuming a large amount of psychology's accumulated knowledge and addressing basic issues of psychology. With a masterful reduction of data into a few general principles, Duffy's theoretical views resemble those of Calkins and Washburn. Like her pioneer predecessors, Duffy's teaching included the encouragement of laboratory research by her undergraduate women students. In many respects, Polly Duffy was indeed a "throwback" to the great women psychologists of the twenties—she was a scholar, a researcher, a respected member of the profession, but most of all, she was a teacher. Her influence, like the others, will live primarily in the memories of her devoted students.

LEARNING FROM DOLLS
Pauline Snedden Sears (1908-   )

Best known for her research on aggression in children as manifested by doll-play and that on the topic of aspiration level, Pauline Sears has been an accomplished and innovative clinical and developmental researcher for forty years. Like many of the women included in this chapter, her most famous studies were completed early in her career, particularly during World War II, but her productivity has been maintained at a high level and shows considerable diversity.

Life and Career

Pauline Snedden was born on 5 July 1908, in Fairlee, Vermont. She then travelled across the country to Stanford University, where in 1930 she earned her A.B.[63, 64, 65] While at Palo Alto, Pauline met Robert Richardson Sears, a fellow psychology student who shared many professional interests. She returned to the East to study at Columbia's Teachers College. There she took courses in child development, clinical psychology, and cultural anthropology, and earned the M.A. in 1931.[63]

In 1932 Pauline married Robert Sears. They are still married, have had two children, and live in Menlo Park, near Stanford.[63, 65] Robert, who had just received his Ph.D. from Yale, accepted a position as an instructor at the University of Illinois and the family spent four years in Urbana, Illinois. Pauline's professional career was put on "hold" and she was a full-time housewife until Robert was invited to Yale and the family moved again. He became an assistant professor and she a graduate student at Yale in 1936.[63, 64]

Pauline Sears received the Ph.D. in psychology from Yale University in 1939. Her career, for twenty-seven years, was typical of the psychologist-wife as we have come to know it. Despite her excellent and well-known research studies early in her career, some in collaboration with her husband and some with the Yale specialists in anthropology and sociology, Sears filled a series of low-status positions. Her husband's career had top priority and when he advanced in his career, Pauline and the family, of course, accompanied him. From 1936 to 1942 Pauline was a clinical instructor at Yale, from 1942 to 1949 she was a research fellow at the University of Iowa (her husband was director of the Child Welfare Station), and then from 1949 to 1953 she had the position of research associate at Harvard (he was a professor of education and psychology and the director of the Laboratory of Human Development).[64]

In 1953, the two moved to Stanford University, he as a professor of psychology and she as an assistant professor of education. Stanford has consistently been amicable to women of psychology. This is the school that added Lillien Jane Martin to form a two-person psychology department in 1898. Martin landed the position through her friend, David Starr Jordan, and, more than seventy years later, Robert Sears became a David Starr Jordan Professor in 1970. Pauline Sears was advanced to the rank of full professor as well. In 1973 he was granted emeritus status and in 1974, Pauline was also.[63]

Contributions

In 1939 five Yale faculty members published the now-famous book, *Frustration and Aggression*. Included in the book was an observational study of a five-month old infant conducted by Pauline and Robert Sears (Robert Sears was one of the book's authors). Pauline Sears was very productive during the Yale years, conducting the now-classic studies on level of aspiration and publishing many journal articles on the procedure. She found that this independent variable, expectations of future performance which are often quite unrealistic, may operate like a "self-fulfilling prophecy." Level of aspiration has been found to be associated with self-concept, classroom behavior of both children and teachers, and academic goal attainment.

As early as 1937, Pauline Sears was involved in research on various aspects of the concept of aggression in children. This area of research made an impact on psychology and brought her fame after she developed the doll-play technique for testing aggression, especially with a series of studies following World War II. With Margaret H. Pintler, she published "Sex-difference in Doll-play Aggression" (1947); with Pintler and Robert Sears, "Effect of Father Separation on Preschool Children's Doll-play Aggression" (1946); and her most influential work, a monograph, "Doll-Play Aggression in Normal Young Children: Influence of Sex, Age, Sibling Status, Father's Absence," was published in 1951.

In 1958, Sears received a rare honor for women when she was asked to write the chapter on "Developmental Psychology" for the ninth volume of the *Annual Review of Psychology*.

More recently, Pauline Sears has published technical papers on such topics as teaching techniques in the nursery school, the effects of computerized teaching machines, psychological effects of accelerated mathematics programs, self-concept in children, and childrearing practices. She is today happily retired and best remembered for her early research studies and for her twenty years as an influential professor at Stanford University.

PARTICIPANT-OBSERVER
Florence Rockwood Kluckhohn (1905–   )

Florence Kluckhohn, sociologist and cultural anthropologist who for years lived in the shadow of her more famous husband, is now growing in prominence and influence because of her work on feminist issues, published almost thirty years ago. Florence Kluckhohn's analysis of the problems facing the dual-career woman has become a classic and she has belatedly joined Margaret Mead and Georgene Seward as intellectual ancestors of the feminist movement.

Life and Career

Florence Rockwood was born in Illinois on 14 January 1905, the daughter of Homer Garfield and Florence McLaughlin Rockwood. She received the

A.B. from the University of Wisconsin in 1927. On 15 October 1932, she married Clyde Kluckhohn, who became one of America's leading anthropologists, an expert on the American Indian, and extremely influential in social sciences generally.[66] She seemed content to run the rather chaotic household, care for their son, Richard, and accompany Clyde on field trips when this was possible.[67]

They moved to Cambridge where Clyde achieved a brilliant career at Harvard and as his prestige increased, Flo became an extraordinary hostess of their famous parties. Since she was a large, flamboyant, attractive, and outspoken extrovert, she was a well-known person in her own right in the high-powered social science community. She took courses, off and on, for years and conducted a spectacular study of Spanish-Americans in New Mexico. This was a participant-observation study and to gain entrance into the community Florence rented a general store and lived in a backroom while she operated the store. Clyde was also conducting a field trip, in Arizona, and the two compared notes on an occasional weekend visit. At this time Florence, a young woman with long raven-black hair, dark complexion, and fluent Spanish, was so thoroughly accepted as part of the community that when she informed her subjects that she was not really a Latino store operator but a cultural anthropologist collecting data for a study, her subjects argued that she was "loco." They were primarily concerned over where they would find such a competent person to run the store.[67]

Florence joined the staff, as a teacher, at Wellesley College in 1940. Her Ph.D., from Radcliffe College, was obtained in 1941. She remained at Wellesley until 1948, working for one year (1944–45) with the Office of War Information in Washington, D.C. In 1948 she came to Harvard.[66] For twenty years she was a lecturer in the Department of Social Relations and an associate in the Laboratory of Social Relations; this is an interdisciplinary department, including social psychology, cultural anthropology, and sociology, one of whose founders was Clyde Kluckhohn.[66, 67]

Florence Kluckhohn did not complete many studies, but her research was very impressive and her publications were all extremely important and very often cited. In addition to *America's Women* (1952), she published a major work on the historic changes in the family, *The American Family, Past and Present*, in 1952. Her most influential work (published with Fred Strodtbeck in 1961) was *Variations in Value Orientations*, an outstanding theoretical contribution. Similar to (some say, "borrowed from") Clyde's concept of "cultural orientation" and to Ruth Benedict's "pattern of culture," Florence's theoretical elaboration expanded and greatly improved the previous constructs. She was able to demonstrate that members of "subcultural" groups, that is, identified social groups that are separate from the WASP "dominant" culture of America, may hold a pattern of values that is "variant" from the "dominant" values.

Never receiving the recognition that her achievements deserved, Florence retired in 1968. She had been widowed for several years and married George Taylor that year. They moved to Seattle, Washington. In 1974 Florence was made an "honorary affiliate professor of anthropology" at the University of Washington.[66] It is only in the past few years that her reputation as a leading social and political critic and social scientist has been established; she has recently been honored by feminist writers with a sense of history.

DOCTOR, PSYCHIATRIST, PSYCHOLOGICAL TESTER, ANTHROPOLOGIST, SOCIOLOGIST, PUBLIC HEALTH EXPERT, INDIAN-AFFAIRS SPECIALIST, SOCIAL PSYCHIATRIST ... AND NOT RETIRED YET!
Dorothea Cross Leighton (1908–   )

Dorothea Leighton is a well-known cultural anthropologist, the 1978 recipient of the Distinguished Scholarship Award of the Southwestern Anthropological Association. This award recognizes her well-received and respected research on the American Indian, oft-cited studies conducted in collaboration with Clyde Kluckhohn, her former husband Alexander Leighton, and others. Most people familiar with her anthropological work are not aware that she, like Alexander Leighton, was trained in psychiatry. In fact, Dorothea is competent in medicine, the social sciences, chemistry, and psychological testing, and some of her best work, in social psychiatry, was not begun until she was close to sixty years of age. This woman, proficient in four separate disciplines, is still professionally active and publishing today.[68]

Life and Career

Dorothea Cross was born on 2 September 1908, in Lunenburg, Massachusetts, the daughter of Frederick Cushing Cross and Dorothea Farquar Cross.[69] She attended Bryn Mawr College, majoring in chemistry and biology, and received her A.B. in 1930. She was elected to Phi Beta Kappa.[68, 69]

For two years following graduation, Dorothea worked at Johns Hopkins Hospital as a chemistry technician assigned to the Pediatrics Department. She then entered Johns Hopkins Medical School, obtaining the M.D. in 1936. Her internship was at the Baltimore City Hospital. On 17 August 1937, she married Alexander Hamilton Leighton, a classmate at Johns Hopkins. They had two children, Dorothea and Frederick, and for thirty years worked and travelled together. They published four books together and a number of journal articles. In October 1965, they were divorced.[68, 69]

Dorothea Cross Leighton was a resident in psychiatry at the Phipps Clinic, Johns Hopkins, from 1937 to 1942. She and her husband took one year off, (1939-40), when they each received a Social Science Research Council Post-doctoral Training Fellowship. They spent three months taking anthropology courses at Columbia University, five months doing field work among the Navaho, and three months doing field work among the St. Lawrence Island, Alaska, Eskimos.[68] From that time on, both Dorothea and Alexander Leighton gained prominence in both anthropology and social psychiatry.

From 1942 to 1945, Dorothea Leighton was a special physician with the U.S. Office of Indian Affairs. She participated in a study, conducted jointly by Indian Affairs and the University of Chicago, on Indian education, where among her duties was personality assessment through the use of projective tests.[68] In 1945 Dorothea worked for the Office of War Information, Foreign Morale Analysis Division. Following this she and her husband each received a Guggenheim Fellowship to complete the Indian Education study.[68]

In 1944, the Leightons published *The Navaho Door*, and Dorothea published, with Clyde Kluckhohn, *The Navaho* in 1946 and also *Children of the People* in 1947. Again with her husband she published *Gregorio the Hand-trembler*, 1949, and articles on the Indian Education studies. It was not until 1966 that she and John Adair published her book on the Zuni Indians, *People of the Middle Place*.

The Leightons then moved to Cornell University, where Dorothea was made a professor in the prestigious home economics department, a position which she held from 1949 to 1952.[69] In 1952 Dorothea moved to the Social Psychiatry Program of Cornell's Department of Anthropology and Sociology; she served as a research associate and then senior research associate, until 1965 (as happens so frequently, she saw her husband appointed director of the program, from 1955 to 1966).[69]

While at Cornell, Dorothea (at times with other members of the staff, including Alexander Leighton) published articles, such as "The Distribution of Psychiatric Symptoms in a Small Town" (1956) and "Psychiatric

Findings of the Stirling County Study" (1963), and two books, *The Character of Danger: Psychiatric Symptoms in Selected Communitites* (1963) and *Psychiatric Disorder Among the Yoruba* (1963). The work of the Cornell group tended to demonstrate that emotional disturbance is related to disintegration of social systems: human striving, they observed, tends to be blocked when a community, an ethnic group, or a subcultural group no longer has survival value for its individual members, who become more acutely "at risk" for emotional disturbance.

Beginning in 1963 Dorothea Leighton became involved in teaching, at Cornell a course in medicine and anthropology and after her divorce, full-time at the University of North Carolina. In Chapel Hill, pursuing a career independent of her ex-husband, who was to go to Harvard, Dorothea was an associate professor in the school of public health (from 1965 to 1972) and then became a full professor and chairperson of the department, until her retirement. She was granted emeritus status at UNC in 1974.[68]

As she noted, Leighton never did any solo research until 1965—although she had a number of solo publications prior to that date—and after that date, she became a spokesperson for the sociocultural approach to medicine. Her later publications include "Poverty and the Individual" (1966), "The Public Health Nurse as a Mental Health Resource" (1968), "Psychiatric Disorder in a Swedish and a Canadian Community" (1968), "The Empirical Status of the Integration-Disintegration Hypothesis" (1971), "Cultural Determinants of Behavior: A Neglected Area" (1972), "Insinuating Social Sciences Into Medical Thinking" (1975), and "Sociocultural Factors in Physical and Mental Breakdown" (1978).[68]

In 1974, at age sixty-six, Dorothea Cross Leighton "retired" to Berkeley, California—she is still writing and conducting research and is associated with the University of California at San Francisco as a lecturer in the Department of Epidemology and International Health. Chemist, psychiatrist, anthropologist, and psychologist, Dorothea will probably always be remembered as a collaborator of Clyde Kluckholn and confused in bibliographic references with her ex-husband. Ironically, perhaps her most important work, on measuring the level of stress, which she completed in the early seventies, is hardly ever mentioned. This work, for which she was involved with several psychiatrists, is a potentially valuable apporach to establishing "risk factors" and developing preventive programs and here she was able to demonstrate the objective, scientific orientation that characterizes the work of the women of psychology included in this chapter.

A VARIED, DIVERSE, AND BRILLIANT CAREER
Eugenia Hanfmann (1905–)

One of the most brilliant individuals in the history of psychology, Eugenia Hanfmann has had a varied career with diverse research interests. A native of Russia, she was a major figure at the Russian Research Center at Harvard and during World War II was on the staff of the now-famous Assessment Program of the Office of Strategic Services. Known primarily for fifty years of competence in personality assessment and clinical research, Hanfmann was a highly regarded teacher, associated particularly with Brandeis University, where she worked for twenty years and with Abraham Maslow helped form the psychology department when the school was in its infancy. Hanfmann has been a colleague of and collaborator with many of the great names in modern psychology: Kurt Koffka, Kurt Lewin, Tamara Dembo, Kurt Goldstein, Andras Angyal, Henry Murray, Robert W. White, Maria Rickers-Ovsiankina, Fritz Heider, and Abraham Maslow. She has also been associated professionally with Clyde Kluckhohn.

Life and Career

Eugenia Hanfmann was born on 3 March 1905, in St. Petersburg, Russia. She studied psychology, education, philosophy, and philology at the University of Jena in Germany. In 1927 she received the Ph.D. in psychology, at age twenty-two, and joined the staff at the Psychological Institute at Jena as an assistant. While in this position, from 1928 to 1930, she participated in laboratory teaching, research, and testing. Her first publications, when she was at the Institute and quite young, prior to her early work with schizophrenics, were concerned with Gestalt psychology and children's play. She published two articles before she was twenty-five, "Die Entstehung visueller Assoziationen" ("The Origin of Visual Associations") and "Ueber das Bauen der Kinder" ("On Childraising").[70]

Hanfmann involved herself in the Gestalt movement and was part of Kurt Koffka's retinue, which came to the United States and settled at Smith College. She remained at Smith for two years, from 1930 to 1932, as a research associate at the Research Laboratory of Psychology which had been set up for Koffka, conducting research on child development and visual perception. Many of her earliest papers were published in the *Psychologiche Forschung*, of which Koffka was one of the founders.[70]

In 1932 Hanfmann went to Worcester State Hospital, where, although hired as a research psychologist, she was involved in mental testing, especially with children. She met Tamara Dembo, who was to become a leading social psychologist, here and the two of them collaborated on a few minor studies with hospital patients; they remained friends for several years. It was at Worcester State Hospital that Hanfmann began her best-known research, on the disturbance of concept formation in schizophrenics.[70]

She left Worcester in 1936, when she received a grant from the Masonic Foundation to continue her research on schizophrenia. She developed the Concept Formation Test, a germinal instrument for the measurement of schizophrenic thought disturbance, and collected data at the Rhode Island State Hospital and at Michael Reese Hospital in Chicago.[70] She wrote ten articles on the disturbance in conceptualization of schizophrenia, the most comprehensive being a special monograph in 1942, with J. Kasanin, published by *Nervous and Mental Disease Monographs.*

By the time she was gaining prominence as a clinical researcher, Hanfmann had joined the faculty at Mt. Holyoke College, first as an instructor, 1939, and then as an assistant professor. She taught in the Department of Psychology and Education until 1944, the year that her monograph with Kurt Goldstein and Maria Rickers, "Case Lanuti: Extreme Concretization of Behavior Due to Damage of the Brain Cortex," was published as an entire issue of *Psychological Monographs.* From 1944 to 1946 Hanfmann was on leave from Mt. Holyoke to work for the OSS, as a psychodiagnostic tester with the Assessment Program. She was one of the authors of *Assessment of Men*, 1948, and although she wrote several articles and monographs, did not publish her second book for another fifteen years.[70]

Hanfmann did not return to Mt. Holyoke, but instead accepted a position at Harvard in the Department of Social Relations, at a reduction in rank. She was a lecturer on clinical psychology and a research associate in the Laboratory of Social Relations there from 1946 to 1952. She worked with Henry Murray, Robert W. White, and George E. Gardner in her clinical work and with Florence and Clyde Kluckhohn, among many others, in the Laboratory. During her years in Cambridge, Hanfmann was able to reestablish ties with the Gestaltists since Kurt Lewin and his followers were involved in important work at the Massachusetts Institute of Technology. Hanfmann was a consultant at MIT in 1947 and again worked with Tamara Dembo. Being at Harvard also allowed her to make a unique, special contribution to the science of psychology—from 1950 to 1954 she was associated with the Russian Research Center. During part of 1950 and 1951 she interviewed Soviet Displaced Persons in Munich, Germany. She also worked part-time at Judge Baker Guidance Center doing psychotherapy with children; George Gardner, its director, was a colleague of hers at Harvard.[70]

In 1952 Hanfmann joined Maslow at Brandeis University, which was then a small, new college and the fledgling psychology department was also tiny. She was hired as an associate professor and director of the Student Counseling Center. Her on-going research on a variation of the sentence-completion method was applied to the authoritarian personality, "Authoritarian Personality Studied by a New Variation of the Sentence Completion Technique" (with R. J. Dorris and D. J. Levinson), in 1954, and she published a major monograph on her work in Munich, "Interpersonal Attitudes of Former Soviet Citizens as Studied by a Semi-projective Method" (with J. W. Getzels), in *Psychological Monographs*, 1955.[70]

Brandeis, then, got a clinical psychologist with a background in philosophy and experimental psychology who had made contributions to experiments on perception, anthropology, clinical research on schizophrenia, personality assessment including instruments she herself originated or revised, and neuropsychology. Hanfmann stayed at Brandeis until 1972; she had been made a full professor and when she retired, professor emeritus.

Hanfmann has published two books, *Psychological Counseling in a Small College*, Schenkman, 1963, and *Effective Therapy for College Students*, Jossey-Bass, 1978, and continues to write. In fact, with time to meditate and integrate, Hanfmann is now in her most productive period. She is also in private practice.[70]

ON CHILDREN, DEVELOPMENT OF SEX ROLES, AND PERSONALITY
Ruth E. Hartley (1910-   )

For more than forty years, Ruth Hartley has been prominent in clinical psychology, child development, educational psychology, and social psychology. She is the author of several well-known textbooks and has worked in several states, including New York, Hawaii, and Wisconsin, and in Australia and New Zealand. Her primary research interests have been in cognitive development, projective techniques, sex role development, early childhood education, and personality development.

Life and Career

Ruth was born on 26 May 1910, in New York City. She received her B.A. from Cornell University in 1930 and her M.A. from Teachers College of Columbia University in 1932.[71, 72] Shortly after receiving her degree, she met Eugene L. Hartley, two years her junior, who was then a graduate

student in social psychology at Columbia, and the two were active partici-
pants in the heady social life at Columbia. They were married in 1935. A
year later he received his Ph.D. and she retired briefly to manage the
household and rear their two children.

In 1936-37 Ruth Hartley was an assistant regional supervisor of the
New York State Department of Education and in 1939 a clinical psychologist for the Family Service Society of Yonkers. In 1944 she received the
Ph.D. in psychology from Columbia.[72] She was an instructor at Brooklyn
College (1945-46), and the joined Eugene at CCNY (1946-47) (he was
there from 1939 to 1969). The longest Ruth was to stay at any position
was her stint at the Carolyn Zachry Institute, where for eleven years, from
1947 to 1958, she was principal investigator of the project on mental
health and children's play.[72]

Ruth Hartley has held various concurrent positions on research projects,
most often as director. She has also had a varied teaching career: Long
Island University, associate professor of psychology, (1961-63); research
professor, Human Development, University of Hawaii, (1967-68); lecturer at various colleges and universities in Australia and New Zealand,
(1964-67); University of British Columbia, Canada, (1968); visiting
professor of psychology and chairperson of the department, Murdoch
University, Australia, (1975-76); and professor and chairperson of the
Department of Psychology, University of Wisconsin-Green Bay, (1968-77).
In 1977, the well-travelled Ruth Hartley retired, was made professor
emerita of Growth and Development, and now lives in Scottsdale,
Arizona.[72]

Although best-known for her research in clinical and child psychology,
Ruth Hartley has also been involved in research on feminist issues. From
1956 to 1961, for example, she worked on a study of women's roles, with
a grant from the National Institute of Mental Health at CCNY.[72]

THE DOCTOR OF YOUNG WOMEN WHO STARVE THEMSELVES
Hilde Bruch (1904-   )

One of America's best-known women psychiatrists, Hilde Bruch is recognized as the world's leading expert on eating disorders. Her recent books,
Eating Disorders: Obesity, Anorexia Nervosa and Person Within (1973)
and *The Golden Cage: The Enigma of Anorexia Nervosa* (1978), are very
popular and influential (and controversial) books on this specialized area.
She is also the author of an excellent, if less well-known, textbook on
psychotherapy, and has for several years been involved in the training of
psychotherapists.

Above (*left*): Georgene Hoffman Seward; (*right*): Eugenia Hanfmann;
below: Hilde Bruch

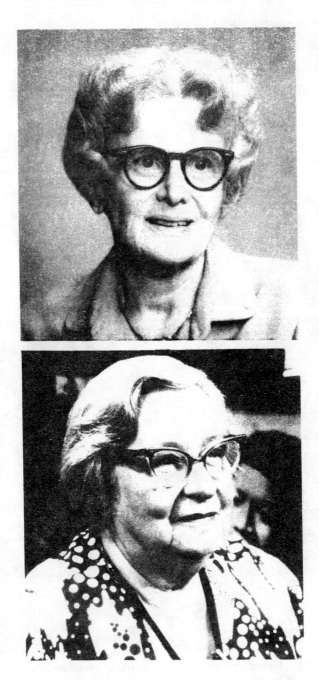

Above: Edith Weisskopf-Joelson; *below*: Marianne Bellak Frostig

Life and Career

Hilde Bruch was born in Duelken, Germany, on 11 March 1904, the daughter of Hirsch Bruch and Adele Rath Bruch. She received her M.D. from the University of Freiburg, Germany in 1929. For the next four years she was active in psychological research and pediatrics at the University Clinics at Kiel and Leipzig. She left Germany, as did many women of psychology, in the face of Nazi occupation, in 1933, and fled to England. Bruch never married, but raised a war-orphan nephew as a son.[73]

Hilde worked at the East End Child Guidance Clinic for one year (1933-34), and then emigrated to America, where she obtained psychiatric training at Johns Hopkins Hospital, from 1941 to 1943, on a Rockefeller Fellowship. She had been an instructor in pediatrics at Columbia University's College of Physicians and Surgeons, from 1934 to 1943, and when she completed her psychiatric residency, she returned to Columbia, where from 1943 to 1964 Bruch was on the clinical staff at the College of Physicians and Surgeons. In 1959, she was made clinical professor of psychiatry at Columbia University.[73]

Bruch completed her psychoanalytic training at the Washington-Baltimore Institute, from 1941 to 1945, and had a private practice in psychoanalysis from 1943 to 1964. She then left New York for Texas and the Baylor College of Medicine in Houston, where she is now professor emeritus of psychiatry. She is still actively engaged in research and writing.[73]

Although Bruch has written books on several topics in psychiatry, such as *Don't Be Afraid of Your Child* (1952), *Studies in Schizophrenia* (1959), and *Learning Psychotherapy* (1974), she became famous through her several writings on eating disorders. One book in particular, *The Importance of Overweight*, which was published in 1957, is very often cited by the popular media. Bruch is often referred to as "the doctor that tells people not to reduce." Hilde Bruch's work on eating disorders has been part of a larger research interest on the concepts of self-awareness and body-image, and some of her admonitions concerning the harmful effects of altering body-image in some patients prone to depression have been exaggerated by the press because it makes "interesting copy."

In the past few years Hilde Bruch has become a much-honored and esteemed woman of psychology. Her earlier works are being reprinted and made more accessible to mass markets, for example, and she has received the following awards: President's Citation for Meritorious Contributions to the Clinical Services, Baylor College of Medicine; William A. Schonfeld Award for Contribution to Psychiatry, American Society for Adolescent

Psychiatry; Gold Doctor Diploma, Medical Faculty, University of Freiburg, Germany; and the Mount Airy Gold Medal Award for Distinction and Excellence in Psychiatry.

CHILDREN, LEARNING, HYPNOSIS, THERAPY
Josephine Rohrs Hilgard (1906–   )

Josephine Hilgard, child psychiatrist, psychoanalyst, research psychologist, teacher, and specialist in the areas of hypnosis and object-loss of children, was one of the few women of psychology to earn both the Ph.D. and the M.D. Her professional experience included many of psychology's most respectable positions—Gesell's Institute at Yale, the Merrill-Palmer School, the Institute for Juvenile Research in Chicago, and Chestnut Lodge in Maryland. Despite her many contributions, she is best known as the wife and collaborator of Ernest Hilgard, who is one of America's leading psychologists and learning theorists. Responsibility for her family early in her career led to a sacrifice of personal achievement and clearly a sacrifice for psychology.

Life and Career

Josephine Elizabeth Rohrs was born on 12 March 1906, in Napoleon, Ohio. An only child, her parents were Henry F. Rohrs, a physician, and Edna Belden Balsley Rohrs, who had obtained an A.B. in music from Oberlin College. Josephine attended Napoleon public schools and graduated from Napoleon High School in 1924.[74]

She went on to Smith College, just before Kurt Koffka arrived there and made the department famous. This was the era of the Gibsons, when most young women attended college to prepare for marriage and child-rearing and a few were to impress with their serious intent and brilliant scholarship. Josephine Rohrs received the A.B. in 1928, elected to Phi Beta Kappa.[74]

She then went to Yale University and received her M.A. in 1930. Between 1929 and 1930, Josephine was a Fellow at the Merrill-Palmer School, where she gathered her data for her thesis on learning and motivation in preschool children.

On 19 September 1931, Josephine Rohrs was married to Ernest Ropiequet Hilgard, who had just received his Ph.D. from Yale. He had been appointed instructor in the psychology department and Josephine worked as a staff assistant in the Clinic of Child Development and began the research for her doctorate. The Hilgards were willing to postpone a family until after Josephine completed her education. She received the Ph.D. in psychology in 1933, working under Arnold Gesell. Her three journal articles in the area of general psychology were written when she was a graduate student and were scientific, experimentally-oriented papers in child psychology.[74]

In 1933 the Hilgards moved to California, where Ernest began a long teaching career at Stanford University. Josephine was able to obtain a position as a research associate in psychology, assigned to Stanford's Department of Neuropsychiatry, (1935–36). This position ended with the birth of Henry Rohrs Hilgard on 9 September 1936. Rather than give up her career, Josephine entered medical school and in 1940 received the M.D. from Stanford University School of Medicine.[74]

Josephine was a fellow and then a staff member at the Institue for Juvenile Research, which was the world's first child guidance clinic when it was founded by William Healy; she was also able to obtain training as an analyst at the Chicago Psychoanalytic Institute (from 1940 to 1942) through a Rockefeller Fellowship. Following her husband, who was involved in the war effort, Josephine joined the staff at Chestnut Lodge Sanitarium in Rockville, Maryland, where Freida Fromm-Reichmann was in residence at the time. She stayed at Chestnut Lodge from 1943 to 1945, and Elizabeth Ann Belden Hilgard was born there on 21 January 1944.[74]

When the family returned to California, Josephine obtained her first "real" position as a professional (prior to this, she had "junior" staff or assistant status). She was made director of the Child Guidance Clinic at Children's Hospital, San Francisco. She served there from 1945 to 1948 and also opened a private practice in psychiatry, which continued from 1945 to 1973.[74]

For seven years (from 1944 to 1951) Josephine Hilgard did not publish in psychology or psychiatry and prior to that, there were only five short articles. Beginning in the early fifties, however, she produced a series of excellent papers in child psychiatry; some representative titles are: "Sibling Rivalry and Social Heredity," (1951); "Strength of Adult Ego Following Childhood Bereavement," (1960); "Early Parental Deprivation in Schizophrenia and Alcoholism," (1963); and "Depressive and Psychotic States as Anniversaries to Sibling Death in Childhood," (1969). Among her contributions was Hilgard's innovative use of peers as "auxiliary therapists" in group therapy with adolescents.[74]

Hilgard has maintained her association with Stanford University; her affiliation with the School of Medicine is reflected in her positions as associate clinical professor of psychiatry (from 1947 to 1962), clinical professor of psychiatry (from 1962 to 1971), and since 1971, clinical professor emeritus.[74] In addition, as befits her dual-degree background, she has been involved with Stanford's Department of Psychology for the past twenty years.

When Ernest Hilgard became director of the psychology laboratory, the Hilgards began their famous collaborative efforts in research on personality factors in hypnosis. It is interesting that the two of them had not worked together until they found a common research interest; for the past twenty years they have produced several papers together. Josephine Hilgard has written only one book, *Personality and Hypnosis: A Study of Imaginative Involvement.*

A grandmother five times, Josephine Hilgard is formally "retired," but writes, "I am still quite active . . . a second edition of my book, *Personality and Hypnosis*, which first appeared in 1970, was published in 1979. I am now working on a monograph reporting my research in the relief of pain in children with cancer through the use of hypnosis."[74]

"YOU CAN GO YOUR OWN WAY"
Edith Weisskopf-Joelson (1910-   )

. . . you can go your own way; then your life will, at times, be painful, but it will be uniquely yours. This is the way I chose to live and I would not want to live any other way.

—Edith Weisskopf-Joelson

Edith Weisskopf-Joelson, who was one of the young idealists of the Bühlers's Vienna salon, has been a leading clinical psychologist, clinical researcher, and professor for forty years. She is best known for her research on projective techniques and transcendental experience. Like Theodora Abel, Weisskopf-Joelson has been both a hard-nosed experimentalist and a researcher in clinical-theoretical areas (especially with the Thematic Apperception Test). Later Weisskopf-Joelson became more clearly identified with the humanist-existential philosophical movement in this country. But most of all, she has been a teacher and in some manner education has always been her primary professional role. Most of her professional career has been spent in Indiana and Georgia.

Life and Career

Edith Weisskopf was born in Vienna, Austria, on 29 November 1910, the daughter of Emil and Martha Guth Weisskopf. She attended the University of Göttingen in 1931–32 and then transferred to the University of Vienna, where she received the Ph.D. in 1937.[75] While in Vienna, Edith had associated both with the Vienna "salon" of the Bühlers at the Psychological Institute, and with the "Vienna Circle" of eminent philosophers.

> When I entered the University I was about twenty years old and it was the first time that I sat in the same classroom with men. The Gymnasium to which I had gone before was not coeducational. Not only did I have to become used to being, as a "mere" women, a second-class citizen at the University, but I also felt that my choice of traditionally masculine subjects (mathematics and physics) detracted from my feminine appeal.
>
> One day I drifted into a psychology class taught by Else Frenkel (who later became Else Frenkel-Brunswik) and was greatly interested in almost everything she had to say. I continued sampling what other psychologists had to offer and decided to drop mathematics and physics and enroll in psychology. As a second field I chose philosophy, specializing in logical positivism (a school related to operationalism); soon I found myself in very close alliance with the famous Vienna Circle.
>
> This is how the Vienna Circle and I became acquainted with each other. At the age of about twenty-two (in the year 1932) I met a member of this circle, Dr. P., at an Alpine winter resort. While going for a long walk with me he told me about logical positivism. He gave several illustrations of the kind of problems upon which logical positivism focused: For example, "When *you* say that an object is red and *I* say that the same object is red, do we see the *same* color red or are our perceptions different from each other? Is this question a pseudo-question, meaning that it can, *in principle*, not be answered? Or could it be answered if we had the medical technology to swap parts of our central nervous systems so that *I* could see the color which *you* call 'red' and vice versa?"
>
> My main point: The conversation was complex, but I followed it with enormous interest.
>
> The Alpine trail was stony and, in addition to listening, I had to watch my step. Then my nose started to bleed. I dabbed my nostrils with a white handkerchief (Kleenex was unknown in Austria at that time), but soon the blood began streaming over my face, my clothes and over the Alpine rocks on the trail. I looked at my companion, hoping he would notice and make helpful suggestions, but my hope was in vain. When we returned to the resort hotel, I was bloody, passionately interested in logical positivism, and wondering whether all members of the Vienna Circle were oblivious of the distress of their fellow humans.[76]

Else Frenkel was Weisskopf's major professor and her dissertation "Wunsch und Pflicht im Laufe des menschlichen Leben" ("Wish and obligation in the course of human life") was part of the research program of the Vienna Psychological Institute inspired by Charlotte Bühler's life-span theories.

> I received my Ph.D. in psychology as a major and philosophy as a minor in 1937, which was a good thing because I could not have received it after 12 March 1938, when Austria became a part of Germany and Jews were banned from the University.[76]

Despite her modesty and her assurances to us that she was immature and interested in looking pretty and attracting men while at the University, Weisskopf was recognized by both the psychology and philosophy faculties at Vienna as an unusually brilliant and outspoken individual. In fact, Moritz Schlick, the leading philosopher of the logical positivists, selected Weisskopf, as his best student, to teach a course at the Vienna Folk University. The Nazis did not allow her to accept this position and she was forced to flee Austria.[76] She emigrated to the United States in 1939 and was an instructor at Briarcliff College in New York State from 1939 to 1942.[76]

In 1942 she moved to Indianapolis, where she was an instructor at Indiana University until 1946. She was then advanced to assistant professor, a position she held until 1949. In 1944, the year she became a naturalized citizen, Weisskopf also worked as a clinical psychologist for Marion County (Indiana) Mental Hygiene Clinic, until 1946, when she moved to Lake County Mental Hygiene Clinic. She accepted a position at Purdue University, Lafayette, Indiana, in 1949, as an associate professor of psychology. On 27 December 1951, she was married to Michael Joelson. Edith advanced to full professor and remained at Purdue until 1965.[75]

Weisskopf-Joelson has conducted research on intelligence and projective tests for forty years. Her most famous investigations were the normative studies of the Thematic Apperception Test, which were very objective and scientific, incongruous perhaps in a woman whose philosophical and literary style is so warm, personal, imaginative, and poetic.

Edith's move from experimentalist to existentialist occurred rather late in her career, after she had been made a full professor at Purdue in 1958.

> When I came up for promotion to full professor around 1956 I was still—at least in part—considered an experimentalist. Thus I was recommended with flying colors by the science committee, but the

recommendation was not accepted by the committee of deans. The reason given for this rejection was the fact that I was married, which meant that I could not possibly give myself hook, line, and sinker to the university. The chairman of the psychology department argued that married men, too, cut grass, paint houses, and drive kids to school, but his argument was in vain. I cannot remember if the committee of deans rejected me once or twice, but I seem to remember that the situation changed when the new dean of the School of Home Economics (a woman) joined the promotion committee.[76]

After one year as a visiting professor at Duke University (1966-67), Weisskopf-Joelson joined the faculty at the University of Georgia, Athens, where she is an esteemed professor emerita of psychology today.

STILL LEARNING AND STILL TEACHING
Marianne Bellak Frostig (1906-   )

No one has done more to increase our understanding of the learning-disabled child than Marianne Frostig. She has not only conducted research and written extensively on the etiology of learning disorders, but has developed diagnostic instruments and comprehensive training programs for the teachers of the learning impaired. Herself her own best example of the valuelessness of formal education, Frostig did not receive her B.A. until she was forty years old.

Life and Career

Marianne Bellak was born in Vienna, Austria, on 31 March 1906, the oldest of three children born to Edda Silberstein and Arnold Bellak.[77] A precocious child, she very early became disillusioned with "governesses, school, and adult authority."[78] Although she only audited courses at the University of Vienna, she became an accepted member of the Vienna salon around the Bühlers. Charlotte Bühler, especially, was a major influence upon Marianne.

She attended the College of Social Work Training but the political upheaval in Austria led to its closing and Marianne transferred to the Hellerau Laxenburg, an institute that emphasized rhythmics, a specialized form of physical education where students get "in touch" with their bodies. It was there that she reestablished her friendship with August Aichhorn, who was to become a leader in psychoanalytically-oriented therapy for adolescents, and made friends with Hans Hoff and Paul

Schilder, soon to become a leading analyst in Vienna and the United States (and the husband of Lauretta Bender.)[78]

In 1924 Marianne was married to Peter Jacob Frostig, a Polish neuropsychiatrist in private practice. From 1929 to 1938, she worked for him as a "psychiatric assistant" first in his practice and then at a small private hospital near Warsaw which he administered. Among other duties, Marianne, who was fluent in English, was his translator.[78]

Without benefit of degree or credentials, Marianne worked in medical laboratories, developed workshops in vocational rehabilitation, and established a form of behavior therapy introduced by a psychiatrist named Simon. She had some success in treating schizophrenia patients. Of course, Frostig had no title and no salary and was able to accomplish her goals through personal relations with the staff.[77]

In 1933, the Frostigs had a daughter, Anna-Marie (who later became a collaborator with her mother). In 1939, the family emigrated to the United States and a son was born. In New York, aware that a degree would be helpful, Marianne enrolled at the New School for Social Research in 1945, needing one year to get her B.A. in 1946.[79]

The family moved to California then and Marianne took a job teaching elementary school. She also enrolled at Claremont Graduate School, where she was influenced by Florence Mater, an expert in mental retardation. She also resumed her relationship with Charlotte Bühler, who had also settled in southern California. Frostig was awarded the M.A. from Claremont in 1948. Her husband died in 1954. She received the doctorate in education from the University of Southern California in 1955; she was forty-nine years old.[78]

In 1947 Charlotte Bühler introduced Marianne to Belle Dubnoff, who became her partner in the development of a school for brain-injured children. Together they established a form of "educational therapy" which was found to be applicable to a wide range of impaired children. Their school, the Marianne Frostig School of Educational Therapy (now the Marianne Frostig Center) was very successful.[78] Dubnoff eventually left to establish her own competing school.[77]

For thirty-five years Frostig has been the established authority on educational therapy. She has published several useful diagnostic tests; the first and best known is the Frostig Developmental Test of Visual Perception. Her teaching techniques, although subsequent research has questioned their validity, are widely applied. She combines an interdisciplinary, eclectic approach meant to convey to the child the "joy of living."[78] Frostig's view of children is holistic, idealistic, and filled with optimism—

she is involved in helping children realize their potentials, no matter what the "realistic" restrictions may be.

Marianne Frostig has never been given the recognition she deserves by her colleagues in psychology. She is one of the most honored and revered women of psychology, as considered by educators and the lay public. Her books; especially *Movement Education*, (1971); *Move, Grow, and Learn*, (1970); and *Learning Problems in the Classroom*, (1973); have had a great influence on special education specialists. Since the late sixties, Frostig has been the recipient of several awards, generally from lay groups.

Today Frostig is the retired director of her center and living in Santa Monica, California. She continues to be involved in research on teaching methods.

> ... I am still learning and am still teaching others what I learn . . . I feel about the present as I have about most of the past: Life is a beautiful gift.[78]

OTHERS

As psychology in general has become more specialized, so have the women of psychology. The following women, presented in alphabetical order, are all well-known and distinguished figures within their respective special fields of interest.

Alexandra Adler (1901–   ) was prepared from early childhood to follow in her father's footsteps and she and her brother Kurt both became psychiatrists. "Ali" was a brilliant researcher and teacher in neurology at Harvard (1935–44) and NYU (from 1956 to 1969) in addition to being a leader of the Individual Psychology movement. She was born in Vienna, Austria, on 9 September 1901.[80] She received the M.D. in 1926 at the University of Vienna and until 1935, when she emigrated to the U.S., she worked at the university hospital. Adler became head of her father's psychiatric group after his death in 1937, was elected president of the International Association of Individual Psychology, and from 1954 has been medical director of the Alfred Adler Mental Hygiene Clinic.[81] She has contributed over 100 scientific papers and books, generally refining Adlerian theoretical concepts, beginning with her first book, *Guiding Human Misfits*, (1938).

Hedda Bolgar (1909–   ) has been involved in the training of clinical psychologists for the past forty years. Since 1974, she has been president and director of the Wright Institute. Born in Zurich, Switzerland, on 19 August 1909, Bolgar received the Ph.D. from the University of Vienna in 1934. She came to Chicago where for several years she was the chief psychologist at Veterans Administration facilities and was involved in clinical training at the University of Chicago. Since 1961, she has worked in California, for several years the chief psychologist at Cedars-Sinai Hospital in Los Angeles, where she once again developed a superior training program in psychology. By virtue of her teaching and her organizational ability, Bolgar has been preeminent in clinical training.[82]

Alice Bryan (1902-   ), by training a librarian, is best known for a series of important research studies dealing with the status of women in psychology. Born in Kearny, New Jersey, on 11 September 1902, she received her Ph.D. in library science from Columbia in 1934. In the forties she collaborated with E. G. Boring and Robert I. Watson on research on the women of psychology that is very often cited (including in the early chapters of this book). She had taught library science at Columbia for many years and is currently professor emeritus of Library Science at Columbia.[83]

Tamara Dembo (1902-   ), one of the so-called "Russians" who followed Kurt Koffka to Smith College in 1930—and one of two in the group who was a native of Russia, is best known for classic studies conducted with Kurt Lewin and his colleagues during the forties. Her two most famous publications are "Frustration and Regression: An Experiment with Young Children" (With R. G. Barker and K. Lewin) in 1941, and "Level of Aspiration" (with K. Lewin, L. Festinger, and Pauline Sears) in 1944. Dembo has been associated with several women of psychology, including Eugenia Hanfmann, Marie Rickers-Ovsiankina, Molly Harrower, Sibylle Escalona, and Pauline Sears. Dembo was born in Baku, Russia, on 28 May 1902, and received her Ph.D. in psychology from the University of Berlin in 1930. In her long career she was affiliated with Harvard, Cornell, and Stanford, but her most important work was completed when Dembo was at Smith College (1930-32), Worcester State Hospital (1932-34), University of Iowa (1935-43), and, of course, Clark University (1952-72). Since 1972 she has been professor emeritus of psychology at Clark.[84]

Annette Lillian Gillette (1909-   ) was for thirty-five years a recognized authority in clinical child psychology. Her best known research was completed in 1936, "Learning and Retention: A Comparison of

Three Experimental Procedures." She was born in Rochester, New York, on 17 December 1907. She received her B.A. from Vassar in 1931 and her M.A. in 1932 and Ph.D. in 1936 from Columbia. From 1947 to 1972 Gillette was the coordinator of psychological services of the Hartford, Connecticut Schools, where she developed a reputation as a leading clinical psychologist with expertise in psychological testing, child development, and school adjustment.[85]

Grace Heider (1903–   ) is a professor emeritus, since 1973, at the University of Kansas. She has been, for many years, a recognized researcher in child psychology, and is particularly well known for early research on language development among deaf children. To many in psychology she is known primarily as Fritz Heider's wife. She was born on 30 November 1903, in Jacksonville, Florida. She received the B.A. from Mt. Holyoke College in 1926 and the M.A. from Smith in 1927. She did not receive her Ph.D. from the University of Kansas until 1959, after she had been involved in several important research studies and had published many significant articles. Her books include *Studies in the Psychology of the Deaf* (1940), *Prediction and Outcome: A Study in Child Development* (1959), and *Vulnerability in Infants and Young Children* (1973).[86]

Karen Machover (1902–   ) is best known for her widely-used psychodiagnostic test, the Draw-A-Person Test, described in her oft-cited book *Personality Projection in the Drawing of the Human Figure*, 1949. Born in Russia on 12 September 1902, Karen was raised, educated, and married in New York City. She received her B.A. in 1928 and M.A. in 1929, from New York University. Machover worked at Bellevue and for several years taught at the New School of Social Research and Long Island College of Medicine. Currently in private practice, Karen was widowed in 1976 after forty years of marriage to Solomon Machover, Ph.D., a prominent New York psychologist. Her unique contribution to projective testing was in presenting her ideas as hypotheses to be tested—this was also notable in her work on child therapy, perception, and personality, where her scientific orientation is also in evidence.[87]

Elsa Margareeta Siipola (1908–   ) was a member of the faculty of Smith College for forty-two years. She is best known for her research on the influence of time pressure on perception, word association, imagination, and coping behavior.[88] Elsa was born in Fitchburg, Massachusetts, on 15 March 1908, and received her A.B. in 1929 and her M.A. in 1931

from Smith College. She was made an instructor at Smith in 1931 and was
an assistant professor there, when in 1939, she obtained the Ph.D. from
Yale. She was married to Professor Harold E. Israel and widowed in 1961.
In 1973 Siipola was made professor emeritus at Smith and continues to
be involved in scientific research and in professional organizations and the
National Science Foundation Committee on Undergraduate Science
Instruction.[89]

Marie Paula Skodak (1910–   ) is best known for her research on children raised in foster homes, generally focusing on the relative effects of
deprivation and stimulation on mental development. These studies were
major contributions to the problem of nature vs. nurture. Born in Lorain,
Ohio, on 10 January 1910, Skodak earned her B.S. and M.A., both in
1931, from Ohio State University. Her Ph.D. is in child psychology from
the State University of Iowa.[90, 91] Although a respected and well-known
clinical child psychologist, who was in private practice from 1946 to 1969
and for many years directed child guidance clinics, Skodak is famous
for her early research studies on foster home placements and such publications as "Children in Foster Homes: A Study of Mental Development"
(1939), "A Follow-up Study of 100 Adopted Children" (1949), and
"Study of Vocational Success of Groups of Visually Handicapped" (1969).
Skodak was married to Orlo L. Crissey in 1966 (and "still am"), retired in
1969, and lives in Michigan.[91]

Notes to Chapter Three

(1) Louise Bates Ames. Personal communication.
(2) Ames, Louise Bates. *Who's Who of American Women* (1977).
(3) Murstein, Bernard, I. "Louise Bates Ames." *Journal of Personality Assessment*, (1974) 38(6):505–506.
(4) "Louise Bates Ames." In *Current Biographies* (1956).
(5) Anastasi, Anne. "Anne Anastasi." In Lindzey, G. (Ed.). *A History of Psychology in Autobiography, Vol. VII.* (1980) San Francisco, Ca.: W. H. Freeman, & Co.
(6) Anne Anastasi. Personal communication.
(7) Anastasi, Anne. "Reminiscences of a Differential Psychologist." In Krawiec, T. S. (Ed.), *The Psychologists, Vol. II.* (1972) New York: Oxford University Press.
(8) Stern, W. "Uber Psychologie der Individuellen Differenzen: Ideen zur ener." *Differentelle Psychologie.* (1900) Leipzig: Barth.

(9) Dunbar, Helen Flanders. *Psychiatry in the Medical Specialities.* (1959) New York: McGraw-Hill.

(10) Powell, Robert C. "Helen Flanders Dunbar (1902-1959) and a Holistic Approach to Psychosomatic Problems. I. The Rise and Fall of Medical Philosophy." *Psychiatric Quarterly,* 1977, 49: 122-152.

(11) "In Memoriam: Flanders Dunbar, 1902-1959." *Psychosomatic Medicine,* Sept.-Oct. 1959, 21:350-352.

(12) (Helen) Flanders Dunbar, in *World Who's Who in Science.*

(13) Cobb, S. "One Hundred Years of Progress in Neurology, Psychiatry, and Neurosurgery." *Archives of Neurology and Psychiatry,* 1948, 59:63-68, 74-75.

(14) Draper, G. *Disease and the Man.* (1930) New York: Macmillan.

(15) Mead, Margaret. *Blackberry Winter.* (1972) New York: William Morrow.

(16) Mead, Margaret. "Margaret Mead." In Lindzey, G. (Ed.). *A History of Psychology in Autobiography, Vol. VI.* (1973) San Francisco: Freeman.

(17) Mead, Margaret. *Coming of Age in Samoa.* (1949) New York: Mentor.

(18) Mead, Margaret. *Sex and Temperament in Three Primitive Societies.* (1950) New York: Mentor.

(19) "Mead, Margaret." In *World Who's Who in Science.*

(20) Miller, J. G. "Margaret Mead." *Behavioral Science,* 1980, 25:1-8.

(21) "Richardson Creativity Award, 1968: Anne Roe." *American Psychologist,* 1968, 23:870-1.

(22) Anne Roe. Personal communication.

(23) Simpson, Elizabeth Leonie. "Occupational Endeavor as Life History: Anne Roe." *Psychology of Women Quarterly,* 1980, 5(1):116-125.

(24) Simpson, G. G. *Concession to the Improbable: An Unconventional Autobiography.* (1978) New Haven, Ct.: Yale University Press.

(25) Roe, Anne. *American Men and Women of Science,* 13th ed. 1979.

(26) Tyler, Leona. "Design for a Hopeful Psychology." Presidential Address presented at the annual meeting of the American Psychology Association, Montreal Canada, August 1973, recorded in *American Psychologist,* 1973.

(27) Tyler, Leona. "My Life as a Psychologist." In Krawiec, T. S. (Ed.). *The Psychologists, Vol. III.* (1978) Brandon, Vt.: Clinical Psychology Publishing.

(28) Tyler, Leona. "The Measured Interest of Adolescent Girls." *Journal of Educational Psychology,* 1941, 32:561-572.

178   *Women of Psychology: Volume II*

(29) Gibson, Eleanor, J. "Eleanor J. Gibson" in Lindzey, G. (Ed.). *A History of Psychology in Autobiography, Vol. VII.* (1980) San Francisco: W. H. Freeman.
(30) Eleanor Jack Gibson. "Distinguished Scientific Contribution Award, 1968." *American Psychologist*, 1968, 23:861–863.
(31) Gibson, Eleanor Jack. *American Men and Women of Science* 13th ed., (1978).
(32) Kendall, Elaine. *Peculiar Institutions: An Informal History of the Seven Sister Colleges.* (1975) New York: G. P. Putnam's Sons.
(33) "Magda B. Arnold." In Averill, J. R. (Ed.). *Patterns of Psychological Thought.* (1976) New York: Wiley.
(34) Arnold, Magda B. *Emotion and Personality.* (1960) New York: Columbia University.
(35) Magda Arnold. Personal communication.
(36) "Arnold, Magda Blondiau" in *Who's Who of American Women* (1958).
(37) Arnold, Magda B. "Physiological Differentiation of Emotional Status." *Psychological Review*, 1945, 52:35–48.
(38) Adorno, T. W., Frenkel-Brunswick, Else, Levinson, D. J., and Sanford, R. N. *The Authoritarian Personality.* (1950) New York: Harpers. (In this reference, as was the style in America, Else's last name if spelled with a "c." We have chosen in the text to use the original spelling, "Brunswik." The name is, after all, her married name and her husband Egon spelled it, almost always, without the "c.")
(39) Levinson, D. J. "Else Frenkel-Brunswick, 1908–1958." In Sills, D. (Ed.). *International Encylopedia of the Social Sciences.* (1968) New York: Macmillan Co. and The Free Press. (5:559).
(40) Heiman, Nanette and Grant, Joan. "Else Frenkel-Brunswick: Selected Papers." *Psychological Issues*, 1974, 8(3): Monograph No. 31.
(41) "Else Frenkel-Brunswick." In Zusne, L. (Ed.) *Names in the History of Psychology.* (1975) New York: John Wiley and Sons.
(42) Lowenthal, Leo. "Else Frenkel-Brunswick. 1908–1958." *American Sociological Review*, 1958, 23(5):585–586.
(43) Murphy, Lois Barclay. "Roots of an Approach to Studying Child Development." In Krawiec, T. S. (Ed.). *The Psychologists, Vol. III.* (1978) Brandon, Vt.: Clinical Psychology Publishing.
(44) Lois Barclay Murphy. Personal communication.
(45) White, R. W. "Vulnerability, Coping and Growth. Review." *American Journal of Orthopsychiatry*, 1978:353–355.
(46) Murphy, Lois Barclay. *World's Who's Who in Science.*
(47) Murphy, Lois Barclay and Moriarty, Alice, E. *Vulnerability, Coping and Growth.* (1976) New Haven: Yale University Press.

(48) Seward, Georgene. "Women as a Minority." In *Psychotherapy and Culture Conflict*. (1956) New York: The Ronald Press.

(49) Georgene Seward. Personal communication.

(50) Seward, Georgene. *Who's Who of American Women.*

(51) Seward, Georgene Hoffman. In Murchison, (Ed.). *The Psychological Register*. (1939) Worcester, Ma.: Clark University Press.

(52) Harrower, Molly. "Changing Horses in Midstream: An Experimentalist Becomes a Clinician." In Krawiec, T. S. (Ed.), *The Psychologists Vol. III*. (1975) Brandon, Vt.: Clinical Psychology Publishing.

(53) Harrower, Molly. Personal communication.

(54) Harrower, Molly. *Who's Who of American Women.*

(55) "Harrower, Molly" in *American Men and Women of Science.*

(56) "Distinguished Contribution to Psychology in the Public Interest Award, 1979: Marie Jahoda." *American Psychologist*, 1980, 35(1):84–81.

(57) Jahoda, Marie. *American Psychology Association Directory* 1951.

(58) McCarthy, Dorothea Agnes. *Who's Who of American Women.*

(59) McCarthy, Dorothea Agnes. *American Men and Women of Science*, 12th ed. (1974).

(60) "Elizabeth Bridgers." Obit. *Greensboro Daily News*, Sunday, December 20, 1970.

(61) Elizabeth Duffy. *Who's Who of American Women.*

(62) Elizabeth Duffy's letter to Dorothy Rethlingshafer, 18 August 1942. Archives of Psychology, University of Akron, Akron, Ohio.

(63) Sears, Pauline S. *American Men and Women of Science*, 13th Ed.

(64) Sears, Pauline. *American Psychology Association Directory.*

(65) Pauline S. Sears. Personal communication.

(66) "Kluckhohn, Florence Rockwood" in *Who's Who of American Women* (1979–80).

(67) Personal observations, 1955–56. The junior author was a student of both Kluckhohns.

(68) Dorothea Cross Leighton. Personal communication.

(69) Leighton, Dorothea Cross. *Who's Who of American Women* (1970–71).

(70) Eugenia Hanfmann. Personal communication.

(71) Ruth Hartley. Personal communication.

(72) "Hartley, Ruth E." *American Men and Women of Science*, 13th ed.

(73) Hilde Bruch. Personal communication.

(74) Josephine Hilgard. Personal communication.

(75) "Weisskopf-Joelson, Edith" in *Who's Who of American Women* (1970–71).

(76) Edith Weisskopf-Joelson. Personal communication.

(77) Marianne Frostig. Personal communication.
(78) Frostig Marianne. "My Slow Path of Learning." In Kauffman, J. M. and Hallahan, D. P. (Eds.). *Teaching Children With Learning Disabilities: Personal Perspectives.* (1976) Columbus, Ohio: Merrill.
(79) Frostig, Marianne. *American Men and Women of Science.*
(80) Adler, Alexandra. *American Men and Women of Science*, 12th ed.
(81) Bottome, Phyllis. *Alfred Adler: A Biography.* (1939) New York: G. P. Putnam's Sons.
(82) Bolgar, Hedda. *American Men and Women of Science*, 13th ed.
(83) Alice Bryan. Personal communication.
(84) Dembo, Tamara. *American Men and Women of Science*, 12th ed.
(85) Gillette, Annette Lillian. *American Men and Women of Science*, 12th ed.
(86) Heider, Grace. *American Men and Women of Science*, 12th ed.
(87) Machover, Karen. *A.P.A. Directory* (1951).
(88) Siipola, Elsa Margareeta. *American Men and Women of Science*, 13th ed.
(89) Elsa Siipola. Personal communication.
(90) Skodak, Marie Paula. *American Men and Women of Science*, 12th ed.
(91) Marie Skodak. Personal communication.

1963—psychology in the era of the absurd.

In **1963**, President John F. Kennedy was assassinated in Dallas, Texas, on November 22. Vice-President Lyndon B. Johnson succeeded to the Presidency.

In **1963**, sexual adequacy became a prominent preoccupation of American intellectuals as the nation entered the "anything goes" era. Popular books were Helen Gurly Brown's *Sex and the Single Girl*, Friedman's *Virgin Wives: A Study of Unconsummated Marriages*, Ellis's *The American Sexual Tragedy*, Mary Calderone's *Release from Sexual Tensions*, and Reich's *The Sexual Revolution*.

In **1963**, Theodora Abel, Therese Benedek, Margaret Mahler, Anna Freud, Grete Lehner Bibring, and Phyllis Greenacre were all affiliated with institutes, working as training analysts. They were all over sixty-five years old.

In **1963**, Dr. Martin Luther King, Jr., wrote a rationale for disobedience of unjust laws. "An unjust law," he said, "is a code inflicted upon a minority which that minority had no part in enacting or creating because it did not have the unhampered right to vote." King wrote these words from the Birmingham, Alabama, city jail, where he had been imprisoned for parading without a permit.

In 1963, the Academy Award for the best motion picture went to *Tom Jones*, a bawdy comedy, and its director, Tony Richardson, was named best director.

In 1963, *Tarzan's Three Challenges* starred Jock Mahoney. His second opportunity to play the ape-man, this feature was filmed in Thailand.

In 1963, William Healy died, ending a collaboration with Augusta Fox Bronner of fifty years' duration.

In 1963, Leona Tyler was a full professor at the University of Oregon, Edith Weisskopf-Joelson at Purdue, and Elizabeth Duffy at North Carolina.

In 1963, UCLA won its very first NCAA basketball championship. They were to repeat this feat nine times in the next eleven years.

In 1963, Betty Friedan published *The Feminine Mystique* (New York: W. W. Norton).

In 1963, the state legislature of Rhode Island passed a law providing for the lending of textbooks to students in private schools.

In 1963, Anne Roe was made a full professor at Harvard, only the ninth woman to be so appointed in its 327 year history.

In 1963, Matina Horner and Sandra Scarr both received their master's degrees.

In 1963, a very popular entertainer was Lenny Bruce, a stand-up comedian who advocated "total freedom from inhibitions." He seldom appeared on television.

In 1963, 200,000 people staged a "Freedom March" on Washington, D.C., to protest discrimination against blacks.

In 1963, the Los Angeles Dodgers beat the New York Yankees in the World Series in four games straight. The Dodgers, perennial losers to the New York team (there was one previous victory, in 1955) when they were in Brooklyn, have not succeeded in World Series competition against the Yankees since.

In 1963, Mary Cover Jones was working at Stanford University on yet another follow-up of the subjects in the Oakland Growth Study, begun in 1932.

In 1963, Roger Staubach, quarterback for Navy, won the Heisman Trophy.

In 1963, in Philadelphia, Timothy Leary delivered a lecture at a meeting sponsored jointly by the Board of Theological Education of the Lutheran Church in America and the American Psychological Association. In his well-received talk, he suggested that "psychedelic foods and drugs . . . can put the subject in perceptual touch with other levels of energy exchanges" and might well facilitate religious experiences.

In 1963, seventy-year-old Charlotte Bühler was involved in the founding of "humanistic psychology."

In 1963, Dorothea Cross Leighton and her colleagues at Cornell published *Psychiatric Symptoms in Selected Communities*, a landmark book in social psychiatry.

In 1963, one of the bestselling books in America was *The American Way of Death* by Jessica Mitford.

In 1963, Magda Arnold was a Fullbright Research Professor teaching for one year at the University of Munich, Marie Jahoda was teaching in England at the University of Sussex, Ruth Hartley was teaching in New Zealand, Bärbel Inhelder at the University of Geneva, and Brenda Milner at McGill University in Canada.

In 1963, Beatrice Gardner began her research on jumping spiders at Tufts University.

In 1963, Eleanor Jack Gibson, who had received her Ph.D. from Yale twenty years earlier, was working as a research associate without pay at Cornell University.

In 1963, Nelson Rockefeller, Governor of the State of New York, was married to Margaretta ("Happy") Murphy, an attractive thirty-six-year-old friend of the family. America was scandalized when "Happy," who had divorced her physician husband only one month before her wedding to Rockefeller, gave her ex-husband custody of their four children. The Governor's popularity plummeted immediately and this marriage possibly led to the nomination of Barry Goldwater as the party's choice to run for President in 1964.

4

Women of Contemporary Psychology

We have called this chapter "Women of Contemporary Psychlogy," (including women born between 1911 and 1940), not because the other women mentioned so far are not still working and producing excellent articles and research reports—many of them still *are*—but because the women in this chapter are less "historical." This chapter spans three decades and, except for Dorothy Adkins (deceased, 1975) and Margaret Harlow (deceased, 1971), all of these women are still alive. It is difficult to know who among these women will eventually become major forces in psychology; therefore, no critical evaluation is made of the work of these women and they are presented with neutral, equal status (that is, alphabetically). This brief review of the life and work of contemporary women psychologists will provide a glimpse of the relevant issues which psychology is currently addresing.

Although the arbitrary assignment of women by birthday was made necessary because of career achievements that often extend over five decades, this can be a bit misleading. As a group female psychologists often have productive professional careers until they are well into their seventies or eighties (or in the case of Helene Deutsch, who is still active at ninety-six, even longer). Another interesting characteristic shared by many of the women of psychology is that they very often experience late-career changes in professional emphasis. Mary Cover Jones, for example, started out as a psychologist interested in child development, but as she matured her concerns turned to gerontology. A greater number of contemporary women have changed the direction of their research interests than in earlier decades.

The women included in this chapter constitute a handful of the most prominent, most productive and, in some cases, most promising psychologists of today, but obviously not all of the women who have made or are making important contributions to psychology are included. In some cases equally prominent and deserving women have had to be omitted

183

merely because, at this writing, adequate biographical material was not available to the authors.

Among the group included in this chapter are two psychiatrists (Stella Chess and Natalie Shainess), two social workers (Virginia Satir and Sophie Freud Loewenstein), a sociologist (Jane Mercer), one college president (Matina Horner), the current president of the American Psychological Association (Florence Denmark), two historians of psychology (Mary Henle and Virginia Sexton), and seven of the leading authorities on the psychology of women (Judith Bardwick, Carolyn Sherif, Sandra Scarr, Janet Spence, Martha Mednick, Matina Horner, and Lois Hoffman).

As the world became more diversified so did psychology itself and the women of psychology along with it. There is no clear-cut pattern among these women professionally. Within this group are basic research psychologists (Natalia Chapanis, Dorothy Jameson, Beatrice Lacey), test developers (Sybil Eysenck, Jane Mercer, Elizabeth Koppitz, Joan Guilford), and child developmentalists (Sybille Escalona, Ina Uzgiris, Bärbel Inhelder).

While theelinocentric research has been undertaken for some time, several of the women of this era are responsible for widely exapnding this area. In fact, if one needed to find one common research interest within this group it would be the psychology of women. However, while this common feminist theme links this group, few of the women are the radical feminists that one hears about in the media, but all seem dedicated to excellence in being women and in being psychologists.

There is also no clear-cut pattern of personal behavior within this group. Some of the women are married (for example, Sybil Eysenck, Elaine Morgan and Jane Mercer) and state that they have no intention of dissolving this relationship at this moment. Similarly, several of the women are divorced or chose not to marry. There are some with children and some without. However, most women indicated contentment with the balance between personal satisfaction and professional growth.

Lastly there is no easily identifiable similarity in types of discrimination which has been experienced by these women. In the prior decade Leona Tyler stated that she had never felt a victim of discrimination. In this era, Mary Henle, similarly states that she has not experienced discrimination. Unfortunately that feeling was not shared by everyone. Ina Uzgiris reports professors' attempts to make her uncomfortable in classes and Sandra Scarr notes that women who want to balance professional life and child-rearing are not taken seriously by colleagues. Although lifestyles are changing, slowly, the difficulties Tracy Kendler experienced were more a function of a traditional orientation—that is, her husband Howard and their children came first—and anti-nepotism rules, than overt discrimination by others.

To this date none of the women of contemporary psychology has attained the stature of a Karen Horney, a Melanie Klein, a Leta Hollingworth, or a Lauretta Bender. But it is clear that any number of the brilliant and competent women included herein one day might. Partly because of the impetus of the current exciting feminist movement and partly because their male counterparts are such a lackluster lot, the women of psychology are today as well-knwon and as eminent as the men, for the first time in the history of psychology.

The women of psychology have more than "come into their own": they have assumed positions of leadership in every area of psychology. Modern female psychologists have established an "old-girls network" that rivals the traditional, all-male "gentleman's club in-group" of psychology. We feel that the current separatism expressed by many women of psychology is both necessary and positive. We expect that women will abandon it when they finally have equal status in psychology, when there are no longer "female psychologists" and "male psychologists," just "psychologists," or perhaps "good psychologists" and "not-so-good" (or even "bad") ones. . .

INTEREST AND ACHIEVEMENT
Dorothy C. Adkins (1912–1975)

The third of the "terrible trio" of women of southern psychology, Dorothy Adkins was chair of the psychology department at the University of North Carolina, Chapel Hill, from 1950 to 1959. Her major fields were statistics and test construction. In 1948–49 Adkins was the president of the Psychometric Society.

Born in Atlanta, Ohio, on 6 April 1912, Dorothy received her B.Sc. and Ph.D. in psychology, from Ohio State University in 1931 and 1937 respectively. From 1936 to 1940 she worked at the University of Chicago, first as a psychological test administrator and then as a research associate. She then went to work for the federal government, where her administrative and research skills led to rapid advancement: for the United States Social Security Board, from 1940 to 1944, she was chief of research and test construction, and for the U.S. Civil Service Commission, from 1944 to 1948, she was chief of social science and administrative testing, policy consultant, and then chief of test development.[1]

In 1948, still only thirty-six years old, Dorothy Adkins was made a full professor at the University of North Carolina. Her research was on interest and achievement testing and she became an expert on the factor analytic technique. Her major interest, however, was teaching and her students remember her as a tough, scientifically-oriented, well-prepared, no-nonsense professor. In 1950, she was appointed chair of the psychology department and during her long term of office assembled a superb faculty of brilliant psychologists and sometimes played second base on the department's softball team. After stepping down as chair in 1959, Adkins remained at UNC until 1965.[1] She is the author of *Factor Anaylsis of Reasoning Tests* (1952), *Test Construction* (1960), and *Statistics* (1964).

In 1965, Adkins married for the first time and moved to Hawaii. From 1965 until her death on 19 December 1975, she was a professor of educational research and educational psychology at the University of Hawaii. She turned her attention to educational research and child development at Hawaii, and conducted studies on affective traits in young children, the development of curricular modules for preschool children, and the evaluation of educational research programs.[1]

FEMININE KNOWLEDGE AND FEMININE EXPERIENCE
Judith Marcia Bardwick (1933–   )

Judith Bardwick is perhaps the finest, most insightful writer on feminine psychology in America today. From her earliest publication, "Investigation into the Effects of Anxiety, Sexual Arousal, and Menstrual Cycle Phase on Uterine Contractions" (1967), through four excellent and influential books, to her latest work, "The Seasons of a Woman's Life" (1980), Bardwick has focused her research and writing on issues important to women.

> I am feminine. It is in my feminine essence that I know life and I know connection. It is the feminine essence of me that creates life and celebrates that life . . . This *knowledge* I share with men; This *experience* I share with women. . . .[2]

Judith Bardwick was born on 16 January 1933, in New York City. She received the B.S. degree in 1954 from Purdue University.[3, 4] While in graduate school at Cornell, she married John Bardwick, an Air Force fighter pilot, on 18 December 1954, and gave birth to three children. This marriage ended in divorce in 1977.[2, 3] She obtained the M.S. in 1955 from Cornell University and the Ph.D. in psychology from the University of Michigan in 1964.[4]

Bardwick joined the faculty at Michigan in 1966 as an assistant professor of psychology. She has been there ever since. During her stay, the psychology department, which once had only two faculty members, Pillsbury and Franz, has become one of the largest and most influential in the world. In addition, the role of women on the faculty has changed radically; where once Martha Colby was a perpetual teaching assistant, the faculty at Ann Arbor has recently included Lois Hoffman, Elizabeth Douvan, Eleanor Maccoby and Martha Mednick, as well as Judith Bardwick.

In addition to her research on women's issues, Bardwick has been a consultant on women in industry, for example, to IBM, Michigan's Graduate School of Business, and Sears, Roebuck and Co.[3, 4] Judith Bardwick is a champion and advocate of feminism, but is not a hostile or militant feminist. She has warned women both against becoming either caricatures of men, excessively competitive and unemotional, or by remaining separatist and idealizing "feminine" traits, failing to become fully productive, self-realizing persons.[2]

One impediment to change, according to Bardwick, is the fear of deviance. Her research on successful men and women led to an explanation of what has been called the "fear of success," for both men and women, as a more general consequence of a fear of being different.[2, 4]

Bardwick has written numerous articles on women's issues and is the author or editor of the four best-known contemporary books on the psychology of women: *Feminine Personality and Conflict* (1970), *Psychology of Women* (1971), *Readings in the Psychology of Women* (1972), and *In Transition* (1979).

THE FEMALE PSYCHOLOGIST OF POPULAR IMAGINATION
Joyce Diane Bauer Brothers (1927-   )

Probably the best known psychologist in all of America today, Joyce Diane Brothers is one controversial psychologist. Traditional psychologists smile subtly when her name is mentioned and they often complain that she actually does more damage than good with her columns and talk shows. On the other hand, most Americans take her advice seriously and, as they trust Ann Landers and Abigail van Buren, people rely on her. Unlike these others, howeer, Joyce Brothers is a trained experimental psychologist with a Ph.D. from Columbia University.

Joyce Diane Bauer was one of two daughters born to Morris K. Bauer and Estelle Rapoport (both of her parents were lawyers and her sister is also an attorney), in Far Rockaway, Queens, New York. Joyce is described as having been a studious person who thrived on "hard work and academic achievement." After graduating from Far Rockaway High School with honors, she entered Cornell where she earned her B.S., with honors, in 1947.[5]

While working on her graduate studies (from 1948 to 1953) at Columbia University (A.M., 1949; Ph.D., 1953), she was a research assistant at Columbia, an instructor at Hunter College and a research fellow on a UNESCO leadership project (from 1949 to 1959).[5, 6] Joyce's dissertation at Columbia was a study of "Anxiety Avoidance and Escape Behavior as Measured by Action Potential in Muscle."[5]

In 1949, after completing her master's thesis, Joyce Bauer married Milton Brothers, a medical student, on July 4. Upon completion of her doctorate, she gave birth to her daughter Lisa.[5]

With what began apparently as a lark, and a chance of removing the family from financial straits, Joyce Brothers entered the quiz show arena. In the mid-50s, quiz shows on TV were new and exciting as was television in general (the senior author has also appeared on a quiz show, during the mid-60s, when they reached their peak of popularity; she was not as fortunate a winner). Joyce appeared as a demure (she is barely five feet tall), female psychologist who knew everything about the sport of boxing. To prepare for her appearance on the show, Joyce memorized a twenty-volume boxing encyclopedia.[5] As any good historian of TV knows, Joyce Brothers won the top prize on "The $64,000 Question." She later was also one of the contestants to be cleared of cheating in the ensuing scandal that surrounded this quiz show.

Joyce Brothers, Ph.D.—experimental psychologist and wife of an internist, now became a full-fledged international celebrity. Her TV career began with "Sports Showcase" in 1956, which she co-hosted. She has had either a radio or TV program ever since and because of her "recognizability," is very often the person picked to portray "the lady psychologist" on episodes of situation comedies. Brothers has also had several syndicated columns, both in newspapers and magazines, for example, a monthly column in *Good Housekeeping.* She is currently a consultant to such firms as Magic Carpet, Sperry and Hutchins, ABC Films, and Greyhound and appears on TV commercials for Kinder Kare.[5, 6] She has also written four non-memorable, but briskly selling books for the mass market.

While totally unappreciated by psychology (she is not even a member of the American Psychological Association), Joyce Brothers has received many honors, particularly from humanitarian and social organizations. Among these are the Woman of Achievement Award, Federation of Jewish Women (1964); Professional Woman of the Year, Business and Professional Women's Clubs (1968); and the Award of the Parkinson Disease Founda-

Joyce Diane Bauer Brothers

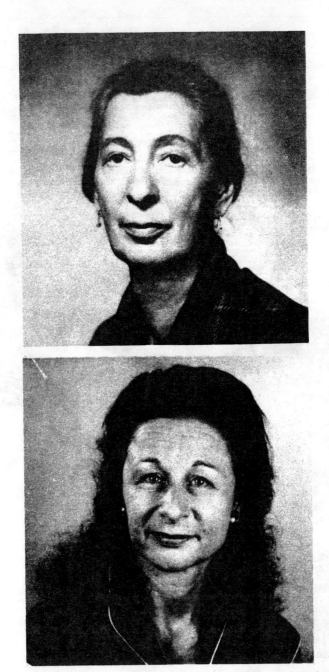

Above: Stella Chess (photograph by Bradford Bachrach); *below*: Sybil
B. G. Eysenck

tion (1971). She has been granted an honorary degree, the L.H.D., from Franklin Pierce College, in 1969.[6] In several polls conducted in the past fifteen years, Joyce Brothers has been listed among the ten most influential or most admired women in the world.

Although Joyce Brothers is the best-known psychologist in America, among the most respected and admired by the public, none of the women with whom we corresponded in collecting data for this book nominated Dr. Brothers as a prominent psychologist. The authors, who refuse to exclude a psychologist out of snobbery, have read several of Joyce Brothers's columns and have found them to be a little dull and textbookish, but much less objectionable, even to our purist selves, than those produced by many other social scientists for popular consumption.

HOPKINS PSYCHOLOGIST
Natalia Potanin Chapanis (1928-   )

Natalia Chapanis, physiological psychologist and clinical psychologist, has been on the faculty of Johns Hopkins School of Medicine since 1966. She is a specialist in neuropsychology and has been long associated with the Cortical Function Laboratory at Hopkins, where she has conducted electrical-stimulation-of-the-brain research. She has also been involved in the Johns Hopkins' research on transsexuals.[7]

Natalia Potanin was born in Brisbane, Australia, on 25 October 1928. She received her B.Med.Sc. in 1951 from the University of Queensland and then spent four years, from 1951 to 1955, at the University of Melbourne, before travelling to Johns Hopkins University, where she received the Ph.D. in psychology in 1958.[7] She worked as a postdoctoral fellow at Hopkins (1958-59), and taught at Goucher College, as assistant professor (1959-60). She then was married to Alphonse Chapanis, a Yale Ph.D., who was a professor of engineering psychology at Johns Hopkins. The newlyweds spent a year in England, where Alphonse served as Science Liaison Officer at the branch office of the Office of Naval Research (1960-61). Natalia spent the year at the Tavistock Institute.[7]

Although Alphonse returned to his faculty position at Hopkins; after a year of unemployment, Natalia had to settle for a research associate position. From 1964 to 1966 Natalia resumed her teaching at Goucher College and then again took a reduction in rank to return to Johns Hopkins, this time as an instructor in medical psychology, form 1966 to 1970. In 1970 she advanced to assistant professor.

Among her many research articles, Natalia has published in a variety of areas: "Cognitive Dissonance: Five Years Later" (1964), "Electrical

Stimulation of the Visual System in Man" (1972), and "Central Phosphenes in Man" (1974).[7]

PROLIFIC CHILD PSYCHIATRIST
Stella Chess (1914-   )

Stella Chess, Professor of Child Psychiatry at New York University Medical School, is the author of twenty-two books and more than one hundred articles and presentations, most of which were collaborative efforts with her husband Alexander Thomas. Best-known for her longitudinal study of children (1956-67), Chess's finding of early differentiable temperament factors which persist and strongly influence later behavior is one of the most important research findings of the past twenty years of psychology.

Stella Chess was born on 1 March 1914, in New York City, to Benjamin Chess and Clara Schwartzman Chess.[8, 9] She received her B.A. from Smith College in 1935 and her M.D. from New York University School of Medicine in 1939, and took psychoanalytic training from the New York Medical College from 1943 to 1946.[8]

In 1938, Stella married Alexander Thomas and they have been colleagues and collaborators ever since. They are the parents of four children, Joan, Richard, Leonard, and Kenneth.[8] In 1939, this busy, productive and energetic woman began psychiatric training at Bellevue Hospital's Children's Psychiatric Ward, where Lauretta Bender was the head of the unit. She also worked at Grassland Hospital and Pleasantville Cottage School.[8]

In addition to her research and clinical work—she was from 1947 to 1956 Coordinating Psychiatrst of the Northside Center for Child Development, of which Mamie Phipps Clark was Executive Director—Stella Chess has had several full-time academic positions. From 1945 to 1964 she was an instructor of child psychiatry and then was advanced to full professor in child psychiatry, 1964 to 1966, at New York Medical College. In 1966 she moved to the New York University School of Medicine, first as an associate professor (from 1966 to 1970) and then as a full professor in child psychiatry (from 1970 to the present).[8]

Although her longitudinal study in collaboration with Alexander Thomas and Herbert Birch is her best known research, Stella Chess has been involved in a series of important large studies since the early fifties, including a study of "infant behavior patterns and child care practices in Puerto Rican families in New York City" (1956-64), a study of the "behaviors of children with congential rubella" (1967-70), and "behavioral development of multihandicapped children" (1977–present). Most of the research has been funded by federal research grants.[8]

In the past several years Stella Chess has been the recipient of numerous awards, including the Family Life Book Award of the Child Study Association of America (1974); Honors Award from the National Society for Autistic Children (1976); The Wilfred C. Hulse Memorial Award of the New York Council on Child Psychiatry (1977); Second Lauretta Bender Annual Lecture (1977); The Richard A. Baum Award for Human Service (1979); the C. Anderson Aldrich Award in Child Development (1979); and the Blanche F. Ittelson Prize for Research in Child Psychiatry (1980).[8]

Among her more important books are *An Introduction to Child Psychiatry* (1959), *Behavioral Individuality in Early Childhood* (1963), *Temperament and Behavior Disorders* (1968), *How to Help Your Child Get the Most Out of School* (1974), *Temperament and Development* (1977), *Daughters* (1978), and *Dynamics of Psychological Development* (1980).

An indication of the high regard in which Stella Chess is held is that for the past twelve years it has been she (and Alexander Thomas) who have been selected to edit the *Annual Progress in Child Psychiatry and Child Development* series. She is, perhaps because of the implications of her work for the understanding of hyperkinesis and early infantile autism, becoming the most oft-quoted and oft-cited woman of psychology.

VERY GIFTED AND BLACK
Mamie Phipps Clark (1917–   )

Mamie Clark was the executive director of the Northside Center for Child Development in New York City for more than thirty-three years. In the thirties and forties she and her husband Kenneth B. Clark conducted the classic studies of racial identification and color preference of black children and during that period they were about the only psychologists interested in doing research on personality development with blacks. We cannot deny that Clark may be said to be the "token" black of this chapter, but among the women in this chapter there is also a "token" Lithuanian and an Australian, and one woman from Wales.

Mamie Phipps was born in Hot Springs, Arkansas, on 18 October 1917. In her senior year at Howard University, she married, on 20 April 1938, a young man from Panama named Kenneth Bancroft Clark, a 1935 Howard graduate and then, a doctoral student at Columbia. Mamie graduated magna cum laude from Howard in 1939 and was elected to Phi Beta

Kappa.[10] She and her husband, who were both interested in social, clinical, and child psychology, began collaborating on their famous research while Mamie was still an undergraduate. They also have had two children.[10] After receiving her M.A. in 1939, also from Howard, Mamie Clark joined her husband in New York. Except for the year when he was president of the American Psychological Association they have lived and worked in New York City. She received her Ph.D. in 1944. After a series of research and clinical jobs, as a research psychologist with the American Public Health Association (1944-45), with the Armed Forces Institute Examination Center at Columbia (1945-46), and a psychologist with the Riverdale Children's Association (1945-46), the Clarks founded the Child Development Center on W. 110th Street in 1946. She was executive director from 1946 to 1979 and he was research director from 1946 to 1966 and for several years acted as chief psychologist.

Mamie Clark's major publications were five articles, all with K. B. Clark, from 1939 to 1950, on self-concept and social identification of young black children. The first of these, "The Development of Consciousness of Self and the Emergence of Social Identification in Negro Pre-school Children," is the best-known of her papers. In 1944, her doctoral research was published as "Changes in Primary Mental Abilities with Age."[10]

Mamie Phipps Clark has received two honorary degrees, the L.L.D. in 1974 from Pratt Institute and the L.H.D. in 1972 from Williams College. She was also a recipient of a Howard University Alumni Award (1958) and a Columbia University Alumni Award (1972).[10]

For the past several years, Mamie Clark has been elected to the board of directors of various companies and institutions, often several simultaneously: The American Broadcasting Company, Mount Sinai Medical Center, Union Dime Savings Bank, Museum of Modern Art, Phelps Stokes Fund, New York City Mission Society, New York City Public Library, and others.[10]

REAL-WORLD ACTIVIST
Florence L. Denmark (1932-   )

The fifth woman to be elected president of the American Psychological Association (1979), Florence Denmark has written extensively in the areas of the psychology of women; minority group achievement; locus of control (or "fate control"); and urban conflict. Despite her articles on evaluation of educational programs, "high-risk" and integration programs, and on the psychology of women and her co-editorship of four books,

Denmark is best known for her political activities; she is the consummate politician and activist, whose list of memberships and offices held is almost as long as Louise Bates Ames's publication list.

Florence Denmark was born in Philadelphia, Pennsylvania, on 28 January 1932. Her A.B., with honors in both history and psychology, in 1952, and the A.M. in psychology in 1954, and the Ph.D. in social psychology in 1958 were all from the University of Pennsylvania. While at Pennsylvania, she was a research assistant, supervisor in the clinical psychology program, and taught, advancing from teaching assistant to instructor.[11]

Denmark moved to New York where she was hired as a lecturer at Queens College, where Ann Anastasi had once organized a psychology faculty during the "idealistic" era. Although it is true that she was only twenty-seven when she joined the faculty, it is amazing that this multi-talented woman remained at Queens for seven years and did not advance in rank. She was also a counselor at Queens's Testing and Counseling Center and was beginning to publish research articles regularly—when she left, however, in 1966, she was still a lecturer. By then, she held a simultaneous position at Hunter College, CUNY.[11]

Joining the faculty at Hunter in 1964 as an instructor, Florence Denmark has been able to advance up the academic ladder of success and she is now a full professor and executive officer of the Doctoral Program.[11] Her research, much of it funded by grants, continues to be large-scale and focused on the psychological effect of social and programmatic changes.

In addition to being the current president of the American Psychological Association, Florence Denmark has been president of Division 35 of the APA (1975–76), chair of the Psychology Section of the New York Academy of Sciences (1975–77), National President of Psi Chi (1978–79), and vice-president of the International Organization for the Study of Group Tensions.[11] She has also been a member, usually an active member and an officer and/or a director of the following organizations: the American Psychological Association, the New York Academy of Sciences, the American Association for the Advancement of Science, the American Association of University Professors, the Metropolitan New York Association for Applied Psychology, Psi Chi, the Association of Women in Science, the Society for the Advancement of Social Psychology, the Association of Women in Psychology, the International Congress of Psychology, the Interamerican Society of Psychology, the International Organization for the Study of Group Tensions, the National Council of Chairs of Graduate Departments of Psychology, the New York State Psychological

Association, and the Eastern Psychological Association.[11] Florence Denmark, by virtue of her motivation, ability, and dedication, has become the preeminent leader of psychology today.

THE PSYCHOLOGY OF THE VERY YOUNG
Sibylle K. Escalona (1915-   )

One of the most often-cited researchers in infant development, Sibylle Korsch Escalona is best known for her studies correlating early test findings with later performance. Although her primary interest has been in normal development in early childhood, Escalona has had varied research contributions, particularly in the area of clinical psychology.[12]

Sibylle was born in Berlin, Germany, on 7 July 1915. Her parents were Karl Korsch and Hedda Korsch. She came to the United States in 1934 and was for many years associated with the Gestalt psychologists. As an undergraduate at Cornell and later at the University of Iowa, she studied under Kurt Lewin and for many years thereafter was engaged in research that resembled that of the Lewinian field theorists. In 1940, having obtained her Ph.D. in clinical child psychology, Sibylle published her important article "The Effect of Success and Failure upon the Level of Aspiration and Behavior in Manic-depressive Psychoses." In 1944 she was married to Edward Escalona, a marriage which later ended in divorce.[12]

After several years at the Child Research Station in Iowa City, Sibylle Escalona went to the Menninger Foundation in Topeka, Kansas. The Menningers were building an impressive research as well as clinical service facility and Escalona was to be the mainstay in the research department for ten years, completing some of her more important studies there. In 1949 she had published, with Bergman, a contribution to the *Psychoanalytic Study of the Child*, "Unusual Sensitivities in Very Young Children," and in 1952, with Leitch, a monograph of the Society of Research in Child Development, "Early Phases of Personality Development: A Non-normative Study of Infant Behavior."

While at the Menninger Foundation, Escalona conducted important longitudinal studies and collaborated with Lois Murphy and Alice Moriarty. Her most important paper was written with Moriarity, "Prediction of School-Age Intelligence from Infant Tests" (1961). "In 1955," she writes, "after a sojourn at Yale University's Child Study Center" she joined the faculty at Albert Einstein College of Medicine; she is now professor of psychiatry and psychology and is affiliated with the Rose Fitzgerald Kennedy Center for Research in Mental Retardation and Human Development.[12]

IN HER OWN RIGHT . . .
Sybil B. G. Eysenck (19??–   )

Although known primarily as the wife and frequent collaborator of Hans Eysenck, one of Great Britain's leading psychologists, Sybil Eysenck is, in her own right, an outstanding research psychologist who has made important contributions to psychology, particularly in the areas of personality research and the psychology of women. She has been a lecturer in psychology at the University of London, and since 1972, senior lecturer.[13]

Sybil Rostal was born in Vienna, Austria, the daughter of Max Rostal, a violinist, and Sela Trau-Rostal, a cellist. Unfortunately, although she and her husband have shared a great deal of personal information, nowhere is her birthdate given. It is known that during her undergraduate days she majored in mathematics and chemistry at London before switching her major to psychology. One of her professors was a young, recently-divorced man, who was born in Berlin, Germany, but in his early thirties was already a well-established and controversial figure in British psychology. Hans Jurgen Eysenck and Sybil Rostal were married on 30 September 1950.[13] They have had three sons and one daughter.

Sybil received her Ph.D. working under Philip Vernon, a close friend of the Eysencks, in 1955. Her thesis was "A Dimensional Analysis of Mental Abnormality."[13] Much of her subsequent work, especially that in collaboration with her husband, has been in the construction and validation of personality scales and other psychological tests. But there was more variety in her research interests and in her publications than most people realize.

Sybil Eysenck has conducted research on women's issues in such studies as "Personality and Pain Measurements in Childbirth of Married and Unmarried Mothers" (1960), "The Personality of Female Prisoners" (1973), and "Physically Attractive Offenders" (1978). She has conducted several psychometric studies with children, as well as with transvestites, prisoners and psychopaths, and neurotic subjects. She has also published a series of cross-cultural studies in which personality scale configurations of British subjects were compared to those from samples from Nigeria (1977), New Zealand (1978), the United States (1978), Yugoslavia (1978), Spain (1978), Greece (1978), and Brazil (1980).[13]

Sybil Eysenck has published almost seventy articles and test manuals, most often co-authored with Hans, and two books, *Personality Structure and Measurement* (1969), and *Psychoticism as a Dimension of Personality* (1976), also with her husbnad.

By marrying her professor, Sybil continued a tradition; among others, so did August Fox Bronner, Charlotte Bühler, Mary Cover Jones, Eleanor Gibson, and the senior author of this book.

WASHOE'S MOTHER
Beatrice Tugendhat Gardner (1933-   )

Best known to a wide audience as "the mother of Washoe," the famous sign-language-communicating chimpanizee, Beatrice T. Gardner is one of the world's most prominent comparative psychologists. With her degrees in psychology and zoology, the very innovative research of Beatrice and Richard Gardner has been a major contribution to understanding language acquisition.

Beatrice Tugendhat was born in Vienna, Austria, on 13 July 1933.[14] She travelled to America for her college education, obtaining her A.B. from Radcliffe College in 1954 and her M.Sc. from Brown University in 1956, both in psychology. She then went to England to study zoology at Oxford; her research was on the behavior of the three-spined stickle-back fish. Her first three articles were on the interruption or frustration of feeding behavior by electric shock and conflict.[15]

In 1959 Beatrice received her Ph.D. in zoology from Oxford. She then accepted a position, instructor of psychology, at Wellesley College, where she remained for four years, until 1963. During this period, she met Richard A. Gardner, whom she married in 1961. He has been her husband and collaborator for almost twenty years.[15] For one year, 1963-64, Gardner worked as a research associate in the biology department at Tufts University, Medford, Massachusetts, where she began a long series of studies on the *Phidippus*, jumping spiders.[15]

In 1964 the Gardners moved to Reno, Nevada, where she was hired as a research associate at the University of Nevada. Here they completed a great deal of significant research on the ability of chimpanzees to acquire language, including eventually the American Sign Language. Although Beatrice was granted a National Science Foundation Fellowship, from 1967 to 1972, and was to become one of America's most recognized psychologists, she was not promoted beyond an instructor until 1973, when she was made a professor at Nevada.[15]

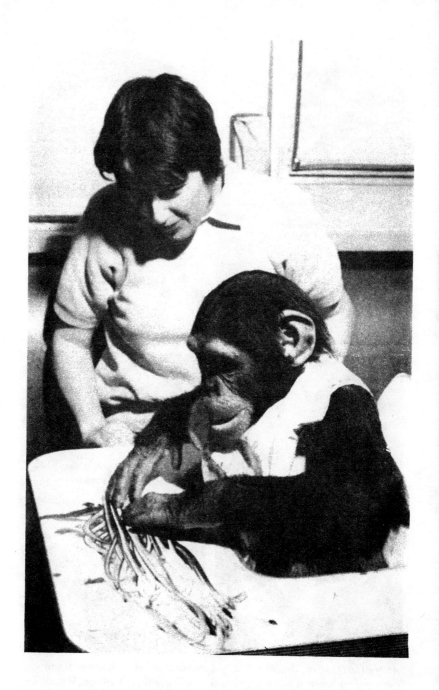

Beatrice Tugendhat Gardner

Above (*left*): Joan Sheridan Guilford; (*right*): Margaret Kuenne Harlow (photograph courtesy of the University of Wisconsin, Madison, Wisconsin); *below* (*left*): Lois Wladis Hoffman; (*right*) Bärbel Inhelder

There is hardly anyone literate in America today who does not know of Washoe and her ability to "speak" to the Gardners using sign language. In several articles and chapters in books, and one film, the Gardners' achievements have been well documented. Beginning with the publication of "Teaching Sign Language to a Chimpanzee" in 1969, the public has closely followed their work, often published in organs available to a mass market, such as the *McGraw-Hill Encyclopedia of Science and Technology, Science, American Scientist,* and *National Geographic Research Reports.*[15]

Beatrice Gardner, eminent comparative psychologist, professor of psychology at the University of Nevada, the woman who "speaks" to chimps, continues to work on language acquisition in primates. Except for her sabbatical leave (1970–71), when she went to Tanzania to observe wild chimpanzees at the Gombe Stream Research Center, Gardner has remained at Nevada for sixteen years.[15]

There have been some doubts expressed recently over whether or not primates can acquire language. A few extremely vocal critic-psychologists have suggested that rather than acquire a language, involving the memory of relationships between symbols and of the rules for combining them, the chimps like Washoe have been merely responding to immediate cues from experimenter-trainers (a process traditionally known in psychology as the "Clever Hans" effect). Among experts who have answered the un-proven charges are the Gardners: "Comment on Terrace's *Linguistic Apes*" (1980), and "Two Comparative Psychologists Look at Language Acquisition" (in press)[15]—the question remains fascinating . . . and open.

PSYCHOMETRIST AND ENTREPRENEUR
Joan Sheridan Guilford (1928-   )

Psychometrist, test developer, and differential psychologist, Joan Guilford has constructed original testing instruments to be used in very important large-scale research, including a two-year study of home accident prevention; elimination of smoking; the relationship of the values of teachers and pupils and its effect upon classroom behavior; and a study of the effect of alcohol on automobile driving. Despite more than twenty years of respectable and superior research and administrative efforts, she is most often identified as J. P. Guilford's daughter, the loyal kid who refined and validated instruments developed by her father and his colleagues, as well as running Sheridan Supply Inc. (now Sheridan Psychological Services; Joan is executive director).

Joan Guilford is an important psychologist in her own right, but her close identification with her father is no secret, especially to those orthodox Freudians like ourselves who have been her good friend for years. Identifying with one's father is certainly no disgrace to the women of psychology, since almost all of the most prominent psychologists readily aver that this was true in their own case; a notable few include Ruth Benedict, Clara Thompson, Helen Flanders Dunbar, Helene Deutsch, Anna Freud, Grace Fernald, and Alexandra Adler. It is so rare for a female psychologist to describe her father with disrespect or dislike, in fact, that we have emphasized it whenever we knew or suspected rejection of the father. Lillien Jane Martin was perhaps the best example of a woman who despised her father and consciously modeled herself after her mother. Joanie Guilford clearly did neither.

Joan Guilford was born in Lincoln, Nebraska, on 28 September 1928, daughter of Ruth Burke Sheridan Guilford, psychologist, housewife and manager of Sheridan Supply, Inc., and J. Paul Guilford, one of America's leading psychologists who became president of the American Psychological Association.[16]

Joan graduated from Marymount High School in Los Angeles in 1945 and took an A.A. from Bradford Junior College in Massachusetts two years later. She found New England to be too conservative socially and politically for an emancipated, ambitious young woman from Los Angeles. Like her father, Joanie is a relaxed, casual person with politically liberal views and, like her father, she returned to Nebraska, where she received her B.A., in sociology, in 1949 (the University of Nebraska, of course, was the school of Leta Hollingworth and H. L. Hollingworth and J. P. Guilford.[16]

In 1949 Joan Guilford entered the graduate program in psychometrics at the University of Southern California, a school whose psychology faculty included her father and Georgene H. Seward. Joan received her M.A. in psychology in 1951; her thesis was a validity study of some of the tests developed by her father and mother. In 1951, Joan married Franklin B. McClung, a clinical psychologist practicing in Los Angeles.[16]

After obtaining her M.A., Joan and her husband went to work for what had become by that time an international company, Sheridan Psychological Services. With her first husband, Joan had three children, and she pursued her doctorate on a part-time basis. This first marriage ended in divorce in 1959. In 1962 she became director of the Los Angeles Office of the American Institute of Research; she completed many important studies under its auspices.[16]

In 1963 Joan Guilford received her Ph.D. from the University of Southern California (this was a slow year for the university; the only other doctorate in psychology conferred at that ceremony was to another of J. P. Guilford's students, the junior author of this book). A few months later, Guilford married Irving J. Budnoff, a fellow graduate student and an instructor in statistics and research design at California State University at Los Angeles. Irv Budnoff was a widower with two daughters. This second marriage ended in 1966.[16]

Joan Guilford had become a leading psychometrician and industrial psychologist when she decided, in 1972, to devote her full energies to Sheridan Psychological Services. Long located in Beverly Hills, the company moved to Orange, California, when Joan Guilford married Frederick L. McGuire, an Orange County psychiatrist.[16]

Although Joan Guilford's publication output includes only two books, *Motivation and Modern Management* (with D. E. Grag, 1970), and *The Guilford-Zimmerman Temperament Survey: Twenty-Five Years of Research and Application* (with J. P. Guilford and W. S. Zimmerman) (1976), she is also the author of sixteen research project reports, each of them as long as a book. Ironically, Joan S. Guilford is recognized mainly as the competent manager who operates and expands the family "business," despite her important and influential independent research which, especially her work on values in school children, itself provides a significant contribution to psychology. Her family ties may have been helpful to her early in her career, but were not necessary for this brilliantly competent woman to succeed in psychology—and ultimately led to her receiving less recognition for her real and important attainments as a psychologist than she deserves.

RECOGNITION, FINALLY
Margaret Kuenne Harlow (1918-1971)

At the 1979 convention of the National Women's Studies Association, Dr. Ruth Bleir, member of the medical faculty at the University of Wisconsin, noted how Margaret Harlow suffered discrimination during her professional career. Both Bleir and Helen LeRoy have described the injustice perpetrated against this brilliant, innovative, and energetic woman, who worked for the University of Wisconsin for twenty-five years without recognition. Margaret Harlow was finally given academic status in 1970, just before her death.[17]

Everyone knows of Harry Harlow and his famous research on terrycloth and wire "mothers." This research, which led to world-wide recognition for Harlow and for Wisconsin's Primate Laboratory, would not have been possible without the contributions of Margaret Harlow, who directed the everyday working of the Laboratory. Yet this eminent researcher, who worked in clinical psychology, child development, and comparative psychology, is generally remembered today only as Harry Harlow's wife and/or the person who established the Publication Office of the American Psychological Association and served as the office's first managing editor.[17]

Margaret R. Kuenne was born on 8 August 1918, in St. Louis, Missouri. She attended Washington University in St. Louis, where she earned the B.A., with election to Phi Beta Kappa, in 1939, and the M.A. in 1940.[17, 18]

Kuenne then went to the State University of Iowa, where she worked at the prestigious Iowa Child Welfare Research Station as a research assistant, while obtaining training as a clinical psychologist. Her dissertation, under Kenneth W. Spence, was hailed as a masterpiece and led to an article in 1946,[19] which, it has been said, anticipated "what would be characteristic of the field in the 1960s" and remains a classic study.[18]

After receiving her Ph.D. in 1944, Margaret Kuenne worked as a clinical psychologist in Pittsburgh and Flint, Michigan, and taught at the University of Minnesota.[17] She then accepted a position as an assistant professor of psychology at the University of Wisconsin in 1946. When she married Harry Harlow in 1948, the promising young psychologist lost her academic position because of anti-nepotism rules.[17, 18]

For the next twenty years, Margaret Harlow was the "director" (there is considerable controversy about her exact title) of the Primate Laboratory at Wisconsin, without tenure and with no academic rank.[17, 18] Meanwhile she also had two children, Pamela, in 1950, and Jonathan, in 1953.[18]

In 1961 Harlow and Harlow's article in *Natural History*, "A Study of Animal Affection," brought the research with rhesus monkeys to a wide audience and their 1962 article in *Scientific American*, "Social Deprivation in Monkeys," made this research famous. Because her husband had been well-established and was much more prominent in psychology during their twenty-three years together, it was generally assumed that Margaret's role was secondary. But that was never a fact. Margaret was involved in the planning of studies and was responsible for the research design, as well as the operation of the laboratory.[17] Despite numerous important publications, Margaret Harlow did not achieve eminence in her field.

In addition to her research on monkeys and children, Margaret Harlow brought her managerial and administrative skills to organizational work; she was executive officer of the Society for Research in Child Development from 1966 to 1971, established the APA Publications Office and was the editor of the *Journal of Comparative and Physiological Psychology* from 1951 to 1962.[17]

In 1965, in the midst of her most important and influential work, Margaret was again allowed to teach at Wisconsin, as a *lecturer* in the School of Education. One of the most significant contributors to psychology, she was made professor of educational psychology in 1970, but died on 11 August 1971, before the beginning of her second year of rank.[17, 18]

ONE OF THE LUCKY PEOPLE
Mary Henle (1913-   )

Mary Henle is one of America's most respected but least-known psychologists. Closely associated with Gestalt psychology, she has been on the faculty of the New School for Social Research, an institution important to the history of psychology, for the past thirty-four years. Long recognized by theoretician colleagues for her incisive analyses of theories and constructs, Mary Henle is today also one of the premier historians of psychology.

Mary was born in Cleveland, Ohio, on 14 July 1913, the daughter of Pearl Hahn Henle and Leo Henle. She describes her childhood as "uneventful save for the fact that I had a twin sister with whom I was always being confused (and sometimes still am). I had a brilliant brother, Paul Henle, the philosopher, who was very influential in setting the standards, and parents who were much interested in the education of their children."[20]

Mary Henle and her twin both attended Smith College. This was the period when Kurt Koffka and the "foreigners" were on campus and Smith was an exciting center of Gestalt psychology. Among her friends at college were several persons prominent in earlier chapters of this book: "Jimmy and Jackie Gibson, Harold Israel, Elsa Siipola, Hulda (Rees) Flynn, Hanna Faterson."[20]

Mary obtained her A.B. in 1934 and the A.M. in 1935 in psychology from Smith College.[20, 21] Her most frequently cited articles, which question tenets of behaviorism on the basis of formal theory construction and basic assumptions, appeared early in her career. Among her important contributions are "An Experimental Analysis of the Law of Effect" (with Hans Wallach) (1941), "A Further Study of the Function of Reward" (also with Wallach) (1942), and "An Experimental Investigation of Past Experience as a Determinant of Visual Form Perception" (1942).

While still a comparatively young experimentalist-theoretician, Mary Henle earned the respect of Edwin Boring, Edna Heidbreder, and Robert Woodworth for her clear statement of Gestaltist positions in such well-received papers as "An Experimental Investigation of Dynamic and Structural Determinants of Substitution" (1942), "The Influence of Valence on Substitution" (1944), "Factors Decisive for Resumption of Interrupted Activities: the Question Re-opened" (1953), "On Activity in the Goal Region" (1956), "On the Relation Between Logic and Thinking" (1962), and "Of the Scholler of Nature" (1971).

In 1939 Henle received her Ph.D. in psychology from Bryn Mawr College. Before joining the faculty at the New School, she was a research associate at Swarthmore College (1939-41), where she was able to work with Wolfgang Köhler, another of the great names of Gestalt psychology. She was then appointed an instructor at the University of Delaware (1941-42), Bryn Mawr (1942-44), and at Sarah Lawrence (1944-46). She was thereupon appointed an assistant professor at the New School for Social Research.[21] Henle's growing reputation as an important figure in theory construction and the philosophy of science was, at this time, combined with a recognition of the excellence of her experimentation. In 1948 she and Donald MacKinnon published *Experimental Studies in Psychodynamics: A Laboratory Manual*, which was the first manual for laboratory studies in human motivation and had a Lewinian orientation.[20]

Henle was an assistant professor from 1946 to 1948, associate professor from 1948 to 1954, and since 1954 has been a professor, Graduate Faculty, of the New School of Social Research. Among her best-known works are "Some Problems with Eclecticism" (1957), in which she takes Woodworth's functionalism to task because the eclectic position reduces the deductive capacity of the alternative theories that are combined, and *Documents of Gestalt Psychology* (1961) which she edited.

More recently Henle has been active in the role of historian, especially with CHEIRON, the international organization of persons interested in the history of the behavioral sciences, of which Henle is a founder. A few of her more notable publications in this area are *The Selected Papers of Wolfgang Köhler* (1971), (with others) *Historical Conceptions of Psychology* (1973), "Max Wertheimer" (1973), "E. B. Titchener and the Case of the Missing Element" (1973), "*Seven Psychologies* Revisited" (1974), "Why Study the History of Psychology?" (1976), "Gestalt Psychology and Gestalt Therapy" (1978), and "Kurt Lewin as Metatheorist" (1978).

Like Florence Goodenough, Henle does not consider herself to be a *woman* psychologist rather than a psychologist. She states, "I suppose you will want to know what being a woman in psychology has meant to me. It has meant being a psychologist in psychology. I have never thought of it any other way." She has not felt herself to be the victim of discrimination. One of the most successful and respected psychologists of her generation, Henle describes herself as content and "lucky": "I like to teach, like to think, like to write. I like to work with students. In short, I am one of the lucky people who have been able to do the work they wanted all their lives."[20]

WOMEN'S CONCERNS UPPERMOST
Lois Wladis Hoffman (1929-   )

Best known for the monumental, two-volume *Review of Child Development Research* (1964 and 1966), which she edited with her husband Martin, Lois Hoffman has been a leading expert on the effects of the employed mother for more than twenty years. She is the author of five books, scores of journal articles, and since 1975 has been a full professor in the psychology department of the University of Michigan.[22]

Almost every woman of psychology has, at one time in her career, addressed women's issues, but Lois Hoffman started out with this research interest foremost in mind. Her 1958 dissertation was titled "Effects of the Employment of Mothers on Parental Power Relations and the Division of Household Tasks."[22] In addition to several journal articles on working mothers, she is the co-author of *The Employed Mother in America* (1963), *The Working Mother and the Family* (1974), and *Women and Achievement* (1975). She has throughout her career, been involved in concerns of women, including several studies on "fear of success" in men and women and the effects of changes in role definitions on children.[22, 23]

Lois Wladis was born in Elmira, New York, on 25 March 1929, daughter of Gustave and Etta Wladis. She received her B.A. from the State University of New York at Buffalo in 1951. Shortly afterward, on 24 June 1951, she was married to Martin Leon Hoffman, with whom she has collaborated on several research studies and books and two daughters, Amy Gabrielle and Jill Adrienne Hoffman.[23]

Lois moved on to Purdue for her M.S. (1953) and then to the University of Michigan for her doctorate (1958). Since 1954 she has been affiliated with this university: research associate with the Institute for Social Research, from 1954 to 1960, lecturer in the psychology department, from 1967 to 1972, associate professor, from 1972 to 1975, and now professor of psychology. From 1962 to 1967 she and her husband prepared, for the Society for Research in Child Development, their two-volume opus; the first volume, published in 1964, was honored with the 1965 Family Life Book Award of the Child Study Association.[22, 23]

Lois Hoffman has been active in organizations devoted to the welfare of children and to the encouragement of research, she has served as a consultant and editor for several institutions and journals, and is currently involved in a large research project. The current research, she says, is an "investigation of the satisfactions, dissatisfactions, and psychological significance of parenthood" and is being conducted in conjunction with investigations in eight other countries.[22]

PRESIDENT HORNER
Matina Souretis Horner (1939–   )

Secure in her varied roles as experimental psychologist, professor, researcher, and administrator, as well as wife and mother, Dr. Matina Souretis Horner succeeded Dr. Mary I. Bunting on July 1, 1972 as president of Radcliffe College, the women's undergraduate affiliate of Harvard University.[24]

Along with Judith Bardwick and Lois Hoffman, Matina Horner has been part of the group at the University of Michigan who independently and sometimes collaboratively conducted research on women's issues. Horner is especially associated with the concept of "fear of success," a generalization derived from her research on achievement motivation of women at Michigan. Fear of success occurs when a person is afraid that success will alter her life to such a degree that her "femininity" will be obfuscated. When her article, "Fail: Bright Women," appeared in the November 1969 issue of *Psychology Today*, Matine Horner became an instant celebrity.[24]

Matina Souretis was born in Roxbury, Massachusetts, on 28 July 1939. Of Greek heritage, Matina was encouraged in academic pursuits, especially by her professor father, and she was recognized as a precocious and special child. In 1957 she entered Bryn Mawr College, where her early interest in achievement motivation was demonstrated by her honors thesis, a study on "need for achievement" in Greek and Jewish groups. She graduated, cum laude, from Bryn Mawr in 1961.[25]

At Bryn Mawr Matina met Joseph L. Horner, a graduate student, who was later to become a Ph.D. physicist with the U.S. Department of Transportation. They were married on 25 June 1961, and have three children, Tia, born in 1964, John, born in 1966, and Christopher, born in 1968.[24] Marriage and motherhood in no way deterred Matina from attaining her goals.

In 1961, she and her husband entered the University of Michigan, where she became the research assistant to John W. Atkinson, a pioneer in the investigation of need for achievement (his colleague in the initial research in the area was David McClelland, a friend of Anne Roe). Horner received her M.Sc. in 1963 and the Ph.D. in 1968.[24, 25]

For the academic year 1968–69, Matina was a lecturer at Michigan. She then moved to Harvard, where for one year she was a lecturer in the Department of Social Relations and from 1970 to 1972 was an assistant professor of clinical psychology.[25] Her papers and articles include "Motivational Implications of Ability Grouping in Schools" (1966), her famous "Fail: Bright Women" (1969), "Femininity and Successful Achievement" (1970), and "Toward an Understanding of Achievement-related Conflicts in Women" (1972).[24]

After one year the search for a president for Radcliffe ended with the selection of Dr. Matina S. Horner, at thirty-three the youngest woman to hold that position in its history. At the same time she was named "dean of Radcliffe" on Harvard's faculty and an associate professor in Harvard's psychology and social relations departments.[24, 25] Horner has received several honorary degrees, among which are the L.L.D. from Dickinson College and Mt. Holyoke College in 1973 and the University of Pennsylvania in 1975 and the L.H.D. from the University of Massachusetts in 1973 and from Tufts University in 1976.[25]

In a 1973 article in the *N.Y. Times Magazine*, Matina Horner described the phenomenon, the elucidation of which had made her famous

[Young men and women] still tend to evaluate themselves and to behave in ways consistent with the dominant stereotype that says competition, independence, competence, intellectual achievement and leadership reflect positively on masculinity but are basically inconsistent or in conflict with femininity.[26]

Later in the same article, commenting upon Horner's selection as president of Radcliffe, Dennis Krebs of Harvard's psychology department was quoted as saying:

She was hired, I think, because she is full of feminine charm, non-threatening, easy to take . . . I think she may surprise them: with the strength and stubbornness that is hers, with her very genuine commitment to her ideas, with her ability to get what she wants.[26]

PIAGET'S RIGHT HAND
Bärbel Inhelder (1913–   )

Best known for innovative and influential work in several aspects of child development, Bärbel Inhelder was the number-one collaborator of the late

Jean Piaget. From 1941 to 1972, she and Piaget worked together and published extensively on the cognitive development of children. She is the author or co-author of fourteen books and scores of articles and chapters of books.[27] One of her early and most important works was her 1948 book, *La géométrie spontanée de l'enfant (The Spontaneous Geometry of Children)* which was co-authored by Jean Piaget and Alina Szemenska.[28] Inhelder's most recent book, with P. Dasen, M. Lavallée, and J. Retschitzki, *Naissance de l'intelligence chez l'enfant baoulé de Côte d'Ivoire, (The Birth of Intelligence in Baoli Children of the Ivory Coast)*, was published in 1978.

Bärbel Inhelder was born on 15 April 1913, in St. Gall, Switzerland. Her father was Alfred Inhelder, Ph.D. in Science. In 1932 she became a student at the University of Geneva, Institute of the Science of Education, where she has remained in some capacity for the past forty-eight years. She took courses in philosophy, psychology, and education. In 1936 Bärbel became an assistant to Jean Piaget; she was then only twenty-three years old. In 1943 she received the Ph.D. from the University of Geneva.[27]

In 1948 Inhelder became a professor of child psychology and genetic psychology at Geneva and upon Piaget's retirement, she was appointed to her mentor's chair at Geneva and became Professeur de Psychologie génétique et expérimentale (professor of genetic and experimental psychology) (since 1971).[27]

Bärbel Inhelder has, on the basis of almost forty years of excellent and important research on child development, received many honors. She is an international figure who has received honorary degrees from such institutions as the Université d'Aix-Marseille (1964), Temple University (1971), Smith College (1975), the Université René Descartes (1976), and the University of Curitiba, Brazil (1979).[27]

Inhelder has also, as befits her international status, been a member or an associate member of learned societies of many countries. She was president of the Société Suisse de Psychologie from 1965 to 1968 and president of the Association de Psychologie scientifique de langue française from 1968 to 1970.[27]

BRIGHTNESS
Dorothea Jameson (1920–   )

The research team of Dorothea Jameson and Leo Hurvich has significantly advanced our knowledge of color vision through a broadly based program of conceptually sophisticated and rigorously conducted experiments. . . . Their very unusual scholarship, technical

*skill, untiring motivation, and contagious enthusiasm for scientific
discovery have set new standards of excellence against which future
experimenters and theorists will be judged.*

Citation, 1972 Distinguished
Scientific Contribution Award

Dorothea Jameson is one of five women up until now who have won the
Distinguished Scientific Contribution Award of the American Psychological Association. The others are Nancy Bayley (1966), Eleanor J.
Gibson (1968), Brenda Milner (1973), and Beatrice Lacey (1976).

Dorothea Jameson was born in Newton, Massachusetts, on 16 November 1920. Educated in local greater Boston schools, she chose Wellesley
College and began her undergraduate work there in 1938. It is interesting
that the original psychology laboratory at Wellesley was founded by
another prominent woman from Newton, Mary Whiton Calkins. There
could be no two psychologists more unalike. Calkins, the theoretician and
generalist, had supported and encouraged the type of scientific young
psychologist, the careful, precise laboratory worker, that Dorothea would
become, but was herself of a temperament unsuited for impersonal,
apparatus-filled work. Like Calkins, Jameson never received her Ph.D.
When Dorothea began college, she had originally intended to go on to
medical school.[29]

Dorothea's plans for a future career were formed while she was an
undergraduate at Wellesley. One of her professors, Michael Zigler, had
interested her in sensory psychology, and a man from the Harvard Business
School's Fatigue Laboratory, Alfred H. Holway, was employed at Wellesley
part-time to supervise student research. She met Holway's friend and
roommate, Dr. Leo M. Hurvich, another native greater-Bostonian, and the
two became collaborators in research, a collaboration that persists to this
day.

The research that Jameson and her colleagues were involved in when
she was an undergraduate had to do with visual fatigue in industry. With
the advent of World War II, the group's research began to include the
phenomena of "stereoscopic and telescopic vision in relation to height
and range finders." Jameson received her A.B. in 1942.[28]

In 1947 the group moved to Rochester, New York, where their research
was underwritten by Eastman Kodak Company's Color Technology Division. In 1948 she and Leo Hurvich were married. After ten years of outstanding work in the investigation of color vision, Jameson and Hurvich

moved to the psychology department of NYU's Washington Square
College; he as a professor and she as a research assistant.[29]

In 1962, their numerous publications and important research having made this research team the recognized leaders in the area of visual
physiology and optics, Hurvich and Jameson went to the University of
Pennsylvania, where again he was appointed professor of psychology
and she was hired as a research assistant. Jameson was able to advance
through the system until, in 1972, she was also made a full professor at
Pennsylvania.[24]

Jameson has been the author or co-author of one book, *The Perception
of Brightness and Darkness* (1966), and close to one hundred articles and
chapters on vision and related subjects. She and Hurvich were selected to
write the 1960 review on color vision for the *Annual Review of Psychology*. In 1971 Jameson and Hurvich were awarded the Howard Crosby
Warren Medal of the Society of Experimental Psychologists and they
became the first couple to win the Distinguished Scientific Contribution
Award.[29] Another married couple, the Laceys, were to repeat this honor—
no research team, no matter how important the attainment or longevity
of the collaboration, has ever won this award if its members were not
married to each other.

"MATURE, INTELLIGENT, AND PERSONABLE WOMAN"
Virginia Eshelman Johnson (1925–   )

Virginia Johnson has had an unsual background for someone who is a
world-wide authority on sexual functioning, the junior partner of "Masters
and Johnson." Daughter of a farmer, from rural Missouri, she has had
several careers, perhaps the most spectacular being that of a country and
western singer. Associated with Dr. William H. Masters since 1957, Johnson is currently co-director of the Reproductive Biology Research Foundation in St. Louis.[30]

Virginia was born in Springfield, Missouri, on 11 February 1925,
daughter of Hershel Eshelman, farmer, and Edna Evans Eshelman. She
began school in Palo Alto, California. The family later returned to Missouri, where she was a precocious and achieving student though somewhat
of an outsider during her school years. She turned to reading and studied
piano and voice. She was to comment on her early years thus: "Everyone
doted on me and I grew up with the sense that accomplishments and talent
were marvelous, but that marriage was the primary goal."[30]

Virginia did indeed marry—four times. She was married in the early
forties to a Missouri politician for two days and to a "much older" lawyer.

From 1950 to 1956 she was married to George V. Johnson, an engineering student at Washington University where they met, and a leader of a dance band. Virginia sang with her husband's band for a while and had two children with him, Scott and Lisa. These three marriages ended in divorce. On 7 January 1971, she married William Masters, which whom she has worked since 1957.

In 1941, Virginia entered Drury College in Missouri, but remained there only one year. She then worked as a part-time clerk with the State Insurance Office in Jefferson City and embarked on a career as a singer. Her mother was a Republican committeewoman and Virginia's career was helped by engagements at political meetings. For several years she appeared on KWTO, a Springfield radio station, on a show sponsored by Gibson Coffee and Virginia assumed Gibson as a stage name. Despite her success as Virginia Gibson, she supplemented her income at St. Louis newspapers and KNOX-TV. She also took classes at University of Missouri and at the Kansas City Conservatory of Music.[30]

Planning to return to school to work for a degree in sociology, Virginia applied for a job with Masters, associate professor of obstetrics and gynecology at Washington University's School of Medicine. He was looking for a "mature, intelligent, and personable woman, preferably a mother" to be his research associate. She has now been working on research on the sexual response and related topics for twenty-three years.[30]

Although she has no academic credentials, Virginia Johnson is one of the most influential women of psychology. Her research and the resultant publications have been of extraordinary import in increasing our understanding of the physiology and psychology of sex. Her books, like her work, were controversial and her methods and conclusions have been questioned, but not refuted. Her three extremely important books, all co-authored with William Masters are *Human Sexual Response* (1966), *Human Sexual Inadequacy* (1970), and *The Pleasure Bond: A New Look at Sexuality and Commitment* (1975).[30]

Johnson and her collaborator have been accused of "dehumanizing sex," of advocating mechanistic and impersonal relationships, of supporting traditional monogamy, and of fostering immorality. What she achieved is a demythification of a natural biological function and a form of recreation and pleasure which provides the cohesive element to a love relationship. She also helped develop a famous form of therapy for sexual problems, a method which has spread throughout the world and has influenced all other forms of sex therapy. From their base in St. Louis, Missouri, Masters and Johnson remain more than ever the most important specialists in sexual research and in prevention and treatment of sexual inadequacy. Virginia Johnson is not the most prolific or best known female sex researcher; she is merely the best, the most scientific, most objective, and has the most common sense of the women who have selected this area of research.

MEDIATING RESPONSES
Tracy Seedman Kendler (1918–   )

Once a competent and accomplished clinical psychologist, Tracy Kendler has become a leading learning theorist, best known for her research on mediating responses and reversal shifts, important contributions to a behavioral analysis of problem solving. She has become a full professor and has been elected into the once all-male Society of Experimental Psychologists. But it was not easy sailing. Documentation of how discriminatory practices and other obstacles placed by society interfered with Tracy Kendler's career advancement is most articulately expressed by Howard H. Kendler, her husband since 1941.

In his 1974 autobiographical sketch, Howard Kendler says of their careers: "Both Tracy and I had similar graduate training and common interests, but it proved much easier for me to pursue mine . . . there are unavoidable conflicts between careers and marriage."[31] Much of what we have to say below of the slights and impediments that Tracy suffered come from Howard's description of events. Many of her most significicnat contributions to psychology were achieved with her husband as collaborator, but her marriage prevented Tracy Kendler from attaining the formal recognition she deserved for twenty years.[31]

Tracy Seedman was born in New York City on 4 August 1918. While attending Brooklyn College, she met Howard Kendler in a logic class. They fell in love and she is given credit for curing the depression that had plagued him since the death of his brother.[31] They were both psychology majors at Brooklyn and completed a joint honors thesis, an "Extension of the Einstellung Problem to the Behavior of Rats."[31] The two of them received their B.A.s in 1940 and went to the State University of Iowa for graduate school.[32, 33]

A few months after Howard received his M.A., they married, on 20 September 1941. That June she received her master's degree and they both received the Ph.D. in psychology from the State University of Iowa in 1943.[33]

For the next several years Tracy was to hold a number of positions, many of them part-time because, with the inadequacy of domestic help, she took on responsibility for the management of the household and the primary caretaker role for their two children. She worked, for example, at Chicago State Hospital as a clinical child psychologist and as a research assistant with the College Entrance Exam Board in 1944 and was a statistician with the U.S. Air Force in 1945–46. For two years she was an instructor at the University of Colorado, from 1946 to 1948, while Harold was an assistant professor on the same faculty.[33]

The two then returned to New York and worked at NYU, Howard as an associate professor and Tracy as a research associate. He moved up to full professor, but for the years that she was at NYU, Tracy did not advance. This despite the fact that she had four important publications during this period, including one highly influential and germinal article, co-authored with Howard, "A Methodological Analysis of the Research Area of Inconsistent Behavior" (1950). It was not until 1955, when Tracy was appointed as an assistant professor of psychology at Barnard College, that she was given a fullfledged academic position, in line with her prior achievements.[32, 33]

At this time, in 1955, she published several articles on the phenomenon of "shifts," a major contribution to our understanding of concept formation, and other important papers on "mediating responses" in problem solving in children. Among the many titles were "Reversal and Non-reversal Shifts in Kindergarten Children" (1959), "Learning, Development, and Thinking" (1960), "Concept Formation" (1961), and "Mediated Responses to Size and Brightness as a Function of Age" (1962).

In 1964, when the Kendlers moved to Santa Barbara, California, they were among the most promising of the younger experimental psychologists and were very conservative behaviorists. Howard accepted a position as professor of psychology and his colleague and collaborator was hired as a research associate! The University of California at Santa Barbara had an anti-nepotism rule and for three years, while continuing her prominent research studies and well-received articles, Tracy Kendler remained in the status of second-class citizen in academia.[31, 32, 33]

When in 1966 the anti-nepotism rule, which had to be temporarily waived each year for Tracy to work at Santa Barbara at all, was "permanently waived" for her, Tracy Kendler was appointed professor of psychology. This was partly in response to Howard's indignant threat to quit the school if the ridiculous indignity to his wife were perpetuated.[31] Tracy Kendler has remained on the faculty at Santa Barbara ever since.

Tracy S. Kendler is the author of a popular textbook, *Basic Psychology* (1971), and more than fifty technical articles in learning theory and child development. She has been president of the Western Psychological Association (1977-78) and served on the executive committee of the Society of Experimental Psychologists, from 1978 to 1980. Like many of her predecessors, Tracy Kendler was saved from anonymity by virtue of her superlative efforts and indominable spirit. In her case, her powerful husband also helped, but this was only just: as Howard Kendler has been the most vocal to assert, if Tracy had not been married, she very likely would have become a recognized leader of psychology sooner, and more easily.[31]

LATE BLOOMER
Elizabeth Munsterberg Koppitz (1919-   )

Recognized as one of the world's leading psychodiagnosticians for children, Elizabeth Koppitz, expert in learning disabilities, lecturer, and writer, is the best example of the "new breed" of mental tester. She combines the sensitivity and intuitiveness of the clinical psychologist and the technical skill of the psychometrist with the careful experimentation of the scientific researcher. Best known for her normative studies and objective scoring system with the Bender Gestalt Test, Koppitz is more recently the creator of an innovative and well-researched instrument, the Visual Aural Digit Span Test (or VADS), a promising test of the "intersensory integration and memory for sounds and symbols" in children.

Elizabeth Munsterberg was born in Berlin, Germany, on 9 February 1919. She earned her B.A. from George Peabody College for Teachers in Tennessee in 1951. She received her M.A. (1952), and the Ph.D. (1955), in clinical psychology, from the Ohio State University. In 1955 she also married Werner J. Koppitz.[34]

She had worked as a clinical psychologist at the Juvenile Diagnostic Center and Children's Mental Health Center in Columbus, Ohio, before moving to New York. Since 1961, she has been a school psychologist with the Special Education Department of the Board of Cooperative Educational Services (BOCES) of Putnam and Northern Westchester County, N.Y. In 1963, she published *The Bender Gestalt Test for Young Children*, the book which established Koppitz as one of America's most influential though least-known, psychologists.

Koppitz's first book details the history of the Bender Gesalt and reports the results of her own and others' research on the test. She also presents an original, empirically determined scoring system for the test and a manual for its use. This book was an instant "hit," a necessary addition to the library of all child psychologists, and has been reprinted five times and translated into German, Spanish, and Japanese.[34]

Elizabeth Koppitz was also the author of *Psychological Evaluation of Children's Human Figure Drawings* (1968), *Children with Learning Disabilities* (1971), *The Bender Gestalt Test for Young Children, Volume 2: Research and Application* (1975), and *The Visual Aural Digit Span Test* (1977). Her work on brain-injured children and those with learning disabilities are of such quality as to make Koppitz the intellectual heir of Lauretta Bender, and her superlative work in test construction and the scientific approach to investigate individual differences in children make her equally the intellectual descendant of Florence Goodenough. Much of Koppitz's significant contributions to psychology, coincidentally, involves the refinement of diagnostic instruments originally developed by Bender and Goodenough. One of the few women of psychology to be a "late bloomer," Elizabeth Koppitz, at sixty-one, has not yet reached her peak as a contributing member of her profession.

LACEY-LACEY
Beatrice Cates Lacey (1919-   )

Beatrice Lacey was the fifth woman to receive, in 1976, the Distinguished Scientific Contribution Award of the APA. She was also the second co-recipient of the award, with her husband, and like Dorothea Jameson, who had been a co-recipient with *her* husband in 1973, Beatrice attained notable success in physiological psychology without ever earning the Ph.D. The Lacey-Lacey citation from their American Psychological Association colleagues suggests that the honor was in part for their contributions to "conceptions of the autonomic nervous system."[35]

Beatrice Lacey delayed her career for fifteen years while she supported her husband's career, managed the family, and followed John from post to post during the war. She was the practical, more empirical, scientific methodologist of the pair. contributing even when she was a full-fledged housewife, and has always been accepted by research psychologists as a competent and brilliant woman and a most important contributor to her husband's career.[35]

Beatrice Cates was born in New York City on 22 July 1919, to Louis H. Cates and Mollie Libowitz Cates.[36] After receiving her early education from New York City public schools, she entered Columbia University's New College (part of Teachers College) in 1935 when she was barely sixteen. During Christmas vacation of 1937, home from her practice teaching in North Carolina, she met John Lacey, a twenty-two-year-old Ph.D. candidate at Cornell, on a blind date. Ten days later they were engaged. When they married in April 1938, Bea Lacey transferred to Cornell, received a B.A. in psychology, cum laude, and then quit school.[35, 36]

In 1941, Beatrice and John published an article in the *American Journal of Psychology*, with a man who had been professor to both of them, Karl Dallenback. This article, "Areal and Temporal Variations in Pain Sensitivity," was written when Beatrice was not yet twenty-one years old; her name did not appear on a publication in psychology again for seventeen years.[35]

Beatrice delayed her career by working to help support the family financially. While a student, she held a job as a statistician with Cornell's College of Agriculture and is credited with being a "hidden collaborator" on Johns' doctoral dissertation. She later worked as a statistician for Standard Oil of New Jersey.[35]

During World War II, rather than resume her education and career, Beatrice followed John, who volunteered his services to the Army and Air Force as a research psychologist, from post to post. While John was able to work in personnel assessment under Col. J. Paul Guilford and to perform very important research, Beatrice worked at post PX's in budget and fiscal offices and sometimes as a a statistician.[35]

The final delay occurred when, after eight years of marriage, the Laceys started a family. Robert was born in 1946 and Carolyn in 1949. Deciding that her children needed a full-time caretaker, Beatrice stayed at home until 1953, when Carolyn was four and able to spend most of the day at school.

Beatrice joined John at the Fels Research Institute for the Study of Human Development, the site of the world's most famous and perhaps most productive longitudinal study. She worked, at first part-time, as a research assistant in the Department of Psychophysiology. In 1956 she was appointed to the Antioch College faculty and in 1958 she received her M.A. in psychology from Antioch (the school where the Fels Research Institute is housed).[35, 36]

Bea Lacey found a marvelous working environment, one which for twenty-seven years has provided her and her collaborator-husband support and encouragement for their pioneering and honored research on the complexities and interrelationships of the autonomic nervous system. The Fels Research Institute and Antioch College have no rules against "nepotism" and recognition is based upon meritorious achievement, not gender. Beatrice has been, since 1972, senior scientist at Fels and, since 1973, professor at Antioch.[35, 36] These are, incidentally, the same titles her husband holds.

From 1958 to 1974 the Laceys produced a series of important articles in psychophysiology, the most prominent being the definitive studies of the autonomic nervous system. They have also contributed to the understanding of the activation system, the limbic system, the physiology of impulsive behavior, cardiac responses, and stress and attention.

> Although they have separate laboratories and offices, they share staff and general facilities, and neither would think of doing an experiment without the close collaboration of the other in design, execution, and interpretation. . . . They share the same scientific goals, and have worked under one grant from the National Institute of Mental Health; the grant is now in its 23d year![35]

THE TAXONOMY OF STRESS
Nadine M. Lambert (1926-   )

Best known for her research on hyperkinesis in children, Nadine Lambert has been an outstanding educational researcher for over twenty years. Her contributions to the early identification of "emotionally handicapped" children, although less well known, have been very important to the establishment of prevention programs for disturbed children as well as the development of special education programs.

Nadine M. Lambert was born in Ephraim, Utah, on 21 October 1926. She received her B.A. in 1948 from the University of California at Los Angeles and then worked in local school systems in the southern California area, first as a kindergarten teacher and then as a guidance counselor. She was working in the latter capacity for the Bellflower Unified School District, from 1953 to 1957, when she received her M.A. from Los Angeles State College (now California State University at Los Angles), in 1955, and got married in 1956.[37]

In 1958 Lambert accepted a position as a research consultant for a major study conducted by the California State Department of Education (1958-61) under Eli Bower. Although most of the publications that evolved from this study, for example Bower, E. M., *Early Identification of Emotionally Handicapped Children in School* (1960), do not list her as an author, she had primary responsibility for the validity studies of the sociometric instruments developed for the project. One of the reasons the authors are aware of Nadine's primary role in this work is that Gardner was one of the psychologists who worked for her, evaluating children in Bellflower schools.

Lambert continued her work on primary prevention procedures in school settings in her doctoral work at the University of Southern California, where she worked under J. P. Guilford, her research supported by grants from the U. S. Office of Education.[37] It was Lambert's contention that school psychologists should be trained to translate psychological test data into specific recommendations to be directly applied in the classroom. Her monograph, "Applications of the Taxonomy of 'Stress' in Specific School Situations" (1964), did much to revise and refine techniques of school psychologists and to establish the school as a major agency for the prevention of emotional disorders. She received her Ph.D. from Southern California in 1965.

Since 1964, Nadine Lambert has been a member of the faculty at the University of California at Berkeley. She is now a full professor of education. At Berkeley she undertook her prominent studies of hyperkinesis. In addition to epidemiological research related to the etiology of this disorder, she and her colleagues have conducted studies and published careful critiques of treatment procedures. Her 1976 article (with Windmiller, Sandoval, and Moore), "Hyperactive Children and the Efficacy of Psychoactive Drugs as a Treatment Intervention," is the most widely quoted scientific paper on this subject.

Nadine Lambert has been involved in a variety of simultaneous studies in educational research. In a few years she has contributed to the areas of primary prevention techniques; early identification of emotional disturbance; educational measurement; non-intellectual attributes associated with learning; adaptive behavior in public school children; and the causes of hyperkinesis.[37]

FROM "FREUD'S GRANDDAUGHTER" TO "SOPHIE LOEWENSTEIN"
Sophie Freud Loewenstein (1924–   )

A staunch, vocal, and erudite feminist, Sophie Loewenstein is currently chairperson of the Human Behavior Department at Simmons College's School of Social Work in Boston. She moved in midlife from a career in social work to teaching, from a psychoanalytic to a systems orientation. She is also Sigmund Freud's granddaughter.[38]

In an unusually candid autobiography, which has the ring of absolute veracity, published, of all places, in the *Harvard Educational Review*,

Sophie eloquently describes the subtle dilemmas she faced on her way to becoming a prominent female professional and mother:

My own depressions were often related to childrearing difficulties. The myth of blissful motherhood has only recently and mercifully been exploded . . . rearing young children is a mental health hazard for some women and . . . employment can be an important mitigator of this stress . . . [But] I have come to the conclusion that both my emotional and professional life would have been impoverished had I chosen to remain childless.[39]

Sophie Freud was born on 6 August 1924, in Vienna, Austria. Her father, Martin Freud, was Sigmund Freud's oldest son; her mother, Esti Drucker Freud, worked full-time as a speech pathologist until she retired at the age of eighty-four. Sophie notes that unlike "other ambitious women who . . . had especially strong bonds with their fathers, my primary identification, both positive and negative, has been with my mother."[39] When the family was forced to flee Austria in 1938, Sophie's parents separated. Her father went to England with her grandfather and Aunt Anna; she and her mother went to France.[38]

In 1942, Sophie and her mother arrived in New York City, but within a few months she left to enter Radcliffe and has lived in the Boston area ever since. On 24 August 1945, she was married to Paul Loewenstein and, she wrote us, "I am still married to him."[38] She received the A.B. in 1946. In 1949, Andrea was born, in 1951, Dania, and in 1955, George. Until 1966 she was employed part-time as a social worker, because she felt restless and also that she had become "overinvolved" with her children. Her primary goal was to be the best mother possible nevertheless and employment had a modern disadvantage—it put the family into a higher tax bracket.[38, 39]

When she was forty-two years old, Sophie Loewenstein found self-fulfillment and maturity through her new career, teaching. Her goal, as she has stated it, is to lead people to greater self-awareness, enhance their professional competence, enrich their lives, and help them establish their own set of values.[39] Since most of her students are women, Sophie's latent feminist sentiments have increasingly found expression during her years of teaching at Simmons.

Part of her emancipation and growing consciousness as a woman involved disavowing psychoanalytic concepts (she had been, she says, a "virtual prisoner" of its values and assumptions) in favor of acknowledging the influence of social forces and "fate." Consistent with her relative denigration of inner factors is her criticism of Matina Horner's conept of "fear of success" on the grounds that it is a "male-oriented concept that assumes that anyone who does not want to play the game by the usual rules is troubled."[39] In her own case, Sophie has an old-fashioned "fear of failure"—of not realizing her potential.

Currently Sophie Loewenstein is developing a mental health advice radio program, similar to Ann Landers's but "more up-to-date."[38]

BROWNING PROFESSOR MACCOBY
Eleanor Emmons Maccoby (1917–   )

One of the most prominent and influential American psychologists today, Eleanor Maccoby has, for thirty years, been an outstanding researcher in the area of human development, well known for her research on child-rearing practices and, more recently, studies of sex differences. Currently Barbara Kimball Browning Professor of Psychology (an endowed chair) at Stanford University and the president of the Society for Research in Child Development, Maccoby has written seven books, three of them among the most important publications in psychology of the past twenty-five years.

Eleanor Emmons was born in Tacoma, Washington, on 15 May 1917, to Viva Johnson Emmons and Eugene Emmons. Eleanor describes her childhood as "odd" and her family as "very independent in its beliefs." Her mother was a folksinger and a follower of astrolgoy. Although she describes her father as a conservative businessman, her parents were vegetarians and members of the Theosophical Society, and believed in reincarnation and other metaphysical ideas.[40]

Sharing the family interest in spiritualism and occult phenomena, Eleanor reports conducting informal ESP experiments when she was in high school. When these obtained negative results, her "convictions were considerably shaken."[40] She was also developing the temperament of an empirical scientist and this was reinforced by her college experiences, especially through the influence of Monty Griffith, a three-hundred-pound early behaviorist at Reed College. Her emerging interest in psychology served to contribute to her adolescent rebellion against her parents' beliefs—she became a political liberal, a materialist, and a person who believed that "human behavior is determined by the events which impinge in this life, and that one can study human behavior in an objective way, just as one could apply science in any other discipline."[40]

Eleanor had completed two years at Reed when, in order to study under Edwin Guthrie, she transferred to the University of Washington in 1937.[41] At Washington, she met Nathan Maccoby, a graduate student in social psychology and a specialist in opinion polling. They married on 16 September 1938, after he had received his M.A.[40] Eleanor obtained the B.A. and was elected to Phi Beta Kappa in 1939.[41] She and Nathan have been married for forty-two years and although they have worked together for a brief time, at Michigan, they have published only a few methodological articles together. They have however produced three children together: Janice, Sarah, and Mark.[40]

During the war Eleanor joined her husband in Washington, D.C., where she worked for the U.S. Department of Agriculture doing studies of public opinion and consumer behavior, from 1942 to 1946. She then went to the University of Michigan, where her research project was relocated and renamed, "Survey Research Center." This time Nathan joined her, a year later, at the Center. They both got their Ph.D.'s in psychology in 1950 from the University of Michigan.[40, 41] By then Eleanor had a series of publications on public opinion polling methodology and was completing one of the earliest studies of children's TV watching behavior.[40]

In 1950, Eleanor Maccoby joined the faculty at Harvard University's Department of Social Relations as an instructor. Although she remained at Harvard for eight years (and Sheldon Gardner testifies that she taught an excellent course in child development), Maccoby was not happy there. She suffered from that school's peculiar brand of gender discrimination, for example, women were not permitted to enter the Faculty Club by the front door or to use the Undergraduate Library.[40] Despite several very important publications, including two near-classic books, *Patterns of Child Rearing* (with R. R. Sears and H. Levin) (1957), and *Readings in Social Psychology* (with T. R. Newcomb and E. Hartley) (1958), Eleanor Maccoby advanced only so far as the rank of lecturer during her eight-year tenure.[40, 41]

When she came to Stanford University in 1958, it was as an associate professor and in 1966 she was made a full professor of psychology at Stanford. Long an international expert in childrearing and socialization—she had, for example, been invited to write the review on "Child Development" for the 1964 edition of the prestigious *Annual Review of Psychology* and one on "Effects of Mass Media" for Hoffman and Hoffman's *Review of Child Development Research*, also published in 1964—Eleanor Maccoby turned her attention to mother-child interactions; the role of women; and finally to gender differences.[40] Despite the fact that the specific topics she chose to investigate, for example, the effect of working mothers on children and gender differences in temperament and cognitive ability, are ordinarily considered to be "women's issues," Eleanor

Maccoby's research and writings in feminism have made her famous—and to some radical feminists, infamous.

Eleanor Maccoby and Carol Nagy Jacklin published *The Psychology of Sex Differences* in 1974. From its earliest reviews, the book, which surveys over two thousand earlier studies, has aroused controversy. Most mainstream psychologists have given the work high praise and the most frequent adjective used to describe it is "excellent." Feminists are divided in their opinions. Since they report the results of hundreds of studies where no differences between genders were found, Maccoby and Jacklin are often said to be correcting a traditional bias in which only significant differences in function had been reported, thus obscuring the more usual finding that there were no differences. Many of the more radical feminists have, however, denounced this book. Freda Salzman, for example, is extremely critical of the work, accuses the authors of over-emphasizing factitious genetic differences, of "buying into patriarchically-oriented" psychology, and, unkindest cut of all, when you consider that Maccoby has been a research methodologist for thirty-five years, of making "such serious methodological flaws as to invalidate their conclusions."[42]

Stanford University has honored Eleanor Maccoby by awarding her an endowed chair; the University of Cincinnati and Russell Sage College have each awarded her an honorary D.Sc., in 1975 and 1977, respectively. Maccoby has more recently been involved in preparing major volumes that include and integrate findings of studies within areas of research of long-standing interest to her, including social development, parental roles, coping behavior, among others.

A SPOKESPERSON FOR THE NEW FEMINIST PSYCHOLOGY
Martha Tamara Mednick (1929–   )

A woman who might well be said to have never realized her full potential as a psychologist, Martha Mednick is establishing a reputation as a leader of the feminist movement in psychology. Having first gained prominence as a clinical researcher and as a scientifically-oriented clinical psychologist, Mednick is best known as an editor; her contributions have primarily been as a compiler rather than as a creative innovator. She is currently a professor of psychology at Howard University.

Martha Mednick was born in New York City on 31 March 1929. She received her B.S. from City College of New York in 1950 and a few months later was married to Sarnoff Andrei Mednick, who had received his M.A. from Columbia that year. Sarnoff is one year older and although the two moved about periodically as their careers advanced, he always remained one step ahead of Martha in their progress. In the case of the Mednicks this was not so much a result of anti-nepotism rules so much as it was due to the responsibility of rearing two children, which of course fell more heavily to Martha Mednick. Since 1968 the Mednicks have lived apart.[43] Martha received the M.A. from CCNY in 1952 and her Ph.D. from Northwestern in 1955. She spent one year at Harvard with a U.S. Public Health Service Fellowship (1956-57), doing post-doctoral work on operant conditioning (now usually referred to as behavior modification) and the next several years engaged in funded research, usually with the title of research associate. She published an article, "Mediated Generalization and the Incubation Effect as a Function of Manifest Anxiety," in 1956. From 1959 to 1964 Martha was a research associate at the Institute of Social Research at the University of Michigan (Sarnoff was appointed an associate professor in the psychology department).[43]

While at Michigan, Martha and her husband edited *Research in Personality*, published in 1962, a very well-received and popular collection of papers that was considered essential in the library of behaviorist-clinical psychologists. From 1964 to 1967 Mednick was an associate professor in the School of Nursing at Michigan and in 1968 she moved to Washington D.C., to accept a position as associate professor at Howard University— Sarnoff, meanwhile, moved to the New School for Social Research in New York as a professor.[43]

For several years Martha Mednick had been interested in the area of creativity and had engaged in studies, usually with college-student subjects, for which she developed a testing instrument, the Remote Associates Tests. A major publication concerning the test and her research was published in 1971. The same year, she was advanced to professor of psychology at Howard.[43]

In the past ten years Martha has become a spokesperson for women of psychology, is a leader of the feminist movement within the profession, and is the Book Review editor of the *Psychology of Women Quarterly*, the APA-sponsored journal, of which she has been an issue editor. She is the author of several journal articles; "Social Psychology of Women: New Perspectives" (1972) is perhaps the best known.

DEMYSTIFYING IQ
Jane Ross Mercer (1924-   )

Jane Ross Mercer is formally a sociology professor and, in person, a charming, attractive, feminine woman, who appears more like the mother of four boys, which she is, than a woman who ignited a social revolution concerning the use of psychological tests and the legal definitions of mental retardation, which she is also. There has never been any conflict in roles in evidence in the case of Jane Ross Mercer; she has established a satisfying synthesis of aspects of her personality and life experiences and has done it seemingly effortlessly: wife, mother, teacher social psychological researcher, reformer, woman. About Jane Mercer, Gwendolyn Stevens, who was her student for two years, has this to say: "If ever there was a woman who is an excellent role model for women psychologists, it is Jane Mercer."

Jane Ross was born in Pittsburgh, Pennsylvania, on 5 December 1924, daughter of Elizabeth Stiteler and Donald R. Ross. She grew up in DuBois, Pennsylvania and entered the University of Chicago in 1944. In 1945, she was married to R. Jack Mercer, musician and high-school band teacher. She writes, "I am still married to Jack and have no current plans to dissolve the relationship." Their son, Robert, was born before she received her M.A. in social science from Chicago in 1948.[44]

The Mercers then moved to Iowa where for nine years (from 1949 to 1958) Jane taught psychology, sociology and "a variety of other subjects" at Creston Community College.[44, 45] While living in Creston, Iowa, the Mercers added Ronald, Raymond and Ross to the family.[44]

In 1958, the thirty-four year old mother of four young boys entered the doctoral program in sociology at the University of Southern California in Los Angeles. The department at that time was small and since Jane was specializing in marriage counseling, the best known program in the sociology department at that time, she was required to take a large number of courses in the psychology department, located directly across the narrow corridor. Mercer took courses in tests and measurement and, of course, at that time, this meant J. P. Guilford and his staff. Jane became interested in the problem of mental retardation and in the labeling process and embarked on a large research project at Pacific State Hospital, where the director of research, Harvey Dingman, was a Guilford-Ph.D. and a personal friend of hers.[44]

Mercer's doctoral dissertation involved interviewing the families of children identified as retarded and she began to question the labeling process and became interested in the "differential perceptions" of their children held by parents from "differing ethnic, cultural, and socioeconomic" backgrounds.[44] This study, like all Mercer's major research, got a spectacular reception: she received the Ph.D., in 1962, became famous; was appointed assistant professor at the University of California at Riverside; published a number of important articles; and received four large research grants to continue her work.[44, 45]

Above: Eleanor Emmons Maccoby (photograph courtesy of Stanford University, Stanford, California); *below*: Jane Ross Mercer

Above: Sandra Wood Scarr (photograph courtesy of J. D. Levine/Yale University); *below* (*left*): Virginia Staudt Sexton; (*right*): Ina Cepenas Uzgiris (photograph by Barbara Karman)

Mercer's most famous research, an interesting survey of all children in Riverside County, California, identified as "mentally retarded," not only found considerable bias in assessment, but discovered a new phenomenon, "the eight-hour retardate." Mercer and her staff collected data from several sources, schools, parents, Boy Scouts, church groups, etc., comparing nominations of retardates. Although there was some agreement when these identifications were collected, she also found a group of children that appeared to be mentally subnormal only during school hours. The fact that trained experts and the testing procedures that reinforce their judgments could frequently isolate children as incapable of benefiting from mainstream educational experience, when no one else who knew the child felt that he or she was not normal, had immediate and dramatic repercussions. It changed the law in California, led to heated debates throughout the United States, and has dealt the psychological assessment establishment a blow from which it has not yet recovered. Mercer's fame is documented by two events that guarantee celebrity status: in 1972 she had an article in the September issue of *Psychology Today* with the rather attention-getting title, "IQ: The Lethal Label" (the magazine chooses the title and prefers something outrageous, provocative, or tawdry), and in the fall of 1974, on a "CBS Special Report" called "The IQ Myth," Jane Mercer was interviewed on national television by Dan Rather.[44]

In 1965 Mercer was made an associate professor of sociology and was quickly promoted to full professor. When challenged to find a substitute for traditional testing in the schools, she developed a new diagnostic instrument, a "System of Multicultural Pluralistic Assessment" or SOMPA, which she first described in 1975 at the Conference Center in Anaheim, California.

Mercer has published numerous journal articles and four books. Her best known work is *Labeling the Mentally Retarded* (1973). She has written three books on her diagnostic technique, which includes parental interviews, assessment of adaptive behavior, and medical reports, as well as more traditional testing; the most comprehensive of the three is *SOMPA: Technical and Conceptual Manual*, 1979.

FOR DISTINGUISHED SCIENTIFIC CONTRIBUTION . . .
Brenda Milner (1918–   )

For outstanding psychological study of the human brain. She and her students have elucidated the role of the prefrontal lobes, previously resistant to analysis; have provided definitive data on the

relation of speech localization to handedness; and have demon-
strated the importance of the right temporal lobe in pattern percep-
tion (visual, auditory, tactual) . . .

Thus begins the citation for the 1973 APA Distinguished Scientifc Contribution Award to Brenda Milner, the fourth woman to have been honored
with this highly prestigious award. It is obvious from the above that,
despite the fact that Brenda Milner is not well known to psychologists who
are not also involved in physiological research, her important brain-localization research has made her one of the most productive and most successful of contemporary psychologists. The citation continues

Of great significance is Milner's study of the function of the hippo-
campus in the consolidation of memory and the devasting effect of
the bilateral loss of the hippocampus on the medial aspect of the
temporal lobe. . . .[46]

Brenda Langford was born in Manchester, England, on 15 July 1918.
She attended Withington Girls' School there and then entered Newnham
College of Cambridge University. She was awarded the B.A. in experimental psychology in 1939. While she originally planned to major in
mathematics, she became interested in human brain function as a result
of the influence of her supervisor, Oliver Zangwill.[46]

Brenda Langford was prepared to start on her graduate program under a
Sarah Smithson Research Studentship at Newnham College when World
War II broke out. The psychological laboratory at Cambridge was diverted
to applied research and for Brenda this meant giving up the study of
brains for devising "perceptual tasks that could be used in the selection of
aircrews." From 1941 until 1944, when she married Peter Milner, who
also became a prominent psychophysiologist, and left for Canada, Brenda
worked as an experimental officer for the Ministry of Supply investigating
different methods of display and control to be used by radar operators.[46]

When Milner arrived in Canada, her scholarship plus a knowledge of
French enabled her to establish a laboratory at the newly-formed Institut
de Psychologie at the University of Montreal. In this setting Milner taught
comparative and experimental psychology from 1944 to 1952. Fortu-
nately for Milner, in 1947 D. O. Hebb arrived at McGill. Hebb's availability
and influence prompted Milner to register for the Ph.D. In 1950 Brenda
was given the opportunity to work with Wilder Penfield's patients at the
Montreal Neurological Institute. She completed the requirements for the
Ph.D. in 1952 with a dissertation titled "Intellectual Effects of Temporal
Lobe Damage in Man."[46]

In 1954 Brenda published her first articles since those reporting her wartime research; the very first was a relatively lengthy article in *Psychological Bulletin* based upon her dissertational research. One year later she and Penfield published their now-classic paper, "The Effect of Hippocampal Lesions on Recent Memory."[46]

She has remained on the staff at McGill and is now professor in the Department of Neurology and Psychosurgery. For thirty years McGill has held a leadership role in psychophysiology and Milner has had the opportunity to collaborate with many illustrious colleagues. Interestingly, Brenda never collaborated with Peter, who, with James Olds, achieved fame through the discovery of the "pleasure centers" of the brain, regions which when stimulated electrically will reinforce behavior. Brenda's research and expertise, although also primarily involved in brain-localization, extended to other topics as well. She wrote on temporal-lobe epilepsy (1958), several articles on memory (1966, 1968, and 1970), and on maze learning (1965), among other subjects.[46]

Brenda Milner has been awarded a Sc.D. from the University of Cambridge (1972); was elected president of the Physiological and Comparative Psychology Division of the APA (1973); was a fellow at Girton College (1971-72); and has received the Kathleen Stott Prize from Newnham College.[46]

PRO-WOMAN AND REVOLUTIONARY
Elaine Neville Morgan (1920-   )

Elaine Morgan was a prize-winning and successful TV scriptwriter and playwright when she produced a brilliant and provocative book, a major contribution to the psychology of women. *The Descent of Woman*, her first and only book, published in the United States in 1972, takes an obscure theory of a marine biologist, Sir Alister Hardy, F.R.S., and turns evolutionary doctrine upside-down in a most convincing and entertaining manner. Born in South Wales and living and working now in Glamorganshire, Wales, Morgan suggests that rather than a liability, the fact that she was not a professional biologist, paleontologist, anthropologist, archeologist, or psychologist, was an asset, it gave her the freedom to let her imagination soar.[47]

The Descent of Woman is much more than a feminist manifesto; it is a genuine and refreshing theoretical achievement, with enough careful scholarship to make it plausible and persuasive. It may be argued that any published work that presents a theory of personality development or describes coping behavior of women or childrearing practices or the interactions between the sexes can be classified as a contribution to psychology. As Morgan herself notes, much of the work of the more highly publicized radical feminists is hollow, outrageous, and lacking factual basis. In the past ten years it has become relatively easy to find a publisher for what Morgan calls "hate literature," the more strident, outrageous, and sparsely-documented, it seems, the better. Morgan's work, in contrast, combines imaginative ideas with solid data and a great deal of common sense and is in no way the polemic diatribe or a worthless political document her critics have accused her of writing.[48]

Elaine Floyd was born on 7 November 1920, in Pontypridd, South Wales, the only child of William Mansel Floyd and Olive Neville Floyd. Her father worked in a mine, as a colliery pumpsman. Elaine won a scholarship to Lady Margaret Hall, Oxford University, and earned the B.A. in 1942.[47, 48]

On 1 April 1945 she married Morien Morgan, who is a schoolmaster in Glamorganshire. Of her marriage Elaine writes, "I've managed to stay married and monogamous: starting when and where I did it was still possible to make it work, though I wouldn't claim easy." One idea that separates Morgan from most of the feminist leaders is her advocacy of the importance and satisfactions of childrearing (Sophie Loewenstein and Judith Bardwick are among the few important feminists who agree with Morgan). Elaine has brought up three sons, John Dylan, Gareth Floyd, and Morien Huw (the last was adopted).[47]

Besides writing, Elaine Morgan has worked as a supply teacher, a lecturer, and as an adult education teacher. She was awarded an honorary M.A. by Oxford University in 1948. Her plays and scripts have won many awards: the Italia Prize for "Joey"; the 1973 Writers Guild Award for "A Pin to See the Peepshow"; the 1976 Christopher Award for "How Green Was My Valley"; and the BFTA Award in 1978 for "Marie Curie."[48]

Morgan is best known in this country for *The Descent of Woman*. Basing her work on Hardy's thesis that the human species evolved, not from tree swinging, hunting apes, but from acquatic mammals, she describes the evolutionary history from the point of view of Ms. Naked Ape. Critics have complained that Morgan is too selective in data presented and serious scientists have insisted that her argument is not convincing. It is possible that her detractors are also prejudiced against the book precisely because it is so gracefully written. In any event, this book presents a clear and well-argued alternative to what she calls "the Tarzan theory," which places the emphasis on the carnivorous, weapon-making, mighty hunter in the evolution of humankind. In Morgan's theory, it is the mother-infant bond, not male-female pair bondings, that is primary and the mother is the food-provider (as she puts it in *The Descent of Woman*): "It would seem that Daddy is brought into the picture only as a last resort, when for some reason or other the job of caring for the young is too exacting for one parent to cope with alone. . . . Where the living is easy he is apt to copulate and then go whistling on his way—anything that happens after that is strictly the female's affair."

Although Elaine Morgan is a member of the Labour Party, her politics, as expressed in her book, tend to be traditional and at variance with radical "liberationists" (her word). She is pro-woman and a revolutionary, but her philosophy suggests wisdom and experience—she does not see the value of hatefully sending men "whistling on their way."

FROM CHILDHOOD TO OLD AGE
Bernice Levin Neugarten (1916–   )

Bernice Neugarten is a professor of Human Development at the University of Chicago. Although she is perhaps the best known gerontologist in this country today, Neugarten has made contributions to the understanding of every aspect of the life cycle. This is reflected in the titles of her books: *American Indian and White Children: A Social-psychological Investigation* (with R. J. Havighurst) (1955), *Society and Education* (1957), *Personality in Middle and Late Life* (1964), *Middle Age and Aging* (1968), *Adjustment to Retirement* (1969), and *Social Status in the City* (1971),[49, 50] and in this excerpt from a *Newsweek* article featuring an interview with the prominent psychologist and sociologist:

> After adolescence, age is no longer a reliable factor in how people feel or act. "Our society is becoming accustomed to the twenty-eight-year-old mayor . . . the fifty-year-old retiree, the sixty-five-year-old father of a preschooler and the seventy-year-old student," observes gerontologist Bernice Neugarten . . . [who] argues that the United States is evolving into an "age-irrelevant society."[51]

Bernice Levin was born in Norfolk, Nebraska, on 11 February 1916. Her parents were David L. Levin and Sadie Segall Levin. She received her B.A. (1936), M.A. (1937) and Ph.D. (1943) in human development, from the University of Chicago. Almost all of her professional career was achieved at Chicago.[55]

On 1 July 1940 Bernice married Fritz Neugarten, a marriage which is now forty years old and still thriving and has produced two children, Dail Ann and Jerrold.[50] From 1937 to 1939 Bernice was a research assistant in the department of education at the University of Chicago and then was made a fellow of the American Council of Education, from 1939 to 1941. She had her first teaching experience at Englewood College in Chicago from 1941 to 1943. After receiving the Ph.D., Bernice took off five years to devote full time to her children.[49, 50]

In 1948 Bernice was hired as a research associate with Chicago's department of human development. She was made an assistant professor in 1951, associate professor in 1960, and a full professor in 1964. In addition to her important research and teaching, she has served as an associate editor of two journals, the *Journal of Gerontology*, from 1958 to 1961, and *Human Development*, from 1962 to 1964.[50] As befits her growing reputation as a leader in various aspects of human development, Neugarten has also been appointed to several commissions and committees, including the National Institute of Child Health and Human Development (1965-69), Committee on University Women (1969-70), the White House Conference on Aging (1971), HEW's Committee on Research on Aging (1975-73), and the National Institute on Aging (1972-76).[51]

Bernice Neugarten has been president of the Gerontological Society (1968-69) and was the recipient of the American Psychological Foundation Teaching Award in 1975, and the Kleemeier Award for Research in 1971.[49, 50]

A WOMAN TO WATCH
Nancy Mayer Robinson (1930-   )

Nancy Robinson has been, since 1974, an associate professor of psychiatry and behavioral sciences at the University of Washington, Seattle. She is a world-renowned expert on mental deficiency; her 1965 book, *The Mentally Retarded Child: A Psychological Approach*, written with her husband Halbert B. Robinson, is the field's definitive and most comprehensive textbook. She is also the editor of the prestigious *American Journal of Mental Deficiency* (her term runs from 1979 to 1984).

Nancy Mayer was born in Houston, Texas, on 30 August 1930. She graduated from Stanford University, B.A., summa cum laude, in 1951 and received her M.A. in 1953 and her Ph.D. in 1958 from Stanford as well. Her training is in clinical psychology and she is an expert in mental testing as well as clinical research. She married in 1951 and is the mother of four children.[51a]

In the past twenty years, Robinson has been able to combine housewife-mother duties with clinical and academic positions, research, and writing; her career showed a spurt of productivity after her children were grown. Her earliest publication, "Bender-Gestalt Performance of Schizophrenics and Paretics," was in 1953, and she did not appear in print again until 1961, when she co-authored three short research articles. It was after her book on mental retardation was published in 1965 that Robinson became well known.

Robinson and her husband were asked to prepare a chapter on mental retardation for Mussen's 1970 revision of *Carmichael's Manual of Child Psychology* and to write the entry on mental retardation for the *World Book Encyclopedia* in 1976. The international reputation of the Robinsons as experts also in early child care is reflected in their selection as editors of an important series of monographs, the *International Monograph Series of Early Child Care*, which has published monographs on child care in Hungary (1972), Sweden (1973), Switzerland (1974), Poland (1978), India (1979), etc. The Robinsons are among the authors of the volume *Early Child Care in the United States* (1974), for the series.[51a]

In 1958–59 Nancy Robinson was a research associate at Stanford and was for one year, 1960–61, a visiting professor at North Carolina College in Durham. She then moved to Chapel Hill where, after four years of temporary positions, she was made lecturer and, from 1966 to 1968, assistant professor of education at the University of North Carolina. She has been at Washington since 1969, and obtained professorial rank in 1974.[51a]

Although her most prominent work has been in mental retardation and the education of the handicapped and of the very young child, Robinson has conducted behavioral research on learning in schizophrenia (1961) and behavior modification in young children (1961), and follow-up research on the efficacy of day care (1971). In addition to her best known book on mental retardation, she is a co-editor of the second edition of *The Biologic Ages of Man: From Conception Through Old Age* (1978), to which she also contributed to ten of the chapters, and a co-author of the sixth edition of *Introduction to Psychology* by C. T. Morgan and R. A. King.[51a] She and her husband have recently published, also with M. A. Darling and G. Holm, *A World of Children: Day-care and Preschool Institutions* (1979).

Nancy Robinson has just turned fifty. If her career follows the pattern of the most prominent women of psychology, she will broaden her horizons, move from her highly specialized area or areas of interest, and begin working on more theoretical and intellectual problems. If the pattern is duplicated exactly, she is ready to transfer to a major university, probably Stanford or U.C. Berkeley, where she will become a major figure in behavioristic child development research. Check back in the 2010 edition of *Women of Psychology*.

PIONEER OF FAMILY THERAPY
Virginia Mildred Satir (1914?-   )

Virginia Satir is a pioneer in the area of family therapy, best known for her 1964 book, *Conjoint Family Therapy*. By training a social worker, Satir has contributed much to our understanding of family dynamics and of the communication and interaction patterns within families. She is Adlerian in orientation. Much of the time today Satir is involved in her popular and dynamic seminars, workshops, and clinics, and is in great demand as the premier trainer of family therapists.

Virginia Pagenkopf was born in Neillsville, Wisconsin, to Reinhold O. and Minnie Wilke Pagenkopf, sometime around 1914. She received the B.E. from Wisconsin State University in 1936 and embarked on a brief teaching career. She taught in the Williams Bay Consolidated School System in Wisconsin (from 1936 to 1938), Ann Arbor, Michigan (from 1938 to 1939) and the Southfield School in Shreveport, Louisiana (from 1939 to 1942).[52]

From 1942 to 1945 Virginia Pagenkopf worked as a social worker in the Homefinding Service of the Children's Service Bureau, Miami, Florida, and from 1945 to 1947 was with the Chicago Home for Girls. In 1948 she received the M.A. from the University of Chicago.[52]

After receiving her M.A., Virginia worked in a series of clinical positions as a psychiatric social worker. In the first of these, at the Community Guidance Center in Dallas, Texas, she also obtained a clinical assistantship at the South Western Medical School (1949-50). Returning to Illinois, Virginia became the supervising counselor at the Association for Family Living in Chicago (1950-53). On 1 September 1951 she was married to Norman Satir (the marriage ended in a divorce in 1961). Her reputation as a family therapist led to her first consultantship, at Leyden Township High School in Illinois (from 1951 to 1955), and a position as an instructor in family dynamics at the Illinois State Psychiatric Institute (from 1955 to 1958).[52]

Virginia Satir then moved to California. In 1959 she was a co-founder of the Mental Research Institute in Palo Alto. This group has been interdisciplinary in outlook and in practice since its inception, attracting sociologists and communication experts as well as persons trained formally as psychotherapists. Although the "establishment" has had considerable trepidation about this "motley crew" and for years expressed concern that unleashing these "wild" therapists would be a danger to public safety, the therapists trained by Satir and her staff have become established as leading family therapists on the west coast.

Along with becoming a respected member of the California mental health profession, Virginia Satir has been a consultant to a great number of private and public mental health facilities; among them Esalen, the San Francisco Mental Health Clinic, the Brentwood Veterans Administration Hospital, the Family Growth Center in Los Angeles, and the following California state hospitals: Mendocino, Napa, Camarillo, and Agnews.[52]

In *Conjoint Family Therapy* Satir elaborates her therapeutic technique which emphasizes the reestablishment of communication patterns between family members. Seeing pathology in terms of distorted communications and interactions, Satir emphasizes social rather than intrapsychic factors. When first postulated, Satir's position was criticized as superficial and simple-minded and her therapeutic techniques for being too exclusively "confrontive." Time has proved Satir both correct and timely: her point of view has become extremely influential and has found general acceptance and she herself has become the leading spokesperson for a therapy that rivals traditional psychotherapy.

RISING STAR
Sandra Wood Scarr (1936-   )

One of the youngest women to appear in this book, Sandra Scarr is best known for her work on the nature-nurture controversy in regard to intelligence. In the past ten years she has been among the most productive, most prolific, and busiest psychologist in the world. Scarr is a Harvard Ph.D. and a full professor at Yale; she has the potential of becoming America's most influential psychologist.

Of all the women included in this chpater, the person most like Scarr is Jane Mercer. Both of them are professors at major universities, they are both physically attractive and have four children each, but more than this, they are both on the same side in the testing controversy and their research has served to discredit widely-used assessment procedures with children from ethnic minorities.

Sandra Wood was born on 8 August 1936, in Washington, D.C., the older of two daughters born to Jane Powell and John Ruxton Wood, M.D. Her father was then a captain in the U.S. Army and Sandra had many of the usual "army-brat" experiences. She entered Vassar in 1954 and received the A.B., in sociology, in 1958.[53]

After an unsatisfying year in a Family and Child Service agency, where she felt that clients were more in need of solutions to socioeconomic problems than of psychotherapy, and a year at the National Institute of Mental Health's Laboratory of Socioenvironmental Studies as a research assistant, Sandra Wood chose Harvard University for her graduate training. Many of the values that guided her subsequent professional career were thus established early; that is, her doubts about traditional treatment of members of ethnic minorities and low socioeconomic groups, her dedication to empirical research, and her willingness to address the major social issues of her time.

Sandra began graduate studies at Harvard's Department of Social Relations in 1960 and reports being involved in the research and political activities of the exciting sixties in Cambridge. In December 1961 she was married to Harry Alan Scarr, who was then a graduate student in sociology in the same department. Sandra was working on her dissertational research, the famous twin study she conducted under Irving Gottesman, when on Christmas Day, 1962, Phillip Ruxton Scarr, their first child, was born. Sandra received her M.A. in 1963 in a ceremony in which her husband received his Ph.D.[53, 54]

The Scarrs moved to Washington, D.C., where Harry became a postdoctoral fellow at the Laboratory of Socioenvironmental Studies and Sandra combined writing her dissertation with caring for baby number one. She accepted a position as a part-time assistant professor at the University of Maryland's Institute for Child Study (from 1964 to 1966).[53, 54]

Sandra Scarr, very conscious of the professional obstacles facing the psychologist-wife, decided, at this time, that she would pursue a "serious career." She writes:

> As a young mother, I wanted very much to work about half-time and to be home with my child[ren]. Unfortunately, it was not possible at that time to be taken seriously as an academic if one worked part-time. As far as I know, it is still not possible; one is always considered less than half a colleague. I wish that my time with my children had not had to be sacrificed to career development, but the reinforcements were so biased that any other choice was suicidal.[53]

Like so many of the women of psychology, Sandra was forced to jeopardize her career and move to Philadelphia when her husband secured a job there. She was, however, fortunate to get a visiting-assistant-professorship of psychology at the University of Pennsylvania (from 1966 to 1967) and at the Graduate School of Education at Pennsylvania (from 1966 to 1967) and at the Graduate School of Education at Pennsylvania (from 1967 to 1970); during the last year she advanced to the rank of associate professor.[53, 54] Her daughters Karen Pelton and Rebecca Blackwell were born in 1967 and 1969, respectively. Scarr conducted her most noted research on race and test performance while at Penn. She also conducted research on "infant distress" with a colleague named Philip Salapatek and became emotionally involved with him.[53]

By the time Sandra, her three children, and Salapatek left Pennsylvania for the University of Minnesota, she had published or had submitted many more important articles, including "Environmental Bias in Twin Studies" (1968), "The Effects of Birthweight on Later Intelligence'" (1969), and (with Salapatek) "Patterns of Fear Development During Infancy" (1970). She was appointed an associate professor at Minnesota (1970–73), and advanced to the rank of professor (1973–77). In 1971 she married Philip Salapatek, in 1973 their daughter Stephanie was born, and in 1976, Sandra reports, this marriage had "fallen apart once and for all."[53]

By the time in 1977 that Sandra Wood Scarr accepted the position as professor of psychology at Yale University, she was a divorced woman with four children, ages seventeen. thirteen, eleven, and six. She was also a famous psychologist who had several notable publications in such journals as *Science* and had written articles for such popular magazines as the *Saturday Evening Post* and *Psychology Today*.

Sandra Scarr has served on a number of task forces, committees, and boards of ten different professional and scientific organizations and has provided consultation to scores of organizations that are involved in humanitarian and social action programs. In addition she has edited eight journals, including *Developmental Psychology* of which she is currently editor.[53]

Among her many publications are two books, (with P. Salapatek) *Socialization* (1974), and *IQ: Race, Social Class and Individual Differences* (1979). Her resarch interests are reflected in the titles of her most influential articles: "Unknowns in the IQ Equation" (1971), "Heredity and Behavior Development" (1971), "Race, Social Class, and IQ" (1971), "The Effects of Early Stimulation on Low-birth-weight Infants" (1973), "Some Myths about Heritability and IQ" (1974), "Comment on Developmental Behavior Genetics: A Theory in Search of Data" (1975), "The War over Race and IQ: When Black Children Grow Up in White Homes"

(1975), "Blood Group, Behavioral, and Morphological Differences among Dizygotic Twins" (1976), "Genetic Determinants of Infant Development: An Overstated Case" (1976), and "IQ Test Performance of Black Children Adopted by White Families" (1976).

TURNING HER ATTENTION TOWARDS THE HISTORY OF WOMEN IN HER FIELD
Virginia Staudt Sexton (1916-   )

On 18 May 1980, Virginia Sexton was granted an honorary degree, the L.H.D., from Cedar Crest College. Among the contributions of this remarkable scholar noted in the citation read in her honor were her many publications in the history of psychology, particularly her work on the history of women in psychology; her leadership in the American Catholic Psychological Association, of which she was president in 1965; her long and illustrious teaching career; and her research on the psychology of women. Today she, along with Mary Henle, is best known for her role as a leading historian in psychology, with five books published in this area.[55]

Virginia Staudt was born on 30 August 1916, in New York City, the daughter of Philip Henry Staudt and Kathryn Burkard Staudt.[55, 56, 57] She has lived and worked in New York all her life. With a B.A., cum laude, from Hunter College (1936) in classics, Virginia worked as an elementary school teacher at St. Peter and St. Paul's School in the Bronx from 1936 to 1939.[56]

While studying for the M.A. in psychology, granted by Fordham University in 1941, Virginia was employed as a clerk with the New York City Department of Welfare (from 1939 to 1944). She then accepted a position as a lecturer at Notre Dame College of Staten Island and during this very busy period was director of guidance at the college, taught courses at other colleges in the region, and worked on her doctorate at Fordham. Virginia received her Ph.D. in psychology in 1946 with a dissertation that led to two articles, "The Relationship of Testing Conditions and Intellectual Level to Errors and Correct Responses in Several Types of Tasks among College Women" and "The Relationship of Certain Personality Traits to Errors and Correct Responses in Several types of Tasks among College Women under Varying Test Conditions," published in 1948.[55]

Virginia, who also obtained postdoctoral training at both Fordham and Columbia, stayed at Notre Dame until 1952, having attained the rank of associate professor and been appointed chair of the psychology department.[55, 57] In 1953 she began her long affiliation with the City University of New York (CUNY): she was an instructor (1953-56); assistant professor (1957-60); associate professor (1961-66); and professor (1967-68), at Hunter College and from 1968 to 1979 was a professor of the Herbert H. Lehman College of CUNY. She is currently professor emeritus at Lehman and is a professor of psychology at St. John's University, Jamaica, New York.[55]

On 21 January 1961, Virginia was married to Richard Joseph Sexton, an English professor at Fordham with whom she had collaborated on a series of articles on "business communication." When they married he was a widower with four children, Nancy, Georgina, Mary, and Richard E. Her husband is also currently a professor emeritus.[55]

Virginia Staudt Sexton is today at the peak of a very busy and productive career. She has been very active in professional and learned societies; among her offices held are chair, Section on Psychology, New York Academy of Sciences (1965-66 and 1966-67); president, American Catholic Psychological Association (1964-65); chair, New York Psychological Association (1959-60); and president of the following divisions of the American Psychological Association: Division 24, Philosophical Psychology (1975-76), Division 26, History of Psychology (1979-80), Division 32, Humanistic Psychology (1979-80), and Division 36, Psychologists Interested in Religious Issues (1980-81).[55] She is the current president-elect of the International Council of Psychologists.

Virginia Staudt Sexton is the author of five books on the history of psychology: *Catholics in Psychology: A Historical Survey* (1954); *History of Psychology: An Overview* (1966); *Historical Perspectives in Psychology: Readings* (1971); *Phenomenological, Existential, and Humanistic Psychologies: A Historical Survey* (1973); and *Psychology Around the World* (1976).[56]

Her numerous articles suggest a variety of research interests: the psychogalvanic response (1948); dating and marriage (1950 and 1952); psychology in Italy (1953); treatment outcome (1953 and 1957); business communication (1957, 1958 and 1959); music therapy (1958); history of psychology (1954 through 1980); and adolescence (1965). Since 1968 Sexton has been the author of several major articles on the psychology of women and on the women of psychology. She is the best known specialist on the history of women in psychology and has contributed biographies of several female psychologists, including Mary Calkins, Margaret Washburn, and Karen Horney.[55]

NO MAN'S BUSINESS
Natalie Shainess (1915-   )

Whether compounded of pessimism or a realistic appraisal, the impression persists that the direction in which the culture is moving is toward the creation of male and female 'humanoids,' becoming still more alienated, mechanical, unfeeling, compulsively cruel, asexual but sexually preoccupied. . . . Society . . . has not only veered from the repressive to the expressive—it has lost its humanity along with its superego.

—Natalie Shainess, 1974

For more than ten years, Natalie Shainess, M.D., psychoanalyst, educator, author, and mother, has been an outspoken leader of feminist psychology and a critic of the contemporary "debasement" of sex. She is not a radical extremist and not a militant, but neither is she a conventional advocate of orthodox psychology, as some ultra-radical feminist detractors suggest. She is a gutsy, loving, common-sense spokesperson for the truly liberated woman.

Natalie Shainess was born on 2 December 1915, in New York City. Her parents were Jacob and Clara Levy Shainess. She received the B.A. from New York University in 1936 and the M.D. from the Medical College of Virginia in 1939.[58, 59] She interned at Wilkes-Barre Hospital (1939-40), and Union Health Center, New York City (1940-44).[59]

On 23 April 1944, she married Herbert Spiegel. They had two children, David, who is now a psychiatrist, and Ann, who is now a pediatrician. The marriage, however, ended in divorce.[58, 59] Natalie completed her residency in psychiatry at the New York State Psychiatric Institute (1945 and 1952-54) and obtained her training in psychoanalysis at the William Alanson White Institute (1945-51).[59]

Shainess interrupted her career to be a full-time mother until her children were attending school, a sacrifice which was "certainly compensated in large measure by the evidence of happiness and growth in the child, as well as by the close relationship itself." She has been in private practice, more or less continuously, since 1946. Since 1964 she has been on the faculty at the William Alanson White Institute and since 1966 has been lecturer in psychiatry at Columbia College of Physicians and Surgeons.[58, 59]

Among her many articles on the psychology of women, sexuality and society, and personality development, are "A Re-assessment of Feminine

Sexuality and Erotic Experience" (1966), "Abortion is No Man's Business" (1970), "The Danger of Orgasm Worship" (1970), "Is Motherhood Unnecessary?" (1972), "Is There a Separate Feminine Psychology?" (1970), "How Sex Experts Debase Sex" (1973), "Toward a New Feminine Psychology" (1972), "Women's Liberation and the Liberated Woman" (1973), and "The Effect of Changing Cultural Patterns upon Women" (1974).[58]

REACHING OUT TO OTHER WOMEN
Carolyn Wood Sherif (1922–   )

Best known for her research on small-group interactions and the concept of reference groups, Carolyn Sherif has been a leading researcher and writer on women's issues for almost twenty years. She is a professor of psychology at Pennsylvania State University and is the immediate past president of APA Division 35, Psychology of Women. With twelve books in print, she is one of America's most prominent social psychologists, and in recent years has focused her attention upon the problems of women in this society.

Carolyn Wood was born in Loogootee, Indiana, on 26 June 1922, the daughter of Lawrence Anselm Wood and Bonny Williams Wood.[60, 61] Carolyn earned her B.S., with honors, in general science, from Purdue University in 1943. She then attended the State University of Iowa, where she worked as a graduate assistant, from 1943 to 1944, and earned the M.A. in psychology in 1944. She was then employed for one year at Audience Research, Inc., in Princeton, N.J.[60]

On 29 December 1945, she was married to Muzafer Sherif, who has been a frequent collaborator with her for thirty-five years. They have had three daughters, Sue in 1947, Joan in 1950, and Ann in 1955.[60, 61, 62]

Between 1945 and 1961, when she received the Ph.D. from the University of Texas, Austin, in psychology with a minor in sociology, Carolyn held a series of positions at various institutions. She was a research assistant at Princeton (1945–47), and Yale (1947–49); was a research associate at the University of Oklahoma (from 1959 to 1966), and also taught sociology there (from 1963 to 1965) as an associate professor, and taught at the Medical School (from 1963 to 1965).[60, 61]

During the period 1945 to 1965, when she came to the Pennsylvania State University, Carolyn had a number of important publications, including three books, *Groups in Harmony and Tension* (1953); *An Outline of Social Psychology* (1956); and *Intergroup Conflict and Cooperation* (1961), and fifteen technical articles in journals or chapters in books.[60, 62]

At Penn State Carolyn was a visiting associate professor (1963-65), associate professor (1966-69), and since 1970 has been professor of psychology. During the 1969-70 academic year, she taught psychology and sociology at Cornell.[60, 61]

Her 1961 article "Established Reference Scales and Series Effects in Social Judgment," was, along with her textbooks, perhaps the best known of her early work. Her books have remained within the domain of "traditional" social psychology: for example, *Reference Groups: Exploration into Conformity and Deviation of Adolescents* (1964); *Attitude and Attitude Change* (1965); *Attitude, Ego-Involvement, and Change* (1967); *Interdisciplinary Relationships in the Social Sciences* (1969); and *Social Psychology* (1969); all these were co-authored with Muzafer Sherif. Her 1976 book, *Orientation in Social Psychology*, was her only solo effort.

In her later work, Carolyn Sherif has established her position as the establishment spokesperson for feminist psychology. Beginning with "Woman's Role in the Human Relations of a Changing World" (1964), her articles on women's issues include "Females and the Competitive Process" (1973), "Dreams and Dilemmas of Being a Woman Today" (1975), "Daily Self-reports on Activities, Life Events, Moods and Somatic Changes during the Menstrual Cycle" (1976), "The Social-psychological Study of Women: Why So Long Becoming" (1978), "What Every Intelligent Woman Should Know about Psychology and Women" (1979), and "In Search of the Token Women in Academia" (1980).

It should be noted that Carolyn Sherif has, for more than thirty years, conducted research and written influential articles on most of the issues of usual interest to social psychology. She has, among other topics, addressed the problems of bias; intergroup and intragroup relations; competition and cooperation; attitude measurement and attitude change; self-concept of blacks; social distance; norm setting; deviant behavior; and conflict resolution.

Carolyn Sherif has written that she, like most of her fellow women, has felt alone—she belongs to a pariah group within psychology just because she is a woman. Division 35 of the APA, of which Sherif has been president, has, she asserts, provided a cohesive measure for the women of psychology, a source of support essential for the mental health of the women of this profession.[63]

MASCULINITY AND FEMININITY
Janet Taylor Spence (1923–   )

Best known for several studies with the Taylor Manifest Anxiety Scale, conducted during the fifties, Janet Taylor Spence has made important contributions to several different areas of psychology—clinical experiments, social, and most recently, feminist psychology. Her first article on the psychology of women was "Sex and Anxiety Differences in Eyelid Conditioning" (1965), and her most recent was "Traits, Roles, and the Concept of Androgyny" (1979). She is the author of *Masculinity and Femininity: Their Psychological Dimensions, Correlates and Antecedents* (1978).

Women of psychology today are divided about fifty-fifty on whether or not to assume their husband's name when they marry. Most often when they marry after they have already established a reputation in professional psychology, they retain their maiden name. Janet Taylor is an exception. After her marriage, the well-known clinical psychologist Janet Taylor, who had developed the widely-used Anxiety Scale and was an expert on concept formation in schizophrenia, disappeared, and Janet T. Spence, experimental psychologist and learning theory expert, entered the scene.

Janet Taylor was born in Toledo, Ohio, on 29 August 1923. She obtained her A.B. from Oberlin College in 1945 and then spent one year at Yale studying clinical psychology (1945–46) before admission to a New York State Rotating Internship Training Program (1946-47).[64, 65] She then entered the graduate school at the State University of Iowa, where the clinical program was research-oriented and behavioristic. Janet received the M.A. and Ph.D. in 1949. Her research at that time was very conservative and focused on anxiety and the eyelid response. Kenneth W. Spence, who had pioneered in the use of the eyeblink reflex to explore basic learning processes, especially the temporal sequence of conditioning, was her co-author on three of her first four journal articles.[64]

Janet Taylor was an instructor at Northwestern University from 1949 to 1951. She was made an assistant professor in 1951 and an associate professor in 1956. Her most famous research on anxiety was conducted at this time. Using a true-false questionnaire which she developed from items of the MMPI, Taylor produced an operational definition of anxiety in humans that served her well in her research and was well-received and adopted by scores of her colleagues for research purposes. In 1960 Taylor abruptly left Northwestern and returned to Iowa.[64, 65]

In 1960 she accepted a position as a research psychologist at the Veterans Administration in Iowa City. She was also married to Kenneth W. Spence. Her research for the next few years involved concept formation in schizophrenia and in brain-injured subjects, learning, anxiety, studies with white rats, and, of course, eyelid conditioning research with her husband. When the Spences moved to the University of Texas in 1964, Janet was also developing a reputation as one of America's leading authorities in learning theory. At Texas she worked as a research associate, because of anti-nepotism rules, and was then appointed professor of educational psychology in 1965.[64]

In 1967 Kenneth Spence died. This was the year that Volume 1 of the Spence-and-Spence-edited *The Psychology of Learning and Motivation* was published. Volume 2 was published in 1968, posthumously for Kenneth. Janet Taylor Spence became professor of psychology at Texas in 1967, was chair of the department from 1968 to 1972, and remains active on the faculty today.[64]

In addition to the books with her husband and *Masculinity and Feminitiy*, there are five other books. One of these, Volume 3 of *The Psychology of Learning and Motivation*, she edited with E. Bower. She is a coauthor of *Elementary Statistics* (1976), and co-editor of *Contemporary Topics in Social Psychology* also 1976. Her most prominent book, however, is *Essays in Neobehaviorism*, which she and Howard H. Kendler edited, published in 1971—essays in tribute to Kenneth W. Spence.[64]

In the past several years Janet Taylor Spence has focused her attention upon women's issues, in particular exploring self-concept, role behavior, and achievement motivation of women. She has written several articles on the psychology of women and is the co-author of an important research instrument, the Attitudes Towards Women Scale (AWS)—Spence, in fact, is becoming a prolific writer in this area.

Janet Taylor Spence has been editor of *Contemporary Psychology* and a consulting editor of *Personality: An International Journal*, the *Journal of Abnormal and Social Psychology*, *Journal of Experimental Psychology*, the *Journal of Sex Role Research*, the *Journal of Experimental Child Psychology*, and the *Journal of Abnormal Psychology*. She has been president of the Southwestern Psychological Association (1970), was elected into the Society of Experimental Psychologists, and has been a member of the Council of Representatives and Board of Directors of the American Psychological Association.[64]

DISPLACED PERSON
Ina Cepenas Uzgiris (1937–   )

For fiteen years Ina Uzgiris has been a specialist in the area of the cognitive development of infants. She is very well known for the investigation of Piagetian concepts for which she and her mentor, J. McVickers Hunt, develoed their famous ordinal scales. A full professor since the age of thirty-six, Uzgiris is a most promising child psychologist.

Ina Uzgiris was born in Kaunas, Lithuania, on 2 December 1937. Her mother was a lawyer and her father was a history professor at the university. Ina reports that the women's movement had made considerable headway in her native country and there were no impediments to a woman in pursuing a career. She writes, "In many respects, women had greater equality in public life in Lithuania before World War II than they did until very recently in the U.S."[66]

Political upheaval during the early years of the war led to her family's fleeing Lithuania to avoid "almost certain arrest and deportation into forced labor camps in Siberia." Ina reflects,

As a child, I spent about eight months periodically fleeing from the lines of battle between the Soviet Union's and Germany's armies and four years in a displaced persons camp before being admitted into the United States..."[66]

Although Ina Uzgiris came to the United States when young and has been a citizen since 1957, she still feels like a "political refugee." She is strongly identified with the Lithuanian community in America and involved in such activities as publicizing the violation of human rights in Soviet Lithuania. She is married to a Lithuanian and reports a strong empathy with all groups of political refugees in this country. Being a Lithuanian and a woman, however, had led to discrimination against Uzgiris and a feeling of being "separate" and "it is hard to tell where it is due to my 'foreignness' and where to my 'womanliness.'"[66]

Uzgiris obtained her education at the University of Illinois, Urbana, B.S. (and election to Phi Beta Kappa) (1951), M.A. (1960), and Ph.D., under J. McV. Hunt (1962). Ina, in describing her graduate-student days, comments on the inhospitality of the university at accepting women into its ranks: "I had my share of 'what is a girl like you doing in graduate school,' and professors bemoaning the presence of the lone female in their seminar as an impediment to their joketelling."[66]

It appears on the surface that Uzgiris's career took off rapidly—after all, she received her Ph.D. well before her twenty-fifth birthday and she became an internationally prominent psychologist while still very young. Yet, despite the support and aid of her frequent collaborator, Hunt, she reports problems in establishing herself early in her career. Ina throws additional light on a peculiarly gender-linked phenomenon—the research associateship. For many very important women of psychology, several years were spent at this low-status rank, sometimes with little or even no salary, while they labored on research projects headed by a tenured male faculty member. Uzgiris writes, "When I was looking for a job, faculty positions had a way of turning into research associateships" and notes that interviewers often questioned whether she, as a young married woman, really wanted full-time employment.[66] Uzgiris was a research associate at the University of Illinois during the 1963-64 academic year and was appointed research assistant professor (1964-66), while conducting her most important research studies.

In 1966 Uzgiris moved to Clark University in Worcester, Massachusetts, a school which had once, during the infancy of American psychology, housed one of the most renowned psychology faculties in the world. She was appointed assistant professor of psychology and began to publish. Having had only one publication prior to arriving at Clark, she has produced more than twenty articles and five books in the past fourteen years (all the books have actually been produced in only the last five). She has presented papers during this period also, generally on her research on infants, to scores of learned societies throughout the world.[66]

Ina Uzgiris remains on the faculty at Clark; she was advanced to the rank of associate professor in 1969 and to full professor in 1973. She is still engaged in research in the area of developmental psychology, which, she suggests can provide the answers to broad questions of human existence.[66]

Uzgiris describes her main research interest as being in the area of the "relation between an individual's cognitive competence and appreciation of external constraints in shaping goal-directed activity and, particularly the role that reflection on one's own actions plays in this process."

In this era of controversy with racial overtones over heritability vs. environment in regard to cognitive development and intellectual ability, Uzgiris's long research experience has led to an interactionist rather than a doctrinaire environmentalist position. She sees a child's development as a function of three forces: (a) the individual characteristics of the child, (b) the experiences of the child (in itself an interaction of self-perception and external reality) and (c) societal expectation.

Notes to Chapter Four

(1) "Adkins, Dorothy C." In *American Men and Women of Science*, 12th ed.

(2) Bardwick, Judith M. *In Transition*. (1979) New York: Holt Rinehart and Winston.

(3) Judith Bardwick. Personal communication.

(4) Bardwick, Judith Marcia. *American Men and Women of Science*, 13th ed.

(5) "Joyce Brothers" in *Current Biography* (1971).

(6) "Joyce Brothers" in *Who's Who of American Women* (1978).

(7) "Natalia Potanin Chapanis" in *American Men and Women of Science*, 12th ed.

(8) Stella Chess. Personal communication.

(9) "Stella Chess" in *Who's Who* (1975).

(10) Mamie Phipps Clark. Personal communication.

(11) Florence Denmark. Personal communication.

(12) Sibylle K. Escalona. Personal communication.

(13) Sybil B. G. Eysenck. Personal communication.

(14) "Beatrice T. Gardner" in *American Men and Women of Science*, 13th ed.

(15) Beatrice Gardner. Personal communication.

(16) Joan S. Guilford. Personal communication.

(17) Communication from Helen LeRoy, secretary for 20 years to Harry H. Harlow.

(18) Harlow, Margaret Kuenne. *Child Development*, 1971, 42:1313–1314.

(19) Kuenne, Margaret R. "Experimental Investigation of the Relation of Language to Transposition Behavior in Young Children." *Journal of Experimental Psychology*, 1946, 36:471–490.

(20) Mary Henle. Personal communication.

(21) Henle, Mary. *American Men and Women of Science*, 13th ed.

(22) Lois Wladis Hoffman. Personal communication.

(23) "Lois Wladis Hoffman" in *Who's Who of American Women* (1978).

(24) "Matina Souretis Horner" in *Current Biography* (1973).

(25) "Matina Souretis Horner" in *American Men and Women of Science*, 13th ed.

(26) Matina Souretis Horner interviewed by Vivian Gornick in *New York Times Magazine*, 14 January 1973.

(27) Bärbel Inhelder. Personal communication.

(28) Alina Szemenska was for a long time a co-worker of Piaget's. She co-authored the monumental work *The Child's Conception of Number* (1941). However the English translation inadvertently omitted her name. "[A] deplorable omission in the assigning of

credit for a scientific work of great importance." Francois Bresson in "Alina Szemenska," *American Psychologist*, 1977, 32(5): 383-384.

(29) Dorothea Jameson. Distinguished Service Contribution Awards for 1972. *American Psychologist*, 1973, 28(1):61-64.

(30) "Virginia Eshelman Johnson" in *Current Biography* (1976).

(31) Kendler, Howard H. "The Making of a Neo-behaviorist." In Krawiec, T. S., (Ed.). *The Psychologists, Vol II*. (1974) New York: Oxford University Press.

(32) Kendler, Tracy S. Personal communication.

(33) Kendler, Tracy S. *American Men and Women of Science*, 13th ed.

(34) Koppitz, Elizabeth. Personal communication.

(35) Beatrice Lacey. Distinguished Scientific Contribution Awards for 1976. *American Psychologist*, 1977, 32(1):54-59.

(36) "Beatrice Lacey" in *Who's Who of American Women* (1978).

(37) "Nadine M. Lambert" in *American Men and Women of Science*, 13th ed.

(38) Sophie Freud Loewenstein. Personal communication.

(39) Loewenstein, Sophie F. "The Passion and Challenge of Teaching." *Harvard Educational Review*, 1980, 50(1):1-13.

(40) Eleanor Emmons Maccoby. Personal communication.

(41) "Eleanor E. Maccoby" in *Who's Who of American Women* (1970).

(42) Salzman, Freda. "Aggression and Gender: A Critique of the Nature-Nurture Question for Humans." In Hubbard, Ruth, and Marian Lowie (Eds.). *Genes and Gender II*. (1979) New York: Gordian Press.

(43) "Martha Tamara Mednick" in *American Men and Women of Science*, 12th ed.

(44) Jane Mercer. Personal communication.

(45) "Jane Ross Mercer" in *American Men and Women of Science*. 13th ed.

(46) "Brenda Milner: Distinguished Service Award" *American Psychologist*, 1974:36-38.

(47) Elaine Morgan. Personal communication.

(48) "Elaine (Neville) Morgan" in *Contemporary Authors*.

(49) Neugarten, Bernice Levin. *American Men and Women of Science*, 13th ed.

(50) Neugarten, Bernice Levin. *Who's Who of American Women* (1978).

(51) "When Age Doesn't Matter." *Newsweek*, 11 August 1980, p. 74.

(51a) Nancy M. Robinson. Personcal communication.

(52) "Virginia Mildred Satir" in *Who's Who of American Women* (1970).

(53) Sandra Scarr. Personal communication.

(54) "Sandra Wood Scarr" in *American Men and Women of Science*, 13th ed.

(55) Virginia Sexton. Personal communication.
(56) "Virginia Staudt Sexton" in *Who's Who of American Women.*
(57) "Virginia Staudt Sexton" in *American Men and Women of Science,* 13th ed.
(58) Natalie Shainess. Personal communication.
(59) "Natalie Shainess" in *Who's Who of American Women* (1970).
(60) Carolyn Wood Sherif. Personal communication.
(61) "Carolyn Wood Sherif" in *Who's Who of American Women.*
(62) "Carolyn Wood Sherif" in *American Men and Women of Science,* 13th ed.
(63) Sherif, Carolyn Wood. "Confessions of an Informer." *Division 35 Newsletter,* April 1980, 7(2):1-2.
(64) Janet Taylor Spence. Personal communication.
(65) "Janet Taylor Spence" in *American Men and Women of Science,* 13th ed.
(66) Ina Cepenas Uzgiris. Personal communication.

5
Epilogue

In the past forty years psychology has moved from a minor academic discipline, still an infant among academic fields, to an accepted science and a firmly established profession. Psychology has done well—and so, in the main, has its women. Once relegated to second-class citizenship in the discipline, women are today among the most productive, most influential, and most eminent contributors to the field. But the struggle for influence and recognition has been a difficult one and has been almost totally ignored by psychology's historians, whose narrow focus on Germanic dinosaurs obscured or entirely overlooked the psychologists and the psychological activities and interests that made psychology the accepted and influential field of endeavor it is today.

No Past and Only a Recent History

Boring begins his 1950 edition of *A History of Experimental Psychology* with a quote from Hermann Ebbinghaus to the effect that psychology has a "long past, but only a short history." What is meant, of course, is that although "philosophers" for many centuries had developed formal theories to aid our understanding of human nature, our behavior and values, psychology as an academic discipline was not established until the end of the nineteenth century. Ebbinghaus's simple generalization, though neatly summarizing the formal history of psychology as seen by the academicians, however, like so many male-oriented generalizations, does not apply to the history of women in psychology. Women psychologists are deprived of a past as much as of a history.

Almost all the philosophers and scientists, the great thinkers of the distant past, have been men. The pitifully few women who, until the end of the nineteenth century, were able to gain prominence for intellectual achievement have been held up as oddities, as the "exceptions" to the rule that only men have the intellect and temperament to accomplish anything worthy in the world of ideas.

247

This is the tradition, the "past," which was handed to the women of psychology. It is the background from which emerged a group of singularly brilliant, dedicated, and courageous women. For most of the first hundred years of psychology, if we begin our story with Dorothea Dix, these women had to struggle first for an education and later to be allowed advanced training, and finally for professional acceptance and recognition. In their struggles the women of psychology whom we call "pioneers and innovators" had no traditions of scholarship and life patterns to follow— no "role models" in the currently popular idiom.

Pioneers and Innovators featured such individuals as Maria Montessori, Leta Hollingworth, Margaret Floy Washburn, Augusta Fox Bronner, Ruth Benedict, Lillien Jane Martin, Karen Horney, Mary Calkins, and Melanie Klein. They were the ancestors who preceded the women of psychology who were born in this century. They were giants, extraordinary women who were willing to face extraordinary obstacles, and in most cases, they succeeded, brilliantly, achieving extraordinary careers. Until recently, however, psychology's "foremothers" did not succeed in obtaining the recognition they deserved in its best-known history books.

The earliest women of psychology were denied a tradition because the discipline itself was young and because at that time few women had succeeded in cracking related fields in science and academia; the women of psychology in its *recent* past and today have been denied a tradition by the academician-historians of psychology who have totally ignored the remarkable "foremothers" of that first generation who—despite overwhelming odds—*did* make it.

Birds of Like Feather?

When the pioneering efforts in psychology have been considered serious enough and important enough to warrant critical attention, the earliest female psychologists are generally lumped together and treated conveniently as stereotypes. This is curious since they were birds who never flocked together—it would be hard to find a group of more flamboyantly individualistic women than the earliest female psychologists.

There is almost nothing you can say about the early women psychologists for which there are not several glaring exceptions. For example, most of the early female psychologists were unmarried (Calkins, Washburn, Martin, Downey, and Dix) or had unhappy marriages that were terminated before the women became prominent (Benedict, Klein, Horney, and Woolley). But Lillien Gilbreth, Leta Hollingworth, Augusta Bronner, Fraziska Baumgarten-Tramer, Helene Deutsch, and Christine Ladd-Franklin had no problem in integrating a happy and successful marriage and family life with an equally happy and successful professional life. The stereotypes may be said to be "useful" for criticial analysis—but how can they be useful when they obscure the truth? They really represent sloppy and lazy scholarship, the fact that such sloppiness has been tolerated for so long is another indication that women of psychology have not been thought to merit careful attention.

When applied to their professional accomplishments, such over-simplified generalizations are equally misleading. The achievements of the earliest women psychologists reveal much more diversity and breadth than the stereotypes drawn by the academician-historians would imply. A majority of the women of psychology, it is true, have been involved primarily in the study of child development and education, clinical and social psychology, and in applied areas generally—but so were a majority of the men of psychology.

In the early history of psychology, the dominating interest was to develop and refine the "tools," theoretical and instrumental, which were to be used to further and direct advancement in the science. Women should be commended rather than condemned for their contributions to theory construction and test development in psychology's early days.

There is no doubt that women had been under-represented in those activities which psychology's historians deem most highly valuable—in adademia and in the experimental laboratory. It should be noted, however, that at the end of the nineteenth century very few women were welcome at major universities, not even as students, and almost no women were welcome in the laboratories. Simply to secure permission to participate in the full gamut of psychological research and inquiry had been, in fact, the major struggle of the women who chose to become psychologists in the early years.

That *some* women—without any encouragement from the "gentleman's club" in-group, or influence, or personal contact—became the "exceptions" and made contributions to the male-dominated areas of experimental psychology (as did, for example, Martin, Ladd-Franklin, and Washburn) and academia and created major theories (Horney, Benedict, Klein, Washburn et. al.) is a testament to their persistence and indomitable spirit.

Winning the Battles and Losing the War

During the war years, the women of psychology, like Rosie the Riveter, were accepted into positions previously denied them. They proved their competence and their ability to make significant contributions to all areas of psychology.

Theories previously put forward and widely accepted—such as that women lack mathematical ability or interest in mechanical or electric gadgets or that women are temperamentally best suited for "maternal" activities like psychotherapy—were proved during wartime to be preposterous.

The years 1941 to 1950 were golden ones for psychology. The great theories, the classic tests, the basic techniques were all refined during this period. Psychology as a behavioral science and as a service profession had become so firmly established and respectable that even the antics of its most colorful and reckless practitioners during the sixties could hardly tarnish its image.

From the zenith of status and recognition during the mid-forties, the status of the women of psychology "normalized" after the war; that is to say, they found themselves back on the bottom again.

The histories written during the fifties and sixties indicate the women's historical fate of near-total oblivion. The incredibly important work the women accomplished was just not mentioned. Karen Horney's theory of personality, although sometimes briefly noted, is given the status of a second-rate effort. (Consistently less attention is paid her work than is given to Maslow's highly derivative theory or to Perl's elaboration of a single idea.) The contributions of Wolpe and Bandura are emphasized over that of Mary Cover Jones in the development of behavior therapy, despite the innovation and creativity of her discoveries. Lauretta Bender's contributions to neuropsychiatry and to the understanding of childhood schizophrenia are never mentioned, nor are the contributions of Charlotte Bühler to humanistic psychology; those of Dorothea McCarthy, Nancy Bayley, and Louise Bates Ames to developmental psychology; Helen Flanders Dunbar to psychosomatic medicine; Margaret Kuenne Harlow to our understanding of maternal affection; and Brenda Milner to an explanation of the function of the hippocampus, to mention just a few of the most glaring omissions.

Until recently, when there has been a resurgence of interest in the contributions of women in science, one had the feeling that an invisible hand had erased one hundred years of effort and brilliant accomplishment from the slate of history. But the women's movement of the seventies will undoubtedly assure that the accomplishments of the women of psychology will be written truthfully, clearly—and in indelible ink.

The Women of Psychology, Today

The women's movement of the seventies, despite the excesses of the more militant and radical fanatics, who now appear to be quaint relics left over from the sixties, has given the women of psychology something close to equal status for the first time in history. Women psychologists, in great numbers, feel aligned with the feminist movement and a sense of identity with an oppressed and maligned sisterhood. It is this sense of identity, along with the consciousness "raised" by the contemporary feminist movement, that has led to a successful revolution in psychology.

The women of psychology, who, from the examples of Calkins, Ladd-Franklin, Martin, and Washburn, have shown themselves to be more capable, more dedicated, and more interesting than their male colleagues, are no longer willing to accept second-class citizenship in the profession. They are demanding equal status and when in-roads cannot be made into male-dominated institutions, they have created their own. There are today numerous books on the psychology of women (the newer ones have tended to be more political and sociological than psychological, and none so far can equal Horney's originality and comprehensiveness); women have a few psychological journals (typically more vital and interesting than establishment organs); and a number of organizations for female psychologists have emerged.

If the efforts of today's women of psychology conjure up images of separatism, it is because many feminists, especially the more activist and militant, are, in fact, pressing for separation. In our opinion, the drive to assert the uniqueness of women in psychology, both in their history and today, and to reclaim their unrecognized and unremembered contributions is a necessary and desirable thing. The experience of the fifties teaches us that gains solidly achieved can prove elusive when the atmosphere changes and that misogyny and gender discrimination can endanger what has been won. To separate from what was once a male-dominated power structure and to set up a competing organization, so that there will be temporarily "two psychologies," is probably necessary at this time to make further progress in what is rightly perceived to be a "war."

As mentioned earlier, the jury is still out. Women of psychology have just found their identity, their voice, their muscle. The women included in Chapter Four of this volume are in the middle of successful careers in psychology and most of them are fervently committed to the women's movement. Who can tell which of them will emerge as this generation's five or ten leading psychologists, the Karen Horneys, Lauretta Benders, Leta Hollingworths, Ruth Benedicts, and Margaret Washburns of our time? The jury is still out also in terms of the move towards separatism. Our experience tells us that the dissidents will inevitably—probably in the not-very-distant future—reunite with the main body of psychology. The stakes are too high, the common interests, intellectual and economic are too deeply shared, and the gains already made are too substantial to eventuate in any other result. We share the vision expressed by Dr. Florence Goodenough: Not male psychologists and female psychologists, but one day . . . just psychologists.

BREAKTHROUGH GENERATION

A. *Women who received Ph.D.'s* in Psychology in the nineteenth century.***

Name	Date of Ph.D.	School
Gertrude Buck	1898	University of Michigan
Emily Ida Conant	1891	New York University
Jane Connell	1898	New York University
Gertrude M. Edmund	1892	New York University
Eleanor McC. Gamble	1898	Cornell University
Alice Julia Hamlin	1896	Cornell University
Clara Maria Hitchcock	1900	Yale University
Rose M. Lathrop	1897	New York University
Anna Jane McKeag	1900	University of Pennsylvania
Kathleen Carter Moore	1898	University of Pennsylvania
Alice J. Mott	1899	University of Minnesota
Hannah E. Newman	1894	New York University
Eliza Ritchie	1889	Cornell University
Stella Emily Sharp	1898	Cornell University
Theodate Louise Smith	1896	Yale University
Alma W. Sydenstricker	1895	University of Wooster
Amy Elizabeth Tanner	1898	University of Chicago
Helen Bradford Thompson	1900	University of Chicago
Margaret Floy Washburn	1894	Cornell University
Jeanette Cora Welch	1897	University of Chicago

*Includes Ped.D.'s conferred by NYU when dissertation was clearly psychological in nature.
**Adapted from Eels, W. C., "Doctoral Dissertations by Women in the Nineteenth Century." *American Psychologist*, 1957, *12*:230-231.

B. *Women APA members born in the 1870's and alive in 1967.* *

Name	Birthdate	Year Ph.D.	School Ph.D.
Collins, A. Louise	12- 2-79	1939	Boston
Gaw, Esther A.	12-28-79	1919	Iowa
Gilbreth, Lillian M.	5-24-78	1915	Brown
Kemmerer, Mabel W.	11- 6-78	1903	Iowa
Kent, Grace H.	6- 6-75	1911	George Washington

*Based on Wallin.

THE WOMEN (OF PSYCHOLOGY) AROUND FREUD

C. *Sigmund Freud's first followers were all men; after 1924, a large percentage of them were women. They following list of women were among those who were directly ivolved with Freud.* *

WOMEN IN THE VIENNA PSYCHOANALYTIC SOCIETY, 1930
Lou Andreas-Salome
Helene Deutsch
Anna Freud

WOMEN IN THE BERLIN PSYCHOANALYTIC SOCIETY, 1930
Freida Fromm-Reichmann
Karen Horney
Melanie Klein

WOMEN TO WHOM FREUD GAVE HIS RING

Katherine Jones
Lou Andreas-Salome
Gisela Ferenczi
Ruth Mack Brunswick
Henny Freud

Anna Freud
Marie Bonaparte
Jeanne Lampl-de-Groot
Edith Jackson
Eva Rosenfeld

IDENTIFIED AS STUDENTS OF FREUD

Beata Rank
Eugenia Sokolnicka
Helene Deutsch
Ruth Mack Brunswick

Mira Oberholzer
Hermine von Hug-Helmuth
Marie Bonaparte
Jeanne Lampl-de-Groot

Dorothy Burlingham
Anny Katan

Eva Rosenfeld
Marianne Kris

WOMEN AT THE 1929 OXFORD CONGRESS

Marjorie Brierly
Melitta Schmideberg
Joan Riviere
Mrs. Sandor Rado
Marie Bonaparte
Ruth Mack Brunswick
Barbara Low
Alix Strachey
Mrs. David Eder
Helene Deutsch
Katherine Jones

Mrs. Roger Money-Kyrle
Melanie Klein
Gisela Ferenczi
Karen Horney
Anna Freud
Sybille Yates
Ella Sharpe
Salomea Kempner
Caroline Newton
Edith Jacobson

---

*From Roazen, Paul. *Freud and His Followers* (New York: New American Library, 1971).

THE SECOND GENERATION

D. Forty eminent psychoanalysts of the "Second Generation" who are women.

Lou Andreas-Salome
Lauretta Bender
Therese Benedek
Marie Bonaparte
Berta Bornstein
Marjorie Brierly
Sylvia Brody
Hilde Bruch
Ruth Mack Brunswick
Dorothy Burlingham
Edith Buxbum
Helene Deutsch
Helen Flanders Dunbar
Selma Fraiberg
Anna Freud
Freida Fromm-Reichmann
Elisabeth Geleerd
Phyllis Greenacre
Eugenia Hanfmann
Karen Horney

Hermine von Hug-Hellmuth
Susan Isaacs
Muriel Ivimey
Edith Jacobson
Adelaide Johnson
Anny Katan
Melanie Klein
Marianne Kris
Jeanne Lampl-de-Groot
Dorothea Cross Leighton
Margaret Mahler
Lili Peller
Beata Rank
Joan Riviere
Madelyn Sechehaye
Hannah Segal
Ella Freeman Sharpe
Melitta Sperling
Alix Strachey
Clara Thompson

THE COLUMBIA CONNECTION

E. Women of psychology who received some or all of their education at Columbia University, from Abel to Zucker.

Theodora Mead Abel
Anne Anastasi
Virginia Axline
Estelle De Young Barr
Ruth Fulton Benedict
Lucy Day Boring
Augusta Fox Bronner
Joyce Brothers
Alice I. Bryan
Cora Sutton Castle
Psyche Cattell
Mamie Phipps Clark
Elizabeth Duffy
Helen Flanders Dunbar
Florence L. Goodenough
Ruth E. Hartley
Edna Heidbreder
Leta Stetter Hollingworth
Muriel Irving
Mary Cover Jones

Mirra Komarovsky
Dorothea Cross Leighton
Margaret Mead
Ruth L. Munroe
Lois B. Murphy
Naomi Norsworthy
Dorothy Rethlingshafer
Suzanne Richard
Anne Roe
Pauline Snedden Sears
Georgene Seward
Milicent W. Shinn
Audrey Shuey
Janet Steinberg
Lois Meek Stolz
Ruth May Strang
Margaret F. Washburn
Caroline B. Zachry
Bess Zucker

THE MENTAL TESTERS

F. One of the major areas where women have made contributions to psychology is in test construction and clinical application of psychological tests. The following is a brief list of some of the most prominent testers.

Louise Bates Ames
Charlotte Bühler
Lauretta Bender
Theodora Abel
Molly Harrower
Maud Merrill James
Grace Fernald
Florence Goodenough
Christina Morgan
Elizabeth Koppitz

Francziska Baumgarten-Tramer
Marguerite Hertz
Karen Machover
June Etta Downey
Maria Rickers-Ovsiankina
Helen Thompson Woolley
Leta Stetter Hollingworth
Psyche Cattell
Joan Guilford
Nancy Bayley

Grace Kent
Marianne Frostig
Augusta Fox Bronner
Janet Taylor Spence
Florence Halpern
Gertrude Baker
Thelma Thurstone

Evelyn Hooker
Amanda Rohde
Leona Tyler
Else Frenkel-Brunswik
Anne Anastasi
Dorothy Adkins

HISTORIANS

G. *Not all of psychology's historians have been male. The following are among a growing number of female historians.*

Edna Heidbreder
Mary Sheehan
Laurel Furumoto
Virginia Staudt Sexton
Gwendolyn Stevens
Mary Henle

Nancy Russo
Maxine Bernstein
Marian MacPherson
Ruth Munroe
Alice Bryan
Clara Thompson

Appendix
On Being a Psychologist's Wife

According to research, male psychologists have overwhelmingly found marriage and a family to be beneficial to their career, while female psychologists have found them to be a detriment.

In a series of studies conducted during the late forties, a time when psychologists of both genders were involved in a readjustment of socially prescribed role definitions following the cultural disruptions engendered by World War II, the issues were clearly delineated. Women who attempted to combine the role of professional psychologist with that of a wife and mother explicitly stated that their having been ascribed certain domestic responsibilities handicapped them in becoming productive scientists. They reported that they read less, completed less research, wrote fewer technical articles, and enjoyed less success in maintaining satisfying full-time employment in psychology.

When I became acquainted with the articles concerning the "woman problem" in psychology, I tended to dismiss them. There was nothing in my experience to cause me to empathize with the problems facing the wife-psychologist. My interest in women's issues was entirely intellectual: I was training to be a social scientist and women, as a group, inspired the same curiosity as did the Trobriand Islanders or various tribes of New Guinea. Like most men of that era I was unconsciously insulated as a member of a different, dominant cultural group, with little understanding or sympathy for this querulous group of women psychologists.

HOW ONE LEARNS TO
APPRECIATE THE BENEFITS OF A WIFE

Men in psychology, perhaps men in all Western civilizations until now, have reaped the benefits of role definitions which entrust wives with primary responsibility for childrearing duties, household chores, and home-management functions. The research on this subject demonstrates the consequences of having a wife: Married men are more satisfied, live longer, and are healthier than the unmarried (and this is not generally

257

true of married women as compared to the unmarried!). More to the point: Married male psychologists, in the studies mentioned above, explicitly state that having a Wife* contributes to professional success.

Professor emeritus at the University of Southern California, J. P. Guilford has been a "very successful" psychologist in every sense. He is a psychologist's psychologist, prominent even during his early days at Cornell, where as a graduate student he was made "director" of the psychology clinic. He succeeded also in his career as an Air Force colonel during World War II, as President of APA, and during his long, extremely productive years at USC. Paul Guilford has been one of the most successful men in psychology.

Professor Guilford once told me the secret to his success. He works hard. While preparing the manuscript for his book on personality, he confided, he worked at his typewriter through the night, every night, for months. Guilford is the best example I know of the type of highly productive scientist Anne Roe described; he is the living proof of Roe's dictum that to be a success you need to be dedicated, single-minded, and work long hours.

He is today best known as the author of very influential psychological test instruments and textbooks. J. P. Guilford has produced hundreds of articles and several comprehensive, definitive books; he has completed many large-scale, significant research studies. According to his autobiography in Murchinson, his wife provided him the freedom from the mundane matters of the everyday world that allowed him to succeed.

Those of us who were Guilford's students and assistants were dimly aware of Ruth Burke Guilford. She was to us an almost mysterious figure, always in the background. In fact, I worked for him for six years and have never met her! In addition to housework and childrearing duties, Ruth managed the household and family finances, ran Sheridan Psychological Services, and collaborated on a few research studies with her husband. Although very few persons know it, Ruth Burke Guilford is also a psychologist, but like a good psychologist's Wife, she was content to stay in the background and be a "power behind the throne."

Like most men who grow up in this society, I was conditioned to find a Ruth Guilford. Trained to be ignorant of sewing, cooking, operating a washing machine, and changing diapers, I was prepared to possess one of those wonderful creatures God provides to be a lover, companion, soul-

*"Wife" is capitalized throughout when the term denotes an occupational role, not necessarily coincident with the marital role nor relevant to the gender of the role-assumer.

mate, and, let's be honest, a servant. I learned that a man should not have to wash dishes, dust, or worry about the lawn or the children—at least not if the man intends to be a successful professional. I learned to call this denegrated physical labor "woman's work."

Implications

Before I became the Wife of a professional psychologist, I had no idea of the significant role that housework, childrearing, money management, and other time-consuming tasks play in depriving women of an equal opportunity to compete against men professionally. Housework takes time and energy, both of which might be profitably applied to professional pursuits. A psychologist–Wife does not have hours of delicious, uninterrupted privacy to write up research reports, prepare journal articles, to read the latest monographs, or to just think. It is clearly not easy to prepare a lecture and at the same time band-aid a knee or dry the dishes. There is not enough time to be both a Wife and an outstanding psychologist.

Books on the history of psychology also do not discuss the problem of housework as a deterrent to success in this field. Why should they? The histories are almost exclusively the chronicle of what we men have done— we who have not been stuck with the housework.

THE PSYCHOLOGIST'S WIFE SYNDROME

With the advantage of hindsight and three years of participant–observation, I should like to present the various elements of a syndrome to which I have been given the benefit of considerable ethnological analysis and empirical thinking. I have discovered a syndrome which, if foisted upon a person who happens to be a psychologist, assures them lower professional productivity, less recognition by peers, and a decreased opportunity for fame and success. The components of this syndrome are:

yielding career priority

degeneration of career aspirations

dislocation

loss of role definition

rules against nepotism

unemployment of underemployment

disidentification

second-class citizenship

time-consuming and unwanted task commitments

To some degree all these problems befall every psychologist's wife, perhaps even every Wife. Although there are some real and unique compensations when the Wife is herself (or himself) a psychologist, many of the elements of the syndrome plague us as well if we are forced to carry out Wifely obligations.

I can do more than state that these conditions are unpleasant, demeaning, demoralizing, and time-consuming and that they lead to a devaluation of the worth of the wife and ultimately to a wife's lowered self-concept, I am now in the position to describe how the process works first-hand.

Yielding Career Priority

In almost every psychologist-couple, the husband's career is placed first. The first letter of inquiry to prospective employers is for a position for *him*, not her. He gets the good job; she finds what she can "when we get there."

When the couple collaborates, he is almost always the principal investigator in the research and the senior author when they publish. In every regard he is the primary breadwinner and his work is considered more important.

The psychologist's wife is expected to put her husband's career first. This is precisely what Gwendolyn and I chose *not* to do. Once she received her Ph.D. we were *ipso facto* equals. She could not longer be my assistant, she could not work on a college faculty where I had higher rank and the other members were buddies of long-standing of mine, and she could not be my research assistant/high-level secretary.

It was in 1978, shortly before she received her Ph.D. from the University of California, Riverside, that we decided that I would become a Wife. This decision was based upon the recognition that her ten-year career interruption was extremely unfair. And, after all, I had not been forced to interrupt anything with marriage and raising a family; the situation had actually gotten easier for me. We decided that we would give her career top priority and would relocate wherever she found an academic position that suited her.

The decision was, I suppose, similar to the philosophical position or attitude assumed when a man decides to be a "househusband." But when two persons are members of the same profession and are committed to remaining active in that profession, the situation is more complicated.

There is some potential for rivalry and an intracouple struggle for dominance. In our case, there appeared to be no emotional reservation, no doubt or dread over this initial step in my becoming a Wife.

In one significant sense my career had come "first"—that is, temporally. I had already been a reasonably successful psychologist for several years before we met. In fact, Gwendolyn was only nineteen and unknown to me when I received my Ph.D. in clinical psychology. Later, I had been one of her professors at California State University at Los Angeles. Perhaps a sense of fair play led me to want to "give" Gwendolyn her chance, or maybe I had grown bored with the whole thing—in any event there has been little competition between us.

Degeneration of Career Aspirations

Although I was extremely happy with the position I held in 1978, I knew that there were others available then which were almost as good and for which I was clearly qualified. I had to squelch any fantasies about my career and try not to let my needs influence Gwendolyn in her choice of her first full-time teaching position. I faced what so many women of psychology were forced to face: a possible abandonment of a career in psychology.

We have learned of scores of women who settled for low-paying or even nonpaying jobs on the periphery of established psychology, essentially postponing a brilliant career while they served as Wife to a psychologist. Many times the women's position was obtained for her by her more more esablished, more powerful spouse; in some cases the "extra job" was used as an inducement for the sought-after husband ("Look, honey, there's even a job there for you too, working in the social psychology lab!"). Of course, if the move is to a small town and there are rules against nepotism, the wife may be unable to work in psychology at all.

When I became a Wife, I had little apprehension concerning my career's ending altogether. I felt insecure, yes, but not apprehensive. Surely my resourcefulness, charm, and demonstrated competence would result in my being able to secure a satisfactory position. In this, I was to be proved almost totally wrong.

Dislocation

In the past forty years, career advancement in psychology has usually meant moving on. In almost every case this has worked out in practice to mean moving on to meet the demands of the husband's career advancement. Gardner Murphy goes to Topeka and Lois Murphy goes along; John

Seward goes to LA and Georgene Seward follows him; J. J. Gibson finds what he wants at Cornell and E. J. Gibson brings along the kids. He is the breadwinner; he is more established; his career is given top priority.

In her quest for a good opportunity, a "tenure track," courses she wanted to teach, and a young, aggressive faculty, Gwendolyn turned down offers at large universities, located in major metropolitan areas. Her preferences were little schools in isolated rural places—places I had never heard of. I became really alarmed. Would my career end? I was only forty-four! We were relieved (since my salary was then twice what she was offered) that her first choice, Southeast Missouri State University, also had a position open for a person to teach clinical psychology. After we arrived in Cape Girardeau, however we learned that "SEMO" has this peculiar policy concerning nepotism.

Loss of Role Definition

After years of study and sacrifice, of earning entrance into an established profession, and of working within the limits set by that profession, a person's occupational role plays a very large part in determining and main- taining a sense of identity. Psychology is a particularly demanding profes- sion in this regard. It is based upon scholarship and respect for the values of science; it is idealistic and humanitarian in purpose; it has a strict code of ethics and sanctions to govern professional behavior. Psychology is more than a "job"; it demands dedication; it is a way of life. In 1978 it appeared that this way of life might not be my way of life any longer.

In addition, contributing somewhat less to an immediate loss of role definition was my no longer being the breadwinner. The prospect of having no "gainful" (i.e., paid) employment was a threat to my under- standing of what a man is or should be. Doing nothing "for a living," of course, also meant that I would no longer be entitled to a Wife of my own.

I knew that all this would happen in a small Midwestern town on the Mississippi. I had never lived among the rednecks and beer-drinkers who drive pick-up trucks with the gun rack in the rear window I imagined Cape Girardeans to be. (This stereotype proved to be mainly false; Cape Girar- deans, it turned out, are just like everyone, everywhere.) My image as a respected urbane sophisticate was endangered as well. I would imagine walking up to the rail of some Cape Girardeau tavern, having some guy ask me what I did for a living, and replying, "I used to be a psychologist, but now I'm a housewife!"

Antinepotism Rules

Until only a few years ago, many universities and other institutions had rules against the hiring of more than one member of a family. These rules, apparently developed to prevent a political leader from concentrating power in some sort of family-oligarchy, have traditionally served to discriminate against married women psychologists (and indeed against married women in many fields of endeavor). Before these quaint rules were discarded—and more than 80 percent of all institutions of higher learning have now abandoned antinepotism rules—such prominent psychologists as Eleanor Gibson, Tracy Kendler, and Margaret Harlow were prevented from attaining full status and participation at university settings. Nepotism rules have been a pervasive problem since so many modern women psychologists have been married to psychologists.

The most dramatic, frustrating, and humiliating single event in my education in becoming a wife was to be denied consideration for a position at SEMO because of nepotism. I had been teaching, usually part-time, for eighteen years at major universities and obviously seemed qualified for a position then open on the faculty. I was told that I could not apply for the position. At the time this constituted the most bitter lesson in my education as a psychologist's Wife.

In more civilized parts of the country, where there are several institutions of higher learning, married psychologists could often find academic positions at different universities within commuting distance of their home. This is what happened, for example, when John Seward joined the faculty at UCLA and Georgene Seward, at the University of Southern California. This was, of course, not possible in Cape Girardeau.

Unemployment/Underemployment

After a career of more than twenty years as a psychologist, most often administering clinical training programs in large and prestigious psychiatric clinics and teaching at such schools as UCLA, the University of North Carolina, and Pepperdine University, I now had to find "whatever employment was available in the area." Would I have to go back to selling shoes?

This was a frightening period—reality had finally sunk in—there appeared to be every prospect that I would never again work as a psychologist. I was fortunate finally to land a job at the local mental health center, as a "junior" psychologist, at a salary of exactly half my previous year's.

Compared to many of the psychologist-wife women whom we have studied, I have indeed been fortunate. Some of them were forced to work part-time in low-paying jobs for decades—and still they were able to make important contributions to psychology. One wonders, for example, when, where, and how Christine Ladd-Franklin did her earliest research? Were the subjects for her studies of the horopter guests in her home? Did she make measurements in the living room? The kitchen? I remember a study Gwendolyn conducted on the Müller–Lyre illusion in children when she was a first-year graduate student. We were vacationing at Lake Arrowhead and she used every kid she could find at the lake as a subject. I guess Ladd-Franklin did something like that.

Disidentification

I mentioned earlier that the loss of professional identification was traumatic for me. The relative loss of all selfhood which is suffered when the identity of the Wife is merged with that of the spouse, a more basic and insidious loss of personhood, was perhaps worse.

At the university I am frequently referred to as "Mr. Stevens" and at functions there my name card often reads "Sheldon Stevens." At the supermarket, to students, to the typewriter-repairperson, and to many of the merchants in town, my name is now Stevens. Our medical insurance and credit, obtained by Gwendolyn before I arrived, are in her name.

To be sure, in the staid, conservative, farm community where we live, the fact that Gwendolyn maintains her maiden name leads to even greater confusion. But this has been a common practice among the women of psychology: Anne Anastasi, Margaret Mead, Anne Roe, Augusta Bronner, Elizabeth Duffy, and Lauretta Bender all did so. In Cape Girardeau, however, it is not usual for a married woman to be the "head" of the household.

Since psychologist-Wives often have less prestigious positions, we have lower status socially. We often become an appendage to our spouse; my tag is sometimes "Dr. Stevens and husband." Since she is better known in this college town, it is not uncommon to be approached on the street with, "Say, aren't you Dr. Stevens' husband?"

Second Class Citizenship

For years I had heard that women enjoy second class citizenship. Having once been a full-fledged member of the ruling class and therefore one of the oppressors, I had either doubted the validity of the claim or had refused to appreciate the real implications. Now, I understand. When a couple chooses to put his career first, makes sacrifices for his advancement, and thereby encourages a male inner sanctum to run a profession, a husband never gets the opportunity to understand the humiliation women feel on account of their low status.

Of course I am not a woman. I have no real feeling for what it would be like to suffer a whole life's experience of ascribed low status. However, I am beginning to realize, after a taste of it, what it is to be ignored, to have one's judgment considered less than competent, to sit in the audience, and to experience being the afterthought ("Perhaps Sheldon would like to come along too"). To be devalued, to lose one's respect and one's autonomous identity, especially when this is reinforced by the entire social structure, is a humiliating and frustrating experience. My career as a Wife has been brief thus far (and might persist indefinitely), but nonetheless has been decidedly unlovely.

When Gwendolyn and I began to make arrangements for a major program at the Annual Meeting of the American Psychological Association, we asked several of the most prominent, brilliant, and productive women psychologists to serve on a panel. We were startled to be told that some of these women, among the best in our profession, preferred to be omitted from the program. They would, they informed us, rather not be singled out for their outstanding achievement, but would be there "sitting in the audience." All the women who demurred were married.

Time-Consuming and Unwanted Task-Commitments

The most obvious impediment to success in psychology suffered by Wives is housework. It is time-consuming, boring, and unsatisfying. Household management and what is associated with it—attention to petty details, endless errands, long waits in line, juggling a budget, waiting for repairpersons, constant phone calls, etc.—contribute to discontent and distraction in the life of the psychologist's Wife: Discontent because of the inherent disagreeable nature of the work for which we have primary responsibility; distraction from everything else—like making contributions to science which, however important, can be postponed (whereas, for example, an over-flowing toilet cannot).

In my opinion, if psychologist-wives must involve themselves in the time-consuming, self-defeating tasks that corrode the lives of housewives, they can never achieve equality with male psychologists. *They just do not have the time.*

CONCLUSION: AIN'T WE GRAND

To dispel the notion that I feel boastful about my career as a Wife or even successful or satisfied with it, I should like to state that, except for the learning experience it has offered, being a Wife is, on the whole, a rotten role and I would never choose it again. That is not to say that life itself has not been without its rewards during the past three years. I am not despondent to the point of suicide. It is just that whatever I have achieved during this period has required more effort, more sacrifice, and more personal degradation than I should want to ever again inflict upon myself (or on anyone else—which is the real lesson I have learned from it all).

That so many women included in our book have been able to be both psychologist and Wife and have done so well at it is a commentary on their dedication, competence, single-mindedness, and boundless energy. As for being a Wife? They can have it.

Sheldon Gardner
Cape Girardeau, Missouri

Index

Sanford, Nevitt, 45, 129
Sarah Lawrence College, 12,
    137–138, 153
Santa Barbara, University of
    California, 211
Satir, Virginia, 230–231
Scarr, Sandra W., 231–234
Schilder, Paul, 7, 22, 24–25
Schizophrenia, research on, 24,
    52, 54–55, 162, 167
Schlick, Moritz, 131–132, 170
Schoen, M., 10
Sears, Pauline S., 154–156
Sears, Robert, 155–156
Seward, Georgene H., 139–143
Seward, John, 141, 143
Sexton, Virginia S., 234–235
Shainess, Natalie, 236–237
Shakow, David, 107–108
Sheffield, University of, 21
Sherif, Carolyn W., 237–238
Sherif, Muzafer, 237
Siipola, Elsa M., 175
Simpson, George Gaylord, 106,
    108–109
Skodak, Marie P., 176
Smith College, 120–122, 124, 146,
    166, 174, 175–176, 190, 201
Society of Experimental Psychol-
    ogy, 119, 125, 212
Sorbonne, Institute de Psychologie,
    11
Southern California, University of,
    142, 172, 198–199, 216, 222
Spence, Kenneth, 200, 239–240
Spence, Janet Taylor (see also
    Janet Taylor), 239–240
Spiegel, Patti Keith, 27, 28
Stolz, Herbert R., 65
Stoltz, Lois Meek, 9, 64–66

Strephosymbolia, 23, 28, 101
Strang, Ruth M., 9, 55–57
Stumpf, Carl, 28
Sullivan, Harry Stack, 35–36
Sundberg, Norman, 117, 118

Taylor, Janet, 239
Taylor Manifest Anxiety Scale,
    239
Test development, 9, 22, 26, 30,
    49, 68, 69, 70, 71, 73, 85,
    89–90, 117, 128, 138, 151,
    162, 170, 172, 175, 185–186,
    195, 199, 212–213, 221, 223,
    239, 241
Texas, University of, 237,
    239–240
Thomas, Alexander, 190–191
Thompson, Clara, 8, 31–39, 53
Thurstone, Louis, 7, 67–68
Thurstone, Thelma, 8, 9, 67–68
Titchener, E. B., 7, 12
Toronto, University of, 127
Tyler, Leona, 6, 81, 112–119

Uzgiris, Ina C., 241–242

Vassar College, 10, 13, 35, 39,
    41, 136–137, 175, 232
Vienna Circle (logical positivism),
    131–132, 169–170
Vienna Institute of Psychology,
    27, 29, 31, 130–132, 149,
    169, 171
Vienna Psychoanalytic Institute
    and Society, 18, 19, 53
Vienna, University of, 21, 28–29,
    53, 61, 69, 96, 130–131, 149,
    168–169, 171, 173, 174
Visual cliff, 120